States of enmity

Manchester University Press

STUDIES IN EARLY MODERN EUROPEAN HISTORY

This series aims to promote challenging and innovative research in all areas of early modern European history. For over twenty years it has published monographs and edited volumes that make an original contribution to our understanding of the period and is particularly interested in works that engage with current historiographical debates and methodologies, including race, emotions, materiality, gender, communication, medicine and disability, as well as interdisciplinary studies. Europe is taken in a broad sense and the series welcomes projects on continental (Western, Central and Eastern Europe), Anglo-European and trans-cultural, global histories that explore the world's relationship with Europe during the sixteenth to eighteenth centuries.

Series editors

Sara Barker, Laura Kounine and William G. Naphy

Full details of the series and all previously published titles are available at https://manchesteruniversitypress.co.uk/series/studies-in-early-modern-european-history/

States of enmity

The politics of hatred in the early modern Kingdom of Naples

Stephen Cummins

MANCHESTER UNIVERSITY PRESS

Copyright © Stephen Cummins 2024

The right of Stephen Cummins to be identified as the author of this work has been asserted in accordance with the Copyright, Designs and Patents Act 1988.

Published by Manchester University Press
Oxford Road, Manchester, M13 9PL

www.manchesteruniversitypress.co.uk

British Library Cataloguing-in-Publication Data
A catalogue record for this book is available from the British Library

ISBN 978 1 5261 7107 8 hardback

First published 2024

The publisher has no responsibility for the persistence or accuracy of URLs for any external or third-party internet websites referred to in this book, and does not guarantee that any content on such websites is, or will remain, accurate or appropriate.

Typeset by Newgen Publishing UK

To Katherine

Contents

List of figures and tables	*page* viii
Acknowledgements	ix
Introduction: enmity and peace in the Kingdom of Naples	1
1 Contours of vendetta and violence in the Kingdom of Naples	33
2 The 'abominable traffic': negotiating justice, money, and blood	60
3 The politics of enmity in the provinces	94
4 Banditry and the culture of enmity	117
5 Jesuit missions and the emotional politics of enmity and peace-making	146
6 The politics of hatred in the aftermath of 1647–48	170
Conclusion	189
Bibliography	194
Index	216

List of figures and tables

Figures

0.1 Map of the city of Naples, detail from Alessandro Barratta, *Fidelissimae Urbis neapolitanae cum ominibus viis accurata et nova delineatio* (1670). page 11

0.2 Map of the Kingdom of Naples (1690), published by Domenico Antonio Parrino. 12

0.3 Map of the Kingdom of Naples, published in Giovan Battista Pacichelli, *Il regno di Napoli in prospettiva diviso in dodici provincie* (1703). 14

1.1 Portrait of Pedro de Toledo from Domenico Antonio Parrino, *Teatro eroico, e politico de'governi de'vicere del Regno di Napoli* (Naples, 1692). 40

2.1 The Castel Capuano, Carlo Capuano/Ascanio Luciani, Museo di San Martino, Naples. 61

4.1 Map of Capitanata, from *Geographia Blaviana* (Amsterdam, 1659). 121

4.2 Detail of a map of the Molise, Joan Blaeu (Amsterdam, c. 1640). 137

5.1 An engraving of Capua from Giovan Battista Pacichelli, *Il regno di Napoli in prospettiva diviso in dodici provincie* (1703). 160

6.1 The viceroy Oñate, from Domenico Antonio Parrino, *Teatro eroico, e politico de'governi de'vicere del Regno di Napoli* (Naples, 1692). 182

Table

4.1 Figures of bandits 1675–82 from *Reassunto de servitii ottenuti nel felicissimo Governo dell'Eccellentissimo Sinor Marchese de los Velez* (Naples, 1682). 124

Acknowledgements

It would not have been possible to write this book without great help. I first wish to thank the archivists and librarians of many different institutions who made access to the sources possible, productive, and also illuminated countless matters. I would like to thank the staff of the Archivio di Stato di Napoli. I would like to note the courtesy and help of the staff of the *Sezione Napoletana* and the *Sezione Manoscritti e Rari* in the Biblioteca Nazionale di Napoli. Don Angelo Fanelli welcomed me graciously to Conversano and the rich diocesan archive there. The staff of the Archivio di Stato di Foggia's section in Lucera made it a congenial and rewarding place to work. I also appreciated the help of the archivists of the Archivum Romanum Societatis Iesu.

This book has its origins in a doctoral dissertation written at the University of Cambridge. I owe great thanks to the supervisor of that thesis, Mary Laven. I would not work on early modern Italy without her encouragement. Her advice on historical style and argument has been indispensable then and after. Also at Cambridge, I want to give warm thanks to Melissa Calaresu, who provided timely counsel that I should continue researching southern Italy. Ulinka Rublack was also a great inspiration and provided invaluable guidance at an early stage of this project. During my time at Cambridge other scholars influenced this project's origins through inspiring teaching including Gabriella Ramos, Richard Drayton, John Morrill, and Richard Serjeantson. I also offer my sincere thanks to the examiners of my thesis, Filippo de Vivo and Stuart Carroll. I also want to thank Stuart Carroll for his continuous interest and support during my doctoral research and in the years afterwards.

After Cambridge, my time at the Center for the History of Emotions at the Max Planck Institute for Human Development has been crucial for this project. I thank Ute Frevert, the Center's director, for her generous support over many years. My colleagues at the Center have been irreplaceable companions in scholarship. Out of many wonderful colleagues, I'd like to thank especially Daphne Rozenblatt, Esra Sarioglu, Hannah Malone, Laura Kounine, Francesco Buscemi, and Kerstin Pahl for their friendship and engagement. I would also like to note my appreciation for the support of Kerstin Singer, Philipp von Hugo, Karola Rockmann, Anja Berkes, Daniela Petrosino, and the late Christina Becher at the Center for the History of Emotions.

A whole host of inspiring scholars on the topics of this book and adjacent early modern fields have contributed to my understanding. For various help advice, references and guidance I would also like to thank Silvana D'Alessio, Carlo Vecce, Paolo Broggio, Nikolas Funke, Domenico Cecere, Umberto Cecchinato, James Amelang, Nicholas Terpstra, Lyndal Roper, Alex Walsham, Peter Mazur, Tom Cohen, Peter Burke, Phil Withington, Marco Cavarzere, Regina Schwartz, and Helen Hills. I would also like to thank Edward Muir for his constant interest in and support of my work. A fellowship with the Academy for Advanced Studies in the Renaissance led by Edward Muir and Regina Schwartz was a defining experience for my work. I would like to thank my co-fellows Charlie Keenan, Colin Rose, and Bianca Lopez for their insights and comradeship.

In the preparation of this volume, I would like to thank Meredith Carroll, Siobhan Poole, and Laura Swift at Manchester University Press for their assistance in transforming my project into a book and Victoria Chow for her careful copy-editing. I would also like to thank Sara Barker, Laura Kounine, and William G. Naphy as series editors for *Studies in Early Modern European History*. I would also like to thank the British School at Rome, the AHRC, the Cambridge Italian Renaissance Network, and Christ's College for financial support of my research.

I owe a great debt of gratitude to my friends and family. I am grateful for the unfailing love and constant support I have received from my mother Sandy, my brother Phil, and my late father Bill. My final thanks I offer to my wife Katherine whose love has been the foundation for my work and the bigger adventure of life beyond it.

Introduction: enmity and peace in the Kingdom of Naples

On 8 September 1655 seven men wearing cloaks and masks of white cloth walked into the Salentine town of Presicce.[1] Although dressed as pious *confrati*, they carried harquebuses, swords, and knives under their robes. They reached the town's piazza as Prince Carlo Bartilotti, the feudal lord of Presicce, left the church and crossed the square towards his palace.[2] The men shot the prince and he fell to the ground, mortally wounded. Don Andrea, the prince's brother, rushed to his side and Carlo's wife, the Princess Agnese Vaaz d'Andrada, witnessed this from a window of the palazzo. The attackers fled. Carlo was brought inside his palazzo where he died upon a bed. The next day a trial began under the authority of Giovanni Battista Brancaccio, the regional governor of Puglia.[3] The attackers had been seen travelling unmasked in a carriage past the olive groves outside of Presicce. In subsequent criminal proceedings they were identified by residents of Presicce as Laurenzo de Blasio, Francesco Daniele, Don Angelo Monaco, Giulio Cesare Giurandi, Pietro Pepe, and Francesco Antonio Sforza.[4] In the testimonies given, it was quickly shown that this attack had a long history of hatred.

The enmity between the Prince and Don Angelo Monaco was said to have begun roughly seven years before when Giulio Cesare Monaco, Angelo's brother, was killed. According to a townsman of Presicce the Prince himself had been outlawed for failing to answer a call for interrogation and in 1656 'his mother Maria Ciso Moles was imprisoned, as she was similarly being investigated in the homicide of Monaco'.[5] The Prince also held enmities with the Giurandi (or Giuranno) family. He had been the enemy of Giulio Giurandi, Giulio's father Francesco Giurandi, and Giulio's cousin the *Arciprete* Raffaele Giurandi for many years. The families persecuted 'the one and the other at court' so the enmity was 'known to all the people of this Province'.[6] Pietro Pepe, in turn, was the enemy of the prince because he blamed the Prince for the murder of his father-in-law Giovanni Andrea Alfarano; this murder and the hatred around it had led to his family leaving Presicce and moving to the town of Ugento.[7] Francesco Daniele's goods had been seized by the Prince for an unknown reason. Blasio was the only one whom witnesses did not know had a direct reason to bear hatred against the prince.

Dense webs of hatred united the killers against Don Carlo Bartilotti. When interrogated in the resulting trial, Angelo Calizzo, who was not a native of Presicce, had heard that Carlo bore a 'bad name' among his vassals and had given them many reasons to hate him.[8] In this account he was a tyrant, an example of the feudal lords of southern Italy who repressed their subjects to gain illicit incomes and used abusive force against their enemies. But, according to Carlo's widow, the story was not one of tyrannicide. Her testimony provided a different interpretation. She talked of how she heard the shots of harquebuses ring out and fled down to the piazza where she threw herself at her husband's body, weeping.[9] One point she wished to make most strongly in her testimony was to dispute that which 'went about publicly' concerning the identity of the killers of her husband. Gossip had identified people with whom the Prince had longstanding enmities but had misidentified those involved in the killing. She named the true killers as: Francesco Daniele, Don Carlo Colitto, Colella Valentino, Fra Giuseppe Panico, and Giovanni Montano.

The killing, for Carlo's widow Agnese, was a moment of betrayal, when those she trusted had allied with known enemies. She divided the culpable between those who they had 'always held as dear and true vassals' and those who had long been known to them as 'capital enemies'.[10] Francesco Daniele, Carlo Colitto, and the monk Fra Giuseppe Panico were those who had previously been counted among the loyal. Yet in her story the Giurandi remained the instigators. Two generations of Giurandi were involved, the siblings Francesco and Giulio Cesare and their respective sons, Francesco and Antonio. It was when the Bartilotti brothers had been young boys that the enmity had been born and they had consistently desired to murder them.

The murder was the first success in a history of attempts on the Bartilotti brothers' lives. One morning in August 1648, when much of the Kingdom was in the immediate aftermath of the uprisings of 1647–48, Don Carlo was looking out of a window from his palace when an harquebus was shot at him.[11] The shooter was one Carlo Martino, a bandit who had been outlawed by the *Regia Audienza* of Lecce apparently under the orders and protection of the Giurandi. In response to this attack the Prince and his brother were moved into the convent of the Franciscan Minors *Santa Maria degli Angeli*. A plan was hatched among the Giurandi, Francesco Adamo, and Angelo Monaco to poison them both. Donato Pepe, a relative of the Giurandi, frequented the kitchens of the monastery and poisoned some soup.[12] Apparently, an antidote was administered just in time and the brothers escaped with their lives.[13]

In the telling of his wife, Don Carlo had always been a 'good lord' of his land and it was the desire that the Giurandi and Monaco had to take 'dominion' from him that led them to organize his killing and the previous attempts on his life.[14] A number of those involved in the murder were captured. The kinship networks of the Giurandi were reconstructed and questioned by the *Regia Audienza* but, at least within the span of time covered by the documentation of the trial, they were not found.[15] Was the Prince a feudal lord who murdered, imprisoned, stole goods, made enemies, and was killed by their hands? Or a son and husband who had always been a '*buon padrone*' yet was a victim of assassination attempts throughout his life because of a faction that desired to overturn his *dominio*?[16] In the piazza and streets of Presicce the enmities and factions that united and divided the town were all matter of public discussion and, eventually, royal justice. Family and institutional connections (both royal and ecclesiastical) meant that feudal lands always had connections beyond themselves.[17]

The Bartilotti and the Giurandi subsequently used the law courts of the Kingdom to persecute each other. The relations of local populations with their feudal lord were described with languages of love and hate, enmity and friendship. In the feudal towns of the Kingdom, resident nobles were often deeply embedded in local communities rather than standing outside them. As well as being prominent local actors the politically active men in the Kingdom's communes were interlocutors with the tribunals of the city of Naples. They wrote letters to and received letters from central institutions; most communities were involved in petitions, lawsuits, or other undertakings that saw them connected to the authorities of the centre. One important point is that, for early modern communities in the Kingdom, it was not only the viceregal regime in Naples that they may have been in dialogue with.[18] The plural and febrile jurisdictional ecology of the Kingdom of Naples shaped the consequences of such enmities. When crimes of inimical violence entered the legal system such causes became potential battlegrounds for rivalries between those who held jurisdictions or aspired to do so: including feudal lords, bishops, and the courts themselves. Acts explained by enmity could quickly gain different meanings or significance than what they possessed among the parties involved.

The flows of communication and the attempts of government to regulate how certain *università* operated reveals attitudes about how these institutions were supposed to function; the place of passions of hatred and enmity in communal government. Governance was shaped by attempts to create peace through good administration and mediate between family rivalries that threatened to end in bloodshed or to destroy taxation revenues as communities plunged into deep debt. Involvement of royal administrators in local factional conflicts was an indispensable part of royal governance but also offered local office-holders the chance to instrumentalize royal authority for their own ends.[19] The *università* of the Kingdom were sites of exclusion and conflict, because of the economic and status privileges they offered, and as such they were a main field of enmity.

This violent act even leaves obscured traces in language and folklore. *Mascarani* (dialect for *mascherati*: masked) became a sobriquet for inhabitants of Presicce which survives until today. A current explanation for the name demonstrates the slightly distorted persistence of the event through the exaggerating lens of anti-feudal memory politics. The inherited story claims that Prince Bartilotti exercised the *ius primae noctis* and that the offended groom, hiding his face in a carnival mask, assassinated him by firearm. The mix of truth and fiction in this inherited story provides evidence for the historical power of such incidents, yet also their liability to be shifted into the realm of the curious, antiquarian, and romantic.

The politics of hatred

Behind these and other such acts of violence that proliferated in early modern southern Italy were the politics of enmity. States of interpersonal hostility and the actions that both emanated from and constructed such states were of primary importance in power relations. Enmity was at the heart of the violence that occurred at all levels of the politics of the Kingdom of Naples. States of hostility had both spontaneous and institutional aspects. This book provides a historical examination of the politics of enmity in terms of its characteristics, dynamics, and emotional dimensions. The idea of Naples as notoriously disordered and violent is an old one, identifying fragments of historical truth but, just as the folklore surrounding the *mascarani* of Presicce, often distorting this reality and resting on false explanations of causes and conditions. The new history of violence and enmity in early modern Europe offers the ability to provide accurate context to the proliferation of inimical violence in Italy in general and southern Italy in particular. Focusing rather on the instability of social hierarchy in early modern Italy and disturbances in systems of status, a vision of violence and conflict emerges which does not equate it with backwardness. With a focus on vivid examples drawn from research into trials, petitions, correspondence, and diaries, this book explores these traditional themes of Neapolitan historiography in new ways: especially the relation between centre and province, feudalism, municipal politics, and banditry.

The new history of violence in Europe provides a framework for comparison that highlights how the Kingdom of Naples is a particular example of political and social instability while seeing how the problems it confronted occurred elsewhere in Europe as well.[20] The book is an account of enmity in the seventeenth century, with reference to both earlier and later periods when necessary to elucidate longer-run trends. Moreover, it concentrates on the troubled middle of the seventeenth century. This book traces the impact of 1647–56, from the revolution to the plague of 1656, and provides a new analysis of this period as a point of divergence between southern Italy and other parts of Italy and Europe. The revolution of 1647–48 and its chaotic aftermath led to a retrenchment of elite violence and the lack of capacity for the state to address it adequately. For this reason, this study focuses on the pivotal mid-century moment, understood in large part as a consequence of the crisis of the Thirty Years' War, and its decades-long aftermath.

The present work explores the realities of the discourses and practices behind social conflict and public order in early modern Naples. *States of enmity*, as a title, is therefore intended to be read in two ways. First, the phrase indicates that the internal policy of early modern states in general and the Kingdom of Naples in particular was, in many respects, a question of the artful management of conflict: hatreds were an object of government, needing to be handled well for the maintenance of authority. Enmities set the rhythm and tempo for much of early modern politics, provoking actions and reactions. Second, it argues that such enmities provided structure for many forms of social interaction in the kingdom and, were by no means simply objects of central control. Being a violent and powerful man with many enmities could be as much empowering, in regard to negotiating with higher levels of political power, as it made one a target for repression.

The peace-making or peace-keeping duties of governors and administrators were commonplaces in early modern Italy and major loci of administration. Despite the positive connotations of the vocabulary of peace, such operations were far from necessarily fair or equitable. In practice, peace was often defined in a limited way that prized quiet over justice.[21] The hatreds that existed in cities, towns, villages, or institutions (and which produced lawsuits, assaults, murders, rapes, arson, the killing of livestock, kidnappings) at times became relevant to the administration of justice, the proper functioning of taxation, and general issues of security. They were often addressed through tamping down the worst excesses rather than the dedicated prosecution of crimes. Local politics was often shaped by factionalism, with the administration of municipalities regularly passing between two rival bodies, either two families or two broader kin alliances.[22]

As well as these bipolar formations, a number of other potential players existed in particular local areas: feudal lords, royal ministers, bandit gangs, powerful ecclesiastical figures or groups, and divisions between noble and non-noble elites. The establishment of 'public quiet' could require the settling of interpersonal enmities, the reconciliation of individual enemies, the construction of a new *modus vivendi* for opposed factions or through violent repression of resistance. Local notables, public officials, or clerics often acted as mediators, resolving or limiting conflicts through the use of embassies, pleasing words, a 'good manner', and other rhetorical tools. If repression was not to be the only path, then information on the nature and depth of local hatred had to be garnered, persuasion carried out, and the parties to the conflict reasonably assured of the wisdom of accepting peace in the feud. Hatreds and the actions that constituted them as social facts, therefore, were not simply obstacles to be removed, but key to the sorts of interactions that constituted governance. In religious life enmities were also important because those who had enmities were meant to be excluded from confession. The division of jurisdiction between the two states, civil and ecclesiastical, also strongly shaped the politics of enmity. In many ways, then, enmity was a cornerstone of elaborate social worlds in early modern Naples.

An introduction to enmity

Enmity was used to refer to both a state of hostility and as a category of a relationship. It was a versatile concept, used to categorize all types of prolonged conflict, from engrained dislike to homicidal violence. The potential origins of enmity were vast. Ludovico Antonio Muratori's expansive discussion in his 1708 work *Introduzione alle paci private* of who an enemy might be is instructive. He could be:

> one who has killed a relative of mine, who has accused me of a great misdeed, who gossips about me, who against my will holds either my wife or my relatives in his power, who has said injurious words to me, or threatened me, or in any other way mistreated me, or if he socializes often, and familiarly with my enemies, or he is bound to them, or he is enemy of my brother, or of my kin, or he claims that he regards me with hatred, or he talks badly of my behaviour, or he takes away from me without cause something that is duly mine, or he does any other similar thing that denotes ill-will towards me.[23]

Another person became an enemy when they or their close kin committed injuries to oneself, one's kin, or one's friends. Keen attention to enmity was also a cause of its growth, as reckoning the friend of one's enemy as an enemy indicates.

On a face-to-face scale, enmity could be recognized by behaviour, as Muratori notes: 'we assume enmity between two people, when they do not greet each other, when they stare at each other with malice, when they flee from conversation, discussion, and eating together'.[24] Enmity cut across the normal sociable modes of encounter. Denoting a lapse from neighbourly love, enmity troubled conscientious priests. The famous confessor Paolo

Segneri provided strategies for a priest to deal with those who were wrapped up in enmities. It is unlikely, Segneri tells his priestly readers, that the worst cases will present themselves at confession. These sick souls, these *vendicativi*, 'certain bloodthirsty men, who think always of killing', will only rarely appear at the confessional. Those who come of their own will present subtler cases. They are of two minds: they both want to be confessed but they also don't want to forgive their enemy. They lie and minimize their own hatreds, tucking them away or presenting excuses. They will tell stories like 'a long time ago they forgave their enemies for every injury, and if they found them sleeping in a wood, they would take care to let them sleep, rather than try to hurt them'. He advises the priest to ask specific questions: do you speak with them? Do you greet them? The negative responses will expose the truth of their internal states. This was a serious problem because such 'demonstrations of hatred' should be regarded as already part of vendetta. They give the hated person the occasion to sin themselves by returning and joining in the enmity, therefore they give scandal. Segneri reminds us that enmity – like any other secret of the human heart – is difficult to pin down.

Notwithstanding such difficulties, and in fact often causing more in turn, enmity was used widely in matters of proof and procedure. Such attempts at a legal definition of enmity refracted local realities, creating opportunities for the instrumental usage of such definitions. The Sicilian jurist Francesco Baronio published a lengthy account of the effects of enmity. His treatise, *De inimicitia eiusque causis et effectibus* (also known as *De effectibus inimicitiae*), in two volumes provided a thorough survey of the various facets of enmity, both as a longstanding juridical institution and as a social problem. This treatise was dedicated to the viceroy of Sicily Don Juan Téllez-Girón, Duke of Osuna (son of Pedro Téllez-Girón, Duke of Osuna and viceroy of Naples, 1616–20) and it was framed both as a detailed work of legal theory and as a resource for governance. In his dedication to the 'Dux Excellentissime' Baronio wrote that enmities were like the monstrous Hydra and that if the Duke fights against them he will gain much praise because the unrestrained rule of this monster would lead to massacres.[25]

Enmity's metaphorical form as many-headed monster stressed both its violence but also the difficulty of ever providing a lasting solution to it; it morphed, sprouted, and regrew. The detailed 'effects' of enmity range widely. Baronio's understanding of an effect was broad, including both procedural norms and more general effects. Inheritance was one of the main fields that enmity affected. Families could be unravelled through enmity, breaking the solidarity that was necessary to manage a lineage over generations. A father was not obliged to give a dowry to an ungrateful and inimical daughter and could disinherit his sons for the same offence.[26] If an enmity existed between father and son then the murder of the son by the father should not be deemed parricide.[27] The corrosive power of enmity dissolved what should be lasting bonds.

Baronio's account was only one example of the jurisprudential preoccupation with enmity. The notion of *inimicitia* featured in the works of the Roman jurists. It had a variety of potential effects on legal procedure. Most commonly, enmity precluded certain roles from being carried out. It featured heavily in regulations concerning guardians and wards. This relationship was discussed at length in the institutes and pandects of Roman law.[28] In Roman society, the main role of the guardian or tutor was to safeguard the pupil's property. An inheritance could be squandered or misused by a guardian who had developed an enmity with the father of the child in the time since he had been named as a potential guardian. It was in this context, of oversight over inheritance, that enmity was discussed at greatest length.

Enmity was so important because it imperilled justice. Pietro Follerio, an eminent southern Italian jurist and an *auditor* of the *Regia Audienza* of Basilicata discussed enmity at length in his widely read handbooks on criminal process the *Practica criminalis* (1553) and the *Canonica criminalis praxis* (1557), in which enmity had multiple functions both as evidence towards guilt and as a reasons to be suspicious of testimony and accusations.[29] Prospero Caravita who had been *avvocato fiscale* of the *Regia Audienza* of the provinces of Principato Ultra and Basilicata (a single tribunal served both these provinces in the sixteenth century) also described the procedural place of enmity in his *Commentaria super ritibus Magna Curiae Vicariae Regni Neapolis*. Enmity could bar a witness's testimony but it had to be proved 'capital' or 'serious' [*gravis*].[30]

The widespread litigation in early modern Europe in general, and the Kingdom of Naples in particular, was fertile ground for enmity. As the writer of a *Vita* of a Neapolitan Jesuit noted, when someone was 'litigating in the Tribunals for regaining what is theirs' often 'self-interest, that so greatly dominates Man, for the most part degenerate into hatred' and therefore 'enmities are contracted under the semblance of Justice'.[31] Both increasing rates of litigation and criticism of them was a wider European trend.[32] But there was a common belief that litigation was particularly problematic in Naples. For instance, the viceroy the Count of Medina wrote that 'this Kingdom is so addicted to lawsuits that its inhabitants would rather do without ordinary sustenance than court cases'.[33] Baronio noted the jurisprudential assumption that *inter duos litigantes praesumitur inimicitia* (between two litigants enmity is to be presumed).

Enmity therefore was a relational idiom with strong legal and political meanings. What undergirded these meanings was a close association of enmity with violence. Enmity was an explanation of the causes of violence.

Which enmities were repressed and which were indulged, tolerated, or ignored, provides insights into how the Spanish regime interacted with local power brokers and the different ways in which this (at least two-way) interaction generated political and social changes. Enmities were also political in the sense of being forms of contestation that often had goals, aims, strategies, and tactics. Considering these micro-political meanings of enmities and their violence allows for analysis of the dynamics of local power in the provinces of the Kingdom. Especially how such local events entered into the purview of its administrative organs. This book therefore combines two different perspectives: from, first, the heights of the regime and, second, the localities that made up the *Regno*.

Enmity was central to the experience of communal life. It was an organizing category. John Bossy characterized early modern enmity as 'personal, face-to-face, eyeball-to-eyeball', a 'force' that was a 'formal and public condition'.[34] Homicidal violence was part of such conditions. It was not only familial disputes that were explained by the language of enmity but clashes over material resources, urban factionalism and a diverse variety of other conflicts. Brawls, duels, murders, wounding, thefts, criminal damage, and slander could all be born from, give birth to, or provide fuel to enmities. A wide variety of early modern writers scrutinized what lay beneath performances of goodwill and what peace really meant. In this undertaking they explored notions of authenticity, dissimulation, and what was required to lay aside hatred in a sincere way.[35] Reconciliation required movements of the heart and knowledge of whether this had truly been done was next to impossible. Yet many agreed on the necessity of peace-making to community life; violence would multiply without it.

Enmity sprawled across early modern society and thought. It could be notorious, public, private, or hidden. Both civil and criminal trials could become debates about the nature and reality of hatred. Society and politics were interpreted through these lenses. Conflict between social groups, competition between nations, local factionalism; all of these were discussed with its language. Violence was regularly explained by pre-existing enmity. The word used most often to talk about feud-like behaviour was enmity.[36] Beyond the political and social, enmity was also used as a primary category for understanding the natural world and not only as metaphor. This tendency was especially strong in the Neapolitan philosophical tradition; philosophers such as Giambattista della Porta and the Calabrian Tommaso Campanella held that the whole natural world was animated by forces of amity and enmity.[37]

As a topic of study both enmity and peace-making are deficiently abridged if viewed only through one kind of historical lens. The practices of enmity and its resolution cannot be considered the province of one type of human action or experience: the topic is not wholly legal nor wholly religious, neither solely public nor fully interior. Thematic divides must be crossed to talk meaningfully about enmity. If only the religious aspects of peace-making are considered, the ways in which it was also an active political issue framed by discourse about governance are neglected. If it is regarded as only legal then the procedural effects of enmity's jurisprudential existence and the place of peace as legal instrument stand in for a multifaceted social whole. If it is only seen as an aspect of state formation then the emotional realities and personal contingencies of hating and peace-making are erased in favour of structural, de-personalized frameworks that stress the progress of the state. Yet if we only consider the emotional aspects and ignore the role of authority and policy we are left with isolated accounts of subjective feeling, unmoored from the profound influences of social stratification and power relations, that therefore have little contribution to wider historical assessment.

The Kingdom of Naples in the Spanish period

A tendency towards violence and disorder, animated by a passion for revenge, has long been part of the stereotype of the Italian south. In 1580 a Venetian ambassador summarized this perception of the Neapolitan character: 'the restless nature of these peoples, that also in the most distant times have shown to hunger consistently for the agitation of civil and foreign wars, has given in large part woeful fermentation to many revolutions [*alterazioni*] and disorders'.[38] Not only were they chronically rebellious and liable to unseat their rulers, but in the late sixteenth century an acute disorder was growing too:

> to this ill disposed nature is added the pestilent humours that are daily accumulating in this disordered body, the infirmity is of a contagious sort, and if it is not in fact to be despaired of, at the least the ownership [of this Kingdom] has always been judged dangerous; it has, after many other nations, today fallen to the Spanish nation.[39]

In the later sixteenth century the Dutch revolt showcased the potential instability of Spanish rule, that is, the shakiness of an empire built upon Habsburg matrimonial politics. But even beyond this particular conjuncture of European politics, Naples as a 'disordered body' – an unstable body politic – was a common theme. As part of this account of disorder the Neapolitans as people (both the urban citizens and the inhabitants of the other provinces that made up the Kingdom) were often branded as particularly vengeful and quick to resort to violence.[40]

The Italian Wars had spread the firearm as a common addition to the dagger and the sword as tools of this vengeance. On the tumultuous urban stage of the capital, violent nobles clashed in the streets and piazzas while the expansion of the city was driven by the urban poor, the plebeians or *popolo minuto*, whose imposing presence threatened that rulers could be thrown off with urban risings. Beyond the city, the provinces were perceived as occupied by peasants prone to physical aggression or, in the mostly small urban centres, factions that spilled blood in the piazzas. The countryside was also the home of feudal power, where feudatories who consorted with bandits or oppressed their vassals were commonplace. The encounter with the Americas furnished commentators with a neat comparison: the wilder parts of the provinces of the Kingdom were 'the Indies over here'.[41] Peripheral and near-savage, they were places where reform, or even the basic installation of religion, customs, and justice was said to be needed. Since the medieval period the contrast between the beauty of the Kingdom's terrain and the city's bay with the alleged nature of its inhabitants had been abridged in another slick contrast: Naples was a paradise inhabited by devils. These putatively diabolic cast members – coarse nobles, fierce outlaws, and feuding peasants – were a danger to their Spanish rulers and needed to be kept in check, unless they caused the loss of the Kingdom.

Yet these stereotypes, wrong as they were in their explanations and in many of the details, gestured toward real issues of disorder and violence in the early modern Kingdom of Naples. But these dilemmas did not make the

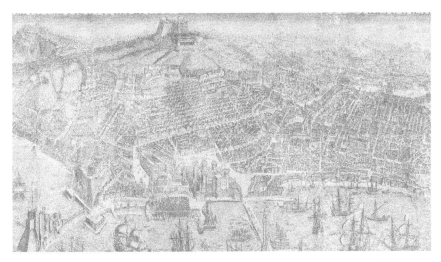

Figure 0.1 Map of the city of Naples, detail from Alessandro Barratta, *Fidelissimae Urbis neapolitanae cum ominibus viis accurata et nova delineatio* (1670). Fondo Antiguo, University of Seville.

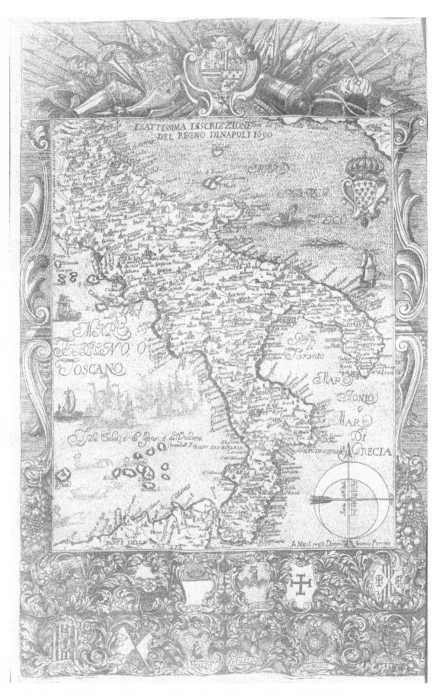

Figure 0.2 Map of the Kingdom of Naples (1690), published by Domenico Antonio Parrino. Fondo Antigo, University of Seville.

Kingdom a prodigal exception, but a region with a particular constellation of features decisively within, not outside of, Italian and European contexts. The problems which concerned the ruling of the provinces of the Kingdom of Naples were the same dilemmas faced in many other regions and typical of early modern state formation. Violence was high in early modern southern Italy, but this was a problem common to large portions of the peninsula.[42] Justice was hobbled by widespread feudal jurisdiction, a relatively weak vicegeral regime, sparse urbanization in many regions outside of the capital, and a lack of imperial interest in reform.

Nonetheless, the divergence between southern Italy and the rest of Italy and Europe has been a dominant theme in historiography. The challenge of histories of violence in southern Italy is to understand divergence without, on the one hand, essentializing or exaggerating such differences and, on the other, ignoring where differences occurred.

Due to the union of crowns, the Kingdom was exposed to harms inflicted by the demands of the Spanish fiscal-military imperial machine. Even after the Italian Wars, the Kingdom was particularly exposed to Spanish–French competition with its debated inheritance and pivotal strategic position. With its long coastlines and dispersed population, it was also exposed to Ottoman attack. Demands for money and men increased with the coming of the Thirty Years' War, leading to the rapid sale of the royal demesne. Such a sale strengthened feudal jurisdiction and weakened the state. The Neapolitan patriciate nobility, due to their crucial role in raising extraordinary taxation, were in many (although not all) ways not pacified or restrained. The effects of these processes are the general field of this book.

Turning to the basic characteristics of the Kingdom, it was constituted by twelve provinces: Abruzzo Ultra and Citra, the Contado di Molise, the Terra di Lavoro, Capitanata, Principato Ultra and Citra, Basilicata, the Terra di Bari, the Terra d'Otranto, Calabria Ultra and Citra. Out of the Italian Wars, the provinces emerged as part of Charles V's empire, his right inherited from his grandfather Ferdinand of Aragon. The capital city of Naples grew immensely in the aftermath of the Italian Wars, with migrants attracted by exemptions from taxation and other economic opportunities. Naples was by far the largest city in all of Italy, let alone the Kingdom. There was a relative dearth of middle-sized cities in the Kingdom exacerbated by poor infrastructure between the capital and the provinces.[43]

Throughout the provinces, the Kingdom possessed just under 2000 *università*. These were settlements with institutional existence, communities with some form of *reggimento* (council). These varied greatly in size, with 144 of them holding the title of *città*. This title did not necessarily imply a particularly large size or varied urban functions, rather, what tended to distinguish them was an area or areas of relatively dense population, churches,

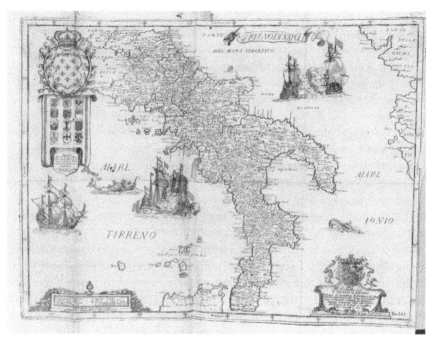

Figure 0.3 Map of the Kingdom of Naples, published in Giovan Battista Pacichelli, *Il regno di Napoli in prospettiva diviso in dodici provincie* (1703). Fondo Antiguo, University of Seville.

or being the seat of a bishopric or archbishopric.[44] Many of the villages, towns and small cities that constituted the early modern *Mezzogiorno* may have been peripheral, but they maintained active relations with central authorities based in Naples and ecclesiastical authorities in Rome.[45]

The provinces also constituted the base of feudal power. The Kingdom of Naples was noteworthy for the force that the feudal nobility held. Unlike other Italian states, which saw a more thoroughgoing – albeit often incomplete – challenge to feudal authority, the Kingdom of Naples remained a state in which many forms of authority lay in the hands of feudal lords. One part of the explanation for this is that the historical inheritance of expansive feudal rights was considerable in the Kingdom of Naples. Another is that Spanish policy was to allow the feudal nobility a large amount of autonomy in exchange for loyalty to the Spanish cause along with regular transfusions of cash from Naples to Madrid. In addition to this, many non-noble wealthy people found it attractive to enfeoff themselves through marriage or the purchase of lands with titles, which was possible both due to indebted nobles selling some of their land-holdings as well as Spain liquidating parts of the royal demesne in order to raise money for the imperial centre. Notable 'stati feudali' were part of this landscape. In lands held by feudal lords, they were normally the most important players in power relations and the local economy. In this way, the enmities of feudatories were often the most salient forms of hatred and preoccupied the central institutions of the Kingdom.

Yet while an increasing number of settlements were part of feudal territory, not all inhabitants of the provinces were vassals of feudal lords. Important larger urban settlements, such as Monopoli in Puglia, were part of this royal demesne. With no feudal lord, they administered first- and second-instance justice communally (although not necessarily equitably). The number of self-governed communities trended downwards during Spanish rule as the Crown alienated the demesne, especially as the costs of the Spanish war machine rose with the outbreak of the Thirty Years' War. In the face of this trend, some communities managed nonetheless to orchestrate the purchase of their own land from its owner and liberate themselves from feudal rule. Protest, whether successful or not, at the point of sale either from demesnial to seigniorial possession or from one feudatory to another was often a flashpoint for conflict. Possession by a feudal lord did not exclude the existence of a patrician nobility, for instance Altamura in Puglia possessed a fractious patrician class while ruled by the Farnese.

The administration of *università* could take one of a set of different constellations. In some, only patrician nobles were allowed to take public office. In others, it was divided between patricians and select non-noble families. It was also possible for only prominent *popolari* families to take part in administration. In many smaller communities, which lacked such hierarchies, all male inhabitants could theoretically aspire to participate. Such institutional structures existed both in feudal and demesnial lands although with potentially more limited administrative faculties in feudal lands. The degree to which such office-holders were subject to control and direction by their lord also varied. In certain *università*, such as Altamura for example, the local elite had considerable power. The control of offices was a major part of power struggles, as they provided proximity to tax revenues and other forms of real and symbolic control. The politics of office-holding were deeply tied up with violence. Resource competition led to violence to secure claims on rights, to push projects of local domination, and could also be a proxy for pre-existing conflicts. Disputes over the distribution of offices and the procedures of governance in *università* were very common, and many towns had mechanisms such as the periodic change of control between kinship groups which aimed, in part, at managing levels of violence. Such attempts at control over the 'reggimento urbano' regularly failed. A certain level of violence was tacitly accepted as a part of local politics but particularly vicious conflicts attracted attention from the Spanish regime and officials could be sent both to punish crimes but also to resettle the regulations and procedures of local governance in an attempt to avoid the 'inconveniences' of violence which were seen to be produced by some of them.

Both the fifteenth and sixteenth century saw extensive violence over control of municipal governments. As Gérard Delille has carefully reconstructed, these conflicts were one of the major reasons that central power intervened in the provinces.[46] Control over the economic privileges and prestige of community governance was often what was fought over in enmities. The capital, Naples, was unique in size and complexity. The provisioning of food was one of the main tasks of urban government. The growth of the city and the increasing number of resident aristocrats, with the urban clashes of pre-eminence that resulted, was a key problem. The town council, the Tribunal of San Lorenzo, was a corporate body formed out of the *seggi*, which were groupings of aristocratic families. By the time of Spanish rule the extant noble seats were the noble seats of Capuana, Nido, Montagna, Porto, and Portanova. When Charles V took Naples, he found that the patrician nobility had excluded the representatives of the non-noble element, the *popolo*, from government. The *eletto del popolo* was restored but remained exposed to control from the viceroy. Membership of a *seggio* was sought-after by aristocratic families. Many notable families existed 'fuori seggio'.

Central government in the Kingdom was divided. The viceroy was the representative of the Spanish monarch in Naples. Most viceroys were Spanish noblemen, who served for a period of around four years. Their court and the *segreterie* were important elements in administration. The viceroy, despite their prestige, was no absolute monarch; Naples was a kingdom and the Kings of Spain were Kings of Naples.[47] One of the viceroy's major tasks was as mediator within the nobility, especially the patrician nobility and other leading *fuori seggio* aristocrats. As the aristocracy could circumvent the viceroy as interlocuter with the crown, there was often delicate balances of power. The viceregal period also witnessed the growing power and influence of the ministerial elites, the *togati*, who staffed the great tribunals and councils of the Kingdom. For instance, viceroys were, often gratefully, guided by the advice of the experienced regents of the Collateral Council and the notarial and archival skills of the chancery. The Collateral Council, had a threefold duty as a consultative organ, deliberative body, and as chancery.[48] It was formed by the viceroy and five regents, but the viceroy was not always present at its sessions. The Collateral Council possessed a chancery (which became the main chancery of the Kingdom) a *segreteria*, and a tribunal. The viceroy could not issue executive acts without the approval of the Collateral. Beyond this, the power of these ministers was also great, due to their long experience compared to the comparatively short tenure of any individual viceroy.

The royal chancery of Naples was one of the major bureaucratic organs that dealt with incoming flows of information and that allowed for decisions to be disseminated. Every day two of the six *scrivani di mandamento* were to read memorials to the regents of the Collateral Council and to record the decrees, provisions and penal orders ordered by the regents.[49] The secretary of the kingdom processed all incoming relations from the *Audienze* and other royal ministers, and after consulting with the *regenti commissarii*, the orders would be formed in session of the Collateral Council, then stamped and registered in the chancery. Then, every Saturday afternoon, all orders would be sent out with the postmasters (*procacci*) of the realm.

The tribunals of the kingdom, most notably the *Gran Corte della Vicaria*, the *Sacro Regio Consiglio*, and the *Sommaria* made up the central organs of jurisdiction. The *Vicaria* was the main criminal and civil tribunal in the kingdom. The *Sommaria* was the chief financial tribunal. The *Sacro Regio Consiglio* was the highest appeal court whose decisions could not be appealed. In the provinces, royal authority was represented with a *regia audienza*, a provincial appeal court that also possessed military functions. Spanish troops were also stationed either permanently or periodically at fortified positions along the coastline and visited local communities as and when it was necessary to remedy situations of special disturbance.

For the Kingdom of Naples, the viceroy had to channel the desires and react to the commands of the Spanish Crown and the Council of Italy. On the fiscal ground, they had to place trust in tax farmers and financiers who tried to enrich themselves as far as possible. In terms of local order, they had to trust barons and other nobility who often trumpeted their – in fact highly contingent – fidelity; on royal agents who were immersed in local interest networks; from troops who had little interest in royal strategy and could join the outlaws they were meant to fight; and municipal or provincial officeholders who could have lost their fortunes or lives by complying too readily to royal decrees.[50] The jurisprudential elite, notably the regents of the Collateral Council and the other major ministers of the realm, had also to exercise power through these compromised and constantly negotiated systems and agents, which they were at the same time embedded within. For inhabitants of the Kingdom this set of personages, institutions, and interest groups felt like a labyrinth that was difficult and costly to navigate. Patronage, favour, or bribes were often indispensable in clearing a path in this institutional forest.

Historiography

Historians of Naples as a society and polity have often focused on lines of schism. Factionalism existed at many different levels, shaping the rhythms of local political projects. The overlapping struggles between viceroy and aristocracy, between the non-noble elite and the nobility, between the newly ennobled and those who claimed ancient blood, between the noble 'of the robe' and that 'of the sword', between the nobles aggregated to the *seggi* and those *fuori seggi*, between ecclesiastical and secular power, between city and province, have all been examined as important parts of the conflictual history of the Italian south.

Paolo Mattia Doria, an aristocrat, in the early eighteenth century composed his *Maxims of the Spanish Government*. This work was intended to reveal the reality of Spanish policy, which, he argued was best exposed through the ancient wisdom *Divide, et impera*. In Doria's telling, the Spanish 'sowed discord between the private nobility, and the Barons, between the superior and inferior Barons, between the people and the private nobility, between the *Popolo civile* and the *Popolo minuto*' and along with this introduction of refracted discord, they provided them with interests in maintaining Spanish dominion.[51] Modern historiography has found much to agree with this description of early modern Naples as a collection of conflicts, even if the exact role of the Spanish Empire in creating or intentionally promoting this situation is often debated. In Giulio Sodano's words, Naples was a 'heterogeneous and disaggregate society, perennially in conflict'. Rosario Villari's monumental study of Naples in the decades before the rebellion of 1647–48 emphasized the role of the preceding 'anarchy'. The rebellions of 1647–48 have been interpreted as the embodiment and apotheosis of this 'dialectic without synthesis' that characterized the history of the Kingdom.[52] The growing power of the ministerial elite (the *togati*), merchants and the wealthy financier class posed some challenge to traditional baronial power. But this new elite increasingly sought access to aristocratic identity through the purchase of feudal lands, due to the prestige and returns that feudal investment offered, enabled through the noteworthy openness of the feudal land market in the Kingdom.

Yet the potentially violent results of such social fragmentation remain only part of the story. Another part was the management of such conflicts through compromises, alliances, and pacts. The story of the negotiation between interest groups can be seen in a variety of ways. The first is how Spanish imperial policy has been characterized as seeking to manipulate rivalries or, in a more positive light, to promote equilibrium between different sectors of Neapolitan society. Studies of Spanish 'good government' have been fundamental to understandings of the ways in which Neapolitan society has been studied. An important example of such analyses is Aurelio Musi's account of how the 'rhythms of compromise between the interests of the monarchy and feudality were given cadence by certain political conjunctures'. He argues that the 'two parties proceeded … across adjustments, readjustments, restructurings of the system of alliance'. A shuttling between confrontation and settlement, underlined by a strong culture of rights, obligations and the recognition that *buone parole* were central to the smooth functioning of the political system.[53] The monarchic–feudal interaction is one of the major themes of Neapolitan history. Similarly, the growth of the *togati* in power and influence as opposed to the 'traditional' aristocracy. Case studies of other examples of equilibrium such as John Marino's study of the management of the *Dogana* have shown the significance of balance in favour of disruptive reform. For the state management of the *Dogana* 'was a problem of keeping the peace' and 'pastoral economics were subordinated to the politics of pacification, and rationalized by the ideology of the literary pastoral' which in Marino's account included keeping elites mollified, managing to feed the population and then taking money for the state from the rest.[54] Giuseppe Galasso, Antonio Calabria, John A. Marino, and others have explored the set of meanings around 'good government' as an idealization of balance and moderation.[55]

But how was this equilibrium put into practice in a society so riven by conflicts? This question is posed by John A. Marino in *Becoming Neapolitan* as: 'How did the early modern city hold together?'[56] Successive viceroys attempted to manage and juggle the various power blocs of the Kingdom with varying intentions and degrees of success. Increasing fiscal demands from the centre of the Spanish empire meant autonomy was given to powerful groups in Neapolitan society in return for their fiscal support.[57] Recent studies have shown how Spanish manipulation of ritual helped to incorporate the divided city into some sort of, often ephemeral, unity.[58] But to answer these questions about equilibrium and good government the politics and practice of pacification must also be reconstructed. In new approaches to these issues historians must consider the politics of communal life, crime, and the place of the judicial (and infra-judicial) system in early modern Naples.

Yet despite the extensive historiography of many aspects of Neapolitan history, in comparison to other parts of Italy the forms that these themes took on a face-to-face level remain quite obscure. In a recent companion to early modern Naples, Tommaso Astarita noted in particular the absence of a chapter on the history of crime and criminal justice. This was attributed to a comparative dearth of research.[59] One explanation for this is the destruction of the majority of the records of the main criminal court (as well as of many other collections), the Grand Court of the *Vicaria*, in the course of the Second World War. No obvious possibility exists for writing equivalent sorts of quantitative studies of crime that have been possible to write, for instance, regarding Bologna.[60] Similarly, work on particular events such as the important book on vendetta and factions in the Friuli by Edward Muir, *Mad Blood Stirring*, is also much rarer for the south of the peninsula.[61] Even putting aside the destructions of the Second World War, the practice of viceregal administration make certain inquiries into justice policy difficult; every viceroy had a secret archive that was kept under their jurisdiction in the viceregal palace and removed with them at the end of their tenure.[62] Nevertheless, recent decades have seen important investigation into aspects of crime, criminal justice, and the socio-cultural worlds revealed by trial documentation in the Kingdom, even if much remains to be done. For the most part these studies have been of ecclesiastical tribunals.[63] Through the usage of trial records previously unused in scholarship, the present book contributes to illuminating the social history revealed by criminal tribunals in early modern southern Italy.

The historiography of enmity and peace-making is also maturing with much profit, but with limited evidence on the southern Italian experience. It has now been well-established that, in Paolo Broggio's words, early modern Italy saw 'the omnipresence of hatred, of conflict, of enmity between lineages and factions, constitutes a fundamental part of the mechanisms of the management of local power (on the field above all of access to public offices) and of the relations between this and central power'.[64] In early modern Naples tackling enmities or containing the effects of such 'plagues of Cities' were major parts of the viceregal and feudal oversight of the villages, towns and cities of the Kingdom.[65]

As Craig Muldrew has written concerning early modern England: 'social conflict and the attempts made to prevent or limit it cannot be considered separately but need to be studied together as intertwined contrapuntal strands of social interaction, both of which constantly affect one another'.[66] This has been established most effectively by anthropologists and historians interested in 'the peace in the feud'; settlement was never simply the antithesis of vengeance.[67] In early modern Italy the making of peace between individuals was a regular practice. Peace-making was neither the sole province of clerics or laity. Injunctions for parish priests to settle enmities recur frequently in synods from the Kingdom.[68] Reconciliation could be arranged by the parties involved or coerced by a variety of officials.[69] Such reconciliations were often notarial or juridical instruments redacted with the help of a notary: forms of the *charta pacis* and similar instruments.[70] The variety of personnel involved also reflects that there was no single discourse of peace; it was a term with complex associations that could be used for different purposes by different people. Peace could signify the absence of conflict, the opposite of war.[71] Yet it also had the more positive meanings of Christian peace; the positive state of human relations offered by faith in God.[72] Similarly the idea of forgiveness – *perdonare* – combined its Christian significance with use in government and personal relations.[73] As Ottavia Niccoli has written acts of peace-making were 'judicial and political, religious and social'.[74]

Italy also possessed the most extensive European literature on peace-making, largely that of the *scienza cavalleresca*.[75] But as Paolo Broggio reminds us, discussion was not solely within the 'idea of nobility and the concept of honour'; the late sixteenth-century genre of works that discussed *paci privati* shows the inventive and exploratory uses that peace was put to in the early modern period. '[T]erms such as "amicizia", "inimicizia", "giustizia", "pace", "onore", "virtù", "quiete pubblica"' formed the conceptual universe of such tracts.[76] Enmity and peace-making were part of a whole array of thought about human nature and society.

A range of studies has introduced us to the histories of peace and peace-making in the medieval and early modern periods. In Italian scholarship, questions about enmity and peace have often been used to understand the development of central state institutions and their relations with communities.[77] Osvaldo Raggio's work on banditry showed how the *paci* made between the kinship groups of the Genoese hinterland created the bonds of solidarity between clans. According to Raggio, the 'political unity of the group of kinsmen was built ... above all on enmities, their settlements'. His investigation of the *paci* was framed as a study of 'the Genoese state as seen from Fontanabuona'.[78] Enmities and peaces in this perspective were raw materials of the social fabric and social sites that central states had to interact with if they wished to extend their authority. Considering how states engaged with the social reality of enmities has complicated the historical understanding of the relationship of centres with peripheries.[79] States arbitrated between factions as a way of increasing their control but this was often by presenting forms of oversight that were welcomed by communities rather than imposing social control.[80]

In British and American scholarship religion has been the main frame for thinking about peace-making. Historians have paid considerable attention to the large-scale preaching of peace and public reconciliations organized by notable Italian preachers such as the Franciscan Bernadino of Siena.[81] Most significant for the early modern period has been the path-breaking synthesis of John Bossy's 1995 Birkbeck lectures. These addressed the post-Reformation churches' engagement with the problem of enmity among their congregations. Bossy saw peace-making as a 'moral tradition' continued by post-Reformation strands of Christianity in varying different ways.[82] This tradition was the addressing of enmity in local communities through reconciliation as an act of charity to promote *pax* and avoid the damaging spiritual and physical results of communal hatred. Bossy argued that continuing this tradition was a key aspect of European churches' engagement with local communities. Like the Italian political history this approach stressed the agency of local communities and their desire for effective resolution, satisfaction and reconciliation. Religion is, of course, a vital field of symbolism that shaped peoples' experiences of interaction in fundamental ways but it did not stand apart from other aspects of society. Nor should it be assumed that religious understandings of peace necessarily dominated juridical or other conceptions.[83] An interest in revenge has also promoted the study of peace, especially for medieval historians.[84] The decline of feuding has often been traditionally mapped on to processes of state formation but recent accounts of the engagement of states with noble violence or provincial factions have complicated these narratives.[85]

A history of enmity and peace-making attuned to the emotions must combine the study of interior states with the way in which passions were represented to and interpreted by authorities; acts of expressing or describing emotions constitute a vital part of the story of the social interactions that spanned conflict and reconciliation.[86] The emotional should be united with the institutional. The history of enmity as a form of social relationship with affective dimensions is inseparable from histories of political and legal institutions, especially those of the viceregal regime, in the early modern period.[87] Love and hatred were intensely political words.[88] They were also deeply connected with cultural frames such as vendetta, faction, and the clan.[89] Love was a political language at the core of feudal relations and persisted in significance perhaps especially in Naples where vassalage to feudal lords and to the Spanish monarchs was the main model of political relationship.[90] It was precisely love and hatred that lay behind the more complex assemblages of enmity, amity, and peace.

Sources

The present work explores the themes of enmity, peace-making, and public order through different sources in order to investigate the social, legal, and emotional worlds connected to them. One body of sources drawn upon is documents produced by the central governing institutions of Naples: the viceroy and the Collateral Council. From the records of the Collateral Council, this work draws upon the collections *Notamenti* that record the discussions of the Collateral Council; incoming correspondence sent to them; the collection *Curiae* which records letters sent under viceregal authority to institutions, communities and personages; the collection *Consulte Originali*; the tribunal upon royal and ecclesiastical jurisdiction *Real Giurisdizione*. All of these furnish important evidence for understanding the view from the heights of the viceregal administration.

Such documentation is supplemented through correspondence from evidence from provincial tribunals and governors. The most extensive single collection of provincial trials analysed in this book is the collection of *processi criminali* produced by the *Regia Audienza* of Capitanata and the Molise. These provide an (at least) double perspective: one is on the event or events that led to the criminal investigation. People, places, and relationships come into focus through the investigations. In another way they reveal the perspective of royal provincial justice and administration, showing the primary manner in which the viceregal regime extended its power into the provinces of the Kingdom. The courts were for the most part engaged in an unending struggle against banditry. I consulted trials from the archepiscopal court of Conversano in the Terra di Bari.

Manuscript sources, both unpublished and published, provide useful supplementary context for these documents. Particularly for the city of Naples, a range of chronicles and journals have been consulted to add details from the perspective of diarists about events and trends in the city and Kingdom. Most utilized are those journals published under the rubric *Giornali di Napoli* in the early twentieth century. These are the journals written by 'Innocenzo Fuidoro' (an alias of Vincenzo d'Onofrio), Domenico Confuorto, and the French publisher Antonio Bulifon. In order to explore the connections between religious orders and local conflict, I have also consulted the records of the Jesuit province of Naples in Rome.

Outline of the work

The chapters, in part, move through the seventeenth century, combining both a chronological and thematic arc in the history of enmity.

The first chapter explores takes two different approaches, the first is a narrative of the politics of enmity from the Italian Wars to the Thirty Years' War. The second is a diachronic exploration of aristocratic violence across the seventeenth century. The two parts of this chapter combine to make a complimentary argument about the history of violence and enmity in the Kingdom of Naples: that is, that the damaging of trust, as Naples became a source of money and men for the Spanish war machine, contributed to an inability to combat the problem of elite violence.

The second chapter examines the relationship of justice and institutions to enmity. I argue that the interrelation between the practice of early modern justice and enmity was very strong. In particular, I look at the interrelation of justice with vendetta in the Kingdom of Naples. Special attention is paid to particular Neapolitan legal institutions and instruments which have not been studied, notably the remission of the offended party and the caution to not offend under the royal word. I explore the connection that early modern Neapolitans made between the nature of their justice system and the ubiquity of violence.

The third chapter focuses on the politics of enmity in the provinces of the Kingdom, with a focus on municipal and institutional politics. I argue that enmity was a primary analytical lens for local politics in the Kingdom of Naples and a form of political action. In particular, the chapter demonstrates the complexities of overlapping municipal, royal, ecclesiastical, and feudal sources of authority and explores how these influenced the politics of enmity.

The fourth chapter explores the characteristics and dynamics of banditry in the seventeenth century. I argue that enmities were central to the problem of banditry. Outlawing was connected to violence due to the previously discussed features of the justice system. In particular, I explore how bandit gangs formed around enmity as one of their major sources of solidarity.

The fifth chapter focuses on Jesuit peace-making missions and enmity. I argue that the Jesuit obsession with enmity and peace-making demonstrates the significance of this category in the history of early modern Kingdom of Naples. Further, I explore the emotional dynamics of enmity and peace-making revealed by the Jesuit sources. I argue that the Jesuit peace-making missions have not yet been understood in the light of the legal and juridical aspects of social conflict in the Kingdom of Naples.

The book ends with a chapter focusing on the rebellions of 1647–48 and its aftermath. I make the argument that the rebellions of 1647–48 can be best understood through the interpretive lens of the politics of enmity. This chapter uses all the previous themes explored to elucidate a particularly important event in the history of the Kingdom of Naples. In particular, it focuses on the events in the Terra di Bari in the aftermath of the rebellion to demonstrate how significant the politics of enmity and reconciliation were.

Any one of these chapters could have been expanded to make the subject of at least a monograph on its own. Therefore this book remains deficient as an extensive treatment of any of its constituent themes. Nonetheless, I hope there is a virtue in drawing these potentially separable topics together. One further limitation deserves direct address: the lack of extensive usage of sources held in Simancas. There would be much further research in Simancas and Naples possible for any of the topics discussed in this book. I focused rather on sources held in Naples and Puglia for this book and plans to extend this were cancelled due to the pandemic. Nonetheless, I hope the book's areas of incompleteness serve rather to signal how much more interesting research can be done on these themes.

When commentators talked about what made the Kingdom of Naples notable, the high incidence of banditry was often signalled. Across the Italian peninsula, and in other parts of Europe also, banditry was a significant social problem but perhaps nowhere else was it a problem of such intractable and endemic quality.[91] Bandits robbed on public roads, burnt crops and houses, kidnapped for ransom, murdered their enemies, could be mobilized as a resource in other private conflicts. When administrators of government discussed public order, banditry was the most salient element of dysfunction. New laws and modes of proceeding against bandits were promulgated with regularity, each new viceroy attempted to tackle the problem with varying levels of personal commitment. But the playbook of tactics and strategies used against bandits was relatively stale, irregular plumes of repressive action that left the social conditions unchanged, and the financing required to pursue repression effectively was lacking until late into the seventeenth century where the administration of the Marquess of Carpio (1683–87) saw major improvements. Clear, identifiable banditry shaded into a more general usage of armed militias in the Kingdom of Naples. Local notables, even bishops or archbishops, possessed gangs of armed men, who were often bandits or near indistinguishable from them.

In the Kingdom of Naples, from the capital to provincial towns and rural areas violent enmities remained strategies for status, emotional satisfaction, and material advancement throughout the seventeenth century. But this was not due to an absence of civic institutions; local political bodies and the broader legal system affected the choices and actions of women and men in the Kingdom. Feudal lords, bishops, and town councils were part of the same local systems of power relations. Rediscovering the vicissitudes yet continuing role of the communes provides a useful addition to seeing the south of Italy as lacking the civic heritage of the north.[92] Administration grappled directly with the sorts of hatreds that were at the same time part of social structures and emotional dispositions. One major way in which people talked about failed institutions or corrupt political processes was the propensity of the bad ordering of institutions to cause enmity. Social peace was also a product of well-ordered institutions. Passions were inseparable from political life.

The politics of enmity were central to the Kingdom of Naples. In the eyes of political authorities in the Spanish Empire, powerful individuals and groups often required reconciliation to avoid disruptions that threatened revenue or outraged royal authority. Enmities could create social capital to press claims for respectful treatment. Even those with lower social status, such as feudal vassals, could form groups who made their enmities potent vehicles for political or juridical claims. The *ancién regime* system of punitive repression was inseparable from these sorts of orchestrated truces and forgiveness. Enmities, therefore, were both phenomena of interpersonal relations and objects of governance or vehicles for grievance. They were narrations of complex relations between people, power, and institutions expressed through the language of the passions. Tracing the contours of this politics of enmity, reconciliation, and public order, as well as providing vivid details of cases of interpersonal hatred to fill in these contours, is the end of this project. The importance of negotiation and pacification to state authority and social relations in early modern Europe is a growing field of interest, there exists no work on southern Italy that investigates enmity and peace-making between people. Beyond simply adding this regional perspective, what follows argues that the politics of enmity is a major key to understanding the history of the Kingdom of Naples.

Notes

1 Archivio di Stato di Napoli (hereafter ASN), *Processi Antichi*, *Pandetta Nuovissima*, busta 1789, fasc. 50092.
2 The Bartilotti family held important titles and were connected to other major families. Their surname is recorded in a variety of forms in documents and subsequent works such as Bartirotti and Bertirotti, however it is clearly Bartilotti in the trial documentation. In 1580 they bought the feud of Castellaneta for 40,000 ducats and embedded themselves in the Neapolitan aristocracy. For this and the origins of the Bartilotti see Giovanni Brancaccio, '*Nazione genovese*': *consoli e colonia nella Napoli moderna* (Naples: Guida, 2001), p. 72 and Elena Papagna, *Sogni e bisogni di una famiglia aristocratica: i Caracciolo di Martina* (Milan: FrancoAngeli, 2002), p. 53. In 1601 Francesca Bartirotti dei Piccolomini d'Aragona, principessa of Castellaneta married Alessandro Mirabello, marchese of Delicto and Duke of Amalfi. Carlo's father Filippo Bartirotti Piccolomini, prince of Castellaneta married Maria Cito Moles d'Aragona and through her he became the prince of Presicce.
3 Archivio di Stato di Napoli, Processi Antichi, Pandetta Nuovissima, busta 1789, fasc. 50092, fol. 168^r.
4 Ibid. fol. 177^r.
5 Ibid., fol. 178^r: 'carcerata Maria Cisamoles sua madre in detta Città di Napoli, come simile inquisita nell'homicidio di detto D. Monaco'.
6 Ibid.: 'persequitandosi con la Corte l'una con l'altra di modo che fra loro inimicitia è stata nota a tutte le gente di questa Provincia'.
7 Ibid., 178^r.
8 Ibid., fol. 182^r.
9 Ibid., fols. 211^r–211^v: 'mi buttai piangendo'.
10 Ibid., fol. 213^r: 'essi vi era qualche inimicitia, et differenza … con li predetti D. Carlo Colitto, et altri prenominati di sopra il predetto principe mio marito, suo fratello, D. Andrea et tutta quella casa è stata sempre in pace e tenuto da veri et cari vassalli'.
11 Ibid. fol. 213^r.
12 Ibid., fol. 213^r: 'minestra attosiccata'.

13 Ibid.
14 Ibid., fol. 213^v: 'buon padrone'.
15 Ibid. fols. 336^r–337^v.
16 Ibid., fol. 213^v.
17 For this point see Tommaso Astarita, *Village Justice: Community, Family, and Popular Culture in Early Modern Italy* (Baltimore: Johns Hopkins University Press, 1999), p. xiv.
18 For this see Angelantonio Spagnoletti, 'Potere amministrativo ed élite nelle "università" del regno di Napoli (sec. XVI–XVII)', in *Congreso internacional espacios de poder: Cortes, ciudades y villas (s.XVI–XVIII)*, ed. by Jesús Bravo (Madrid: Universidad Autónoma, 2001), p. 78.
19 Regarding this topic in the Papal States during the late seventeenth century see Betrand Forclaz, 'Local Conflicts and Political Authorities in the Papal State in the Second Half of the Seventeenth Century', in *Empowering Interactions: Political Cultures and the Emergence of the State in Europe*, ed. by Willem Pieter Blockmans, André Holenstein, and Jon Mathieu (Farnham: Ashgate, 2009), p. 76.
20 Stuart Carroll, *Enmity and Violence in Early Modern Europe* (Cambridge: Cambridge University Press, 2023); Colin Rose, *A Renaissance of Violence: Homicide in Early Modern Italy* (Cambridge: Cambridge University Press, 2019); Krista J. Kesselring, *Making Murder Public: Homicide in Early Modern England* (Oxford: Oxford University Press, 2019) ; Caroline Dodds Pennock, Robert Antony, and Stuart Carroll, eds., *The Cambridge World History of Violence: Volume III 1500–1800CE* (Cambridge: Cambridge University Press, 2020).
21 John Bossy explored this issue in *Peace in the Post-Reformation* (Cambridge: Cambridge University Press, 1998), especially in the sections where he discusses the *pax* and *tranquillitas*, pp. 1–3.
22 For studies on factionalism in early modern Italy see Mathieu Caeser, ed., *Factional Struggles: Divided Elites in European Cities and Courts (1400–1750)* (Leiden: Brill, 2017) and Gèrard Delille, *La maire et le prieur: Pouvoir central et pouvoir local en Méditerranée occidentale (XVe–XVIIIe siècle)* (Paris: EHESS, 2003).
23 Ludovico Antonio Muratori, *Introduzione alle paci private* (Modena, 1708), pp. 82–3: 'Mio nemico eziandio si presumerà chi ha ucciso un mio parente, chi mi accusa d'un misfatto capitale, tende insidie alla vita, ritiene contra mia voglia in suo potere o la moglie, o le parenti mie, mi ha dette parole ingiuriose, o minacciato, o in altra guisa mal trattato, pratica spesso, e famigliarmente co'miei nemici, o è loro collegato, o è nemico di mio fratello, o de'miei congiunti, protesta che mi ha in odio, dice male delle azioni mie, mi toglie senza cagione una cosa a me dovuta, o fa altre simili cose denotanti mal'animo verso di me.'
24 Ibid., p. 83: 'presumeremo inimicizia fra due persone, quando non si rendono il saluto, si guardano di mal'occhio, fuggono il conversare, il ragionare, il mangiare insieme'.

25 Francesco Baronio, *De effectibus inimicitiae, seu de inimicitia eiusque causis, et effectibus* (Palermo, 1656), pp. i–ii: 'Tu etiam, Dux Excellentissime, si hoc volumen aliquando dignabere, legens quot effectus pariant Inimicitiae, eos veluti monstrosa hydrae capita, si forte repullulabunt, fortius ac maiori incensus gloria debellabis, ubi animadvertes quantam tibi laudem conciliaturus sis si ob publicae concordiae studium cum tam horribili, infensoque monstro, ex quo tot strages, tot excidia aggerantur, colluctabere.'

26 Ibid., p. v.

27 Ibid., p. 21.

28 For this see *Institutes* 1.25. 11; *Digest* 27.1. David F. Epstein, *Personal Enmity in Roman Politics, 218–43 BC* (London: Croom Helm, 1987), pp. 12–30.

29 Pietro Follerio, *Practica criminalis* (Leiden, 1556), p. 508.

30 Prospero Caravita, *Commentaria super ritibus Magna Curiae Vicariae Regni Neapolis* (Naples, 1601).

31 Simone Bagnati, *Vita del servo di Dio P. Francesco di Geronimo della Compagnia di Gesu* (Naples, 1705), p. 25: 'Alcune nimicizie si contraggono sotto specie di Giustizia; quando litigandosi ne'Tribunali per riaver il suo, l'interesse, che tanto predomina nell'Uomo, per lo piu traligna in odio'.

32 See Richard Kagan, *Lawsuits and Litigants in Castile, 1500–1700* (Chapel Hill: University of North Carolina Press, 1981), esp. pp. 3–20, 79–127.

33 Quoted and translated by Antonio Calabria, 'The South pays for the North: Financing the Thirty Years' War from Naples, 1622–1644', *Essays in Economic & Business History*, 20 (2002), 1–20 (p. 15).

34 Bossy, *Peace in the Post-Reformation*, p. 100.

35 These topics were explored in a range of genres from jurisprudence, reason of state, moral theology to the obvious candidate of the works concerned with *paci privati*. An overview of these discussions can be found in Paolo Broggio, 'Linguaggio religioso e disciplinamento nobiliare: Il "modo di ridurre a pace l'inimicitie private" nella trattatistica di età barocca', in *I Linguaggi del potere: Politica e religione nell'età barocca*, ed. by Francesca Cantù (Rome: Viella, 2009), pp. 275–317. For one example see Fabio Albergati, *Del modo di ridurre a pace le inimicitie private* (Bergamo, 1587), p. 5: 'che la Pace è una unione: onde quando due, che sono discordi, vengono à far pace, si sogliono toccar la mano, & abbraciarsi, e baciarsi, quasi volendo con questo dar segno, d'essersi uniti. Ma questa unione non basta a formar la pace, di che noi trattiamo; percioche sappiamo, che i cattivi molte volte s'uniscono, e tuttavia non hanno ver pace frà loro'.

36 On 'feud-like' behaviour see Paul R. Hyams, *Rancor and Reconciliation in Medieval England* (Ithaca: Cornell University Press, 2003), p. 7.

37 See Tommaso Campanella, *Del senso delle cose e della magia* (Soveria Mannelli: Rubbettino, 2003), for example, Chapter 13: 'Del senso delle pietre, e metalli: amicizia e nemicizia tra loro'.

38 Published in *Le Relazioni degli Ambasciatori Veneti al Senato*, ed. by Eugenio Alberì (Florence: Società Editrice Fiorentina, 1858), s. II, vol. V, p. 449: 'la natura inquieta di questi popoli, che anco ne'tempi più rimoti ha mostrato di

appetir sempre l'agitazione delle guerre civili e forestiere, ha dato in gran parte miserabil fomento a tante alterazioni e a tanti disordini'.
39 Ibid., pp. 449–50: 'questa mala disposizion di natura aggiunti poi gli umori pestilenti che di giorno in giorno si sono andati vie più accumulando in questo corpo sregolato, l'infermità si è fatta di maniera contagiosa che, se non disperata affatto, almeno pericolosa sempre è stata giudicata la cura sua; la quale, dopo tante altre nazioni, essendo oggidì caduta nella spagnuola, si vede chiaramente che con tutto l'aver estenuato e indebolito mostruosamnete questo corpo, ne vive con gelosia e con sospetto tale, che non assicurandosi di veder ogni membro e ogni spirito suo mortificato ed illanguidito, va tuttavia facendo quanto può perchè non riprenda forza, onde avesse a riescir poi, non che difficile, impossibile ogni medicamento'.
40 Raffaele Colapietra, *Vita pubblica e classi politiche del viceregno napoletano (1656–1734)* (Rome: Edizioni di storia e letteratura, 1961), p. 107.
41 See discussion in 'Introduction' Jennifer Selwyn, *A Paradise Inhabited by Devils: The Jesuits' Civilizing Mission in Early Modern Naples* (Aldershot: Palgrave, 2004).
42 For a statement of the situation see Stuart Carroll 'Revenge and Reconciliation in Early Modern Italy', *Past and Present* 233.1 (2016), 101–42.
43 For an overview of this situation see Gaetano Sabatini, 'Economy and Finance in Early Modern Naples', in *A Companion to Early Modern Naples*, ed. by Tommaso Astarita (Leiden: Brill, 2013), pp. 87–107.
44 Gérard Labrot, 'La città meridionale' in *Storia del mezzogiorno*, ed. by Giuseppe Galasso, vol VIII-1 (Rome: Editalia, 1994), p. 220.
45 This point is made very clear in Astarita, *Village Justice*.
46 Delille, *La maire et le prieur*.
47 Giuseppe Galasso made the point that historians need to be wary in calling the kingdom of Naples a *viceregno* in *Alla periferia dell'impero: il Regno di Napoli nel periodo spagnolo (sec. XVI–XVII)* (Turin: Giulio Einaudi, 1994), p. 15.
48 Aurelio Musi, *Mezzogiorno spagnolo: la via napoletana allo stato moderno* (Naples: Guida, 1991), p. 49.
49 ASN, *Consiglio Collaterale, Affari Diversi*, I, busta 1, f. 352r.
50 For further illustration on the dilemmas of early modern governance see Charles Tilly, 'Invisible Elbow', *Sociological Forum* 11 (1996), 589–601.
51 Paolo Mattia Doria, *Massime del governo spagnolo a Napoli* (Naples: Guida, 1973), p. 31.
52 John A. Marino, *Becoming Neapolitan: Citizen Culture in Baroque Naples* (Baltimore: Johns Hopkins University Press, 2011), p. 113.
53 Musi, *Mezzogiorno spagnolo*, p. 18: 'ritmi del compromesso di interessi fra Monarchia e feudalità sono scanditi da alcune congiunture politiche: quel che risulta con piena evidenza è il fatto che la linea di fondo non viene mai meno. I due soggetti procedono, piuttosto, attraverso aggiustamenti, riaggiustamenti, ristrutturazioni del sistema d'alleanze'.
54 John A. Marino, *Pastoral Economics in the Kingdom of Naples* (Baltimore: Johns Hopkins University Press, 1988), pp. 262–3.

55 Antonio Calabria and John A. Marino, eds., *Good Government in Spanish Naples* (New York: Peter Lang, 1990).
56 Marino, *Becoming Neapolitan*, p. 2.
57 Rosario Villari, *The Revolt of Naples* (Cambridge: Polity, 1993), p. 22.
58 Ibid.; Gabriel Guarino, *Representing the King's Splendour: Communication and Reception of Symbolic Forms of Power in Viceregal Naples* (Manchester: Manchester University Press, 2010); Carlos José Hernando Sánchez, 'Immagine e cerimonia: la corte vicereale di Napoli nella monarchia di Spagna', in *Cerimoniale del viceregno spagnolo e austriaco di Napoli: 1650–1717*, ed. by Attilio Antonelli (Soveria Mannelli: Rubbettino, 2012), pp. 37–80.
59 Tommaso Astarita, *A Companion to Early Modern Naples*, (Leiden: Brill, 2013), p. 6.
60 Rose, *A Renaissance of Violence*.
61 Edward Muir, *Mad Blood Stirring: Vendetta and Factions in Friuli during the Renaissance* (Baltimore: Johns Hopkins University Press, 1993).
62 Luigi Amabile, *Fra Tommaso Campanella ne'castelli di Napoli, in Roma ed in Parigi* (Naples: Cav. Antonio Morano, 1887), p. ix.
63 Important in this regard are: David Gentilcore, *From Bishop to Witch: The System of the Sacred in the Early Modern Terra d'Otranto* (Manchester: University of Manchester Press, 1992); Giovani Romeo, *Amori proibiti: I concubini tra Chiesa e Inquisizione* (Rome: Laterza, 2008); Jean-Michel Sallmann, *Chercheurs de trésors et jeteuses de sorts: La quête du surnaturel à Naples au XVIe siècle* (Paris: Aubier, 1986).
64 Broggio, 'Linguaggio religioso e disciplinamento nobiliare', pp. 289–90: 'l'omnipresenza dell'odio, del conflitto, dell'inimicizia tra lignaggi e fazioni, costiuisce un tratto fondamentale dei meccanismi di gestione del potere locale (sul terreno soprattutto dell'accesso alle cariche pubbliche) e dei rapporti tra quest'ultimo e il potere centrale'.
65 Geronimo Marciano, *Memorie historiche della Congregatione dell'Oratorio* (Naples, 1693), p. 407: 'l'invecchiate inimicitie, che sono le pesti delle Città'.
66 Craig Muldrew, 'The Culture of Reconciliation: Community and the Settlement of Economic Disputes in Early Modern England', *The Historical Journal*, 39 (1996), 915–42 (p. 918).
67 The anthropological insights of the first half of the twentieth century were brought to historians' attention most effectively by Max Gluckman, 'The Peace in the Feud', *Past and Present*, 8 (1955), 1–14.
68 Gaspar Cervantes de Gaeta, *Constitutioni Sinodali della Chiesa Metropolitana di Salerno* (Rome, 1568), pp. 25–6; Gabriele de Rosa, ed., *Clero e mondo rurale nel sinodo di Policastro del 1633* (Venosa: Edizioni Osanna Venosa, 1987), pp. 123–4; Pietro Ebner, *Chiesa, baroni e popolo nel Cilento*, 2 vols (Rome: Edizioni di storia e letteratura, 1982), I, pp. 192–4.
69 For discussion see Marco Bellabara, 'Pace pubblica e pace privata: linguaggi e istituzioni processuali nell'Italia moderna', in *Criminalità e giustizia in Germania e in Italia: pratiche giudiziarie e linguaggi giuridici tra tardo medioevo e prima età moderna/Kriminalität und Justiz in Deutschland und Italien: Rechtspraktiken und gerichtliche Diskurse in Spätmittelalter und*

Früher Neuzeit, ed. by Marco Bellabarba, Andrea Zorzi, and Gerd Schwerhoff (Bologna: Il Mulino, 2001), pp. 189–213.
70 These will be discussed at greater length in the next chapter. Yet see: Bellabarba, 'Pace pubblica e pace privata'; Rosa Maria Dessì, 'Pratiques de la parole de paix dans l'historie de l'Italie urbaine', in *Prêcher la paix et discipliner la société: Italie, France, Angleterre (XIIIe–XVe siècle)*, ed. by Rosa Maria Dessì (Turnhout: Brepols, 2005), pp. 245–78; Daniele Edigati, 'La pace nel processo criminale: il caso toscano in età moderna',in *Stringere la pace: teorie e pratiche della conciliazione nell'Europa moderna (secoli XV–XVIII)*, ed. by Paolo Broggio and Maria Pia Paoli (Rome: Viella, 2011), pp. 369–410; Ottavia Niccoli, 'Giustizia, pace, perdono: a proposito di un libro di John Bossy', *Storica*, 25–26 (2003), 195–207; Ottavia Niccoli, *Perdonare: idee, pratiche, rituali in Italia tra Cinque e Seicento* (Rome: Laterza, 2007); Ottavia Niccoli, 'Pratiche sociali di perdono nell'Italia della Controriforma' in *I linguaggi del potere: politica e religione nell'età barocca*, ed. by Francesca Cantù (Rome: Viella, 2009), pp. 249–73; Antonio Padoa-Schioppa, 'Delitto e pace privata nel pensiero dei legisti bolognesi: brevi note', *Studia Gratiana*, 20 (1976), 269–87; Carmelo Elio Tavilla, 'Paci, feudalità e pubblici poteri nell'esperienza del ducato estense (secc. XV–XVIII)', in *Duelli, faide e rappacificazioni: Elaborazioni concettuali, esperienze storiche: Atti del seminario di studi storici e girudici (Modena 14 gennaio 200)*, ed. by Marco Cavina (Milan: Giuffrè, 2001), pp. 285–318; Massimo Vallerani, *Medieval Public Justice*, trans. by Sarah Rubin Blanshei (Washington, DC: Catholic University of America Press, 2012), pp. 174–227.
71 On the range of meanings to the word peace see Maria Clara Rossi, 'Polisemia di un concetto: la pace nel basso medioevo. Note di lettura', in *La pace fra realtà e utopia* (Sommacampagna: Cierre, 2005), pp. 9–46; For a study of early modern British notions of peace see Phil Withington, 'The Semantics of "Peace" in Early Modern England', *Transactions of the Royal Historical Society*, 23 (2013), pp. 127–53.
72 Kiril Petkov, *The Kiss of Peace; Ritual, Self, and Society in the High and Late Medieval West* (Leiden: Brill, 2003), pp. 3–4.
73 Niccoli, *Perdonare*, pp. 4–7.
74 Ottavia Niccoli, 'Rinuncia, pace, perdono. Rituali di pacificazione nella prima età moderna', *Studi storici*, 40 (1999), 219–61 (p. 245): 'un atto insieme giudiziario e politico, religioso e sociale'.
75 On the European context of the *scienza cavalleresca* see Stuart Carroll, 'The Peace in the Feud in Sixteenth and Seventeenth-Century France', *Past & Present*, 178 (2003), 74–115. See also Claudio Donati, 'Scipione Maffei e la "Scienza chiamata cavalleresca": saggio sull'ideologia nobiliare al principio del settecento', *Rivista storica Italiana*, 90 (1978), 30–7; Francesco Erspamer, *La biblioteca di Don Ferrante: duello e onore nella cultura del cinquecento* (Rome: Bulzoni, 1982), pp. 56–7, 69–73.
76 Broggio, 'Linguaggio religioso e disciplinamento nobiliare', p. 290: 'Termini come "amicizia", "inimicizia", "giustizia", "pace", "onore", "virtù", "quiete pubblica", si rincorrono e si collegano gli uni con gli altri in modo talmente inestricabile da impedire di qualificare questo tipo di trattatistica semplicemente

come uno sviluppo della scienza cavalleresca, rappresentando invece un interessantissimo esempio di come la scienza giuridica abbia potuto fondersi ed integrarsi con la trattatistica sulla Ragio di Stato e con la teologia morale'.

77 For a very useful account of this tendency see Marco Cavarzere, 'At the Crossroads of Feud and Law: Settling Disputes in Early Modern Tuscany'.
78 Osvaldo Raggio, *Faide e Parentele: Lo stato Genovese visto dalla Fontanabuona* (Turin: Einaudi, 1990), p. 176.
79 For some examples see: Andrea Zorzi, *La transformazione di un quadro politico: ricerche su politica e giustizia a Firenze dal comune allo Stato territoriale* (Florence: Firenze University Press, 2008), p. 130; Marco Bellabarba, *La giustizia ai confini: Il principato vescovile di Trento agli inizi dell'età moderna* (Bologna: Il Mulino, 1996); Marco Dedola, '"Tener Pistoia con le parti"': Governo fiorentino e fazioni pistoiesi all'inizio del '500', *Ricerche storiche*, 22 (1992), 239–59.
80 Osvaldo Raggio, 'La politica della parentela: conflitti locali e commissari in Liguria orientale (secoli XVI–XVII)', *Quaderni storici*, 21 (1986), 721–57.
81 Cynthia Polecritti, *Preaching Peace in Renaissance Italy: Bernardino of Siena and His Audience* (Washington, DC: Catholic University of America Press, 2000).
82 Bossy, *Peace in the Post-Reformation*, p. 100.
83 See Lucien Faggion, 'La pacificazione e il notaio nel vicariato di Valdagno nel secondo Cinquecento', *Acta histriae*, 21 (2013), 93–106 (pp. 102–3).
84 Hyams, *Rancor and Reconciliation in Medieval England*; Thomas Benedict Lambet and David W. Rollason, *Peace and Protection in the Middle Ages* (Durham: Durham University, 2009); see the essays in Susanna A. Throop and Paul R. Hyams, eds., *Vengeance in the Middle Ages: Emotion, Religion and Feud* (Farnham: Ashgate, 2010).
85 Stuart Carroll, *Blood and Violence in Early Modern France* (Oxford: Oxford University Press, 2006), p. 4.
86 On the expression of emotions as a form of social interaction see Barbara Rosenwein, 'Problems and Methods in the History of Emotions', *Passions in Context*, 1 (2010), 1–32 (pp. 19–20).
87 On the emotions in institutional history see Victor Morgan, 'A Ceremonious Society: An Aspect of Institutional Power in Early Modern Norwich', in *Institutional Culture in Early Modern Society*, ed. by Anne Goldgar and Robert I. Frost (Leiden: Brill, 2004), p. 134–5.
88 John Bossy, 'Postscript', in *Dispute and Settlements: Law and Human Relations in the West*, ed. by John Bossy (Cambridge: Cambridge University Press, 1983), pp. 287–94.
89 See the work of Edward Muir, such as *Mad Blood Stirring*.
90 Ibid, pp. 293–4.
91 For banditry in Sicily see Bruno Pomara Saverino, *Bandolerismo, violencia y justicia en la Sicilia Barroca* (Madrid: Fundación Española de Historia Moderna, 2011).
92 Edward Muir, 'The Sources of Civil Society in Italy', *Journal of Interdisciplinary History*, 29 (1999), 379–406.

1

Contours of vendetta and violence in the Kingdom of Naples

The ubiquity of violence in sixteenth- and seventeenth-century Italy became a commonplace for foreign visitors. Travellers regularly noted the frequency of murders and the widespread sensitivity to insult that preceded them. One particularly extensive account of this is found in the impressions of the naturalist John Ray (1627–1705) who noted that the Italians suffered from the vice of revenge, writing:

> *Revenge*; they thinking it an ignoble and unmanly thing to put up or pass any injury or affront. Many times also they dissemble or conceal their displeasure and hatred under a pretence of friendship, that they more easily revenge themselves of whom they hate by poisoning, assassinating or any other way; for nothing will satisfie them but the death of those who have injured them: and there be *Bravo's* and cut-throats ready to murther any man for a small piece of money. Besides, which is worst of all, they are implacable, and by no means to be trusted when they say they pardon. Hence they have a proverb among them, *Amicitie reconciliate & minestre riscaldate non furono mai grate*. The women also provoke their children to revenge the death of their fathers by shewing them the weapons wherewith they were murthered, or cloths dipt in their blood or the like, by which means feuds between families are maintaeined and entail'd from generation to generation.[1]

Revenge was not simply a personal inclination, but a matter of inheritance. Other observers of Italy noted the high incidence of violence, George Sandys (1578–1644) recounted that in Sicily 'in their private revenges, no night passe without murder'.[2] It was during the early modern period when accounts of this nation's tendency towards revenge, explaining the high levels of homicide in Italy, entered into the realm of stereotype.[3]

Travellers found that both violence and associated measures to avoid it, affected life in Italy. Guides and language books for travellers at times noted the need to travel with the *procaccio* – postal messengers who travelled with armed horsemen – to avoid the violence of bandits.[4] John Ray also noted, from experience, that it was troublesome to travel with firearms in Italy, because you had to deposit them at city gates, which 'is done to prevent assaults and murthers, which are so frequent in many Cities of Italy'.[5] Fear of becoming victim to acts of violence upon both city streets and while navigating rural provinces affected visitors to the peninsula. Certain figures emblematic of the culture of violence, such as the Italian bandit and the bravo, became figures of European fame by the end of the seventeenth century. The growing fever for the duel in the cities of sixteenth-century Italy was also noted as the continent-wide obsession for Italian fashions increased.

Modern scholarship has confirmed the bulk of the reality of these impressions: many parts of Italy had extremely high levels of violence in this period.[6] The ease in which both minor slights and major offences could spark attacks with blades or firearms, thereby increasing their deadly consequences above fist-fights, marked early modern Italy out. The craze for duelling was only one part of a much broader spectrum of violent encounter.[7] Levels of social tension were markedly high and often resulted in bloody tit-for-tat killings. Nor was this marginal violence: the most dangerous occupation or social identity in many places was being a noble or an office-holder.

The new scholarship on violence in Italy, and Europe more generally, then shows that high levels of interpersonal violence were by no means unique to the south. Nonetheless by the late sixteenth century *vendetta* was remarked by commentators as especially fierce in the south, leading to bloody consequences. A devotion to violence was attributed to the Neapolitan aristocracy who held a notably wide notion of kin obligation to revenge. The use of violence to pursue disputes was common, ranging over a variety of types of conflict, including offended honour of person or clan, clashes over jurisdictions, tumults over benefices, quarrels over borders and many other types of dispute, as well as convoluted admixtures of offence. Violence was therefore part of the practice of politics in general and was also incorporated in various schemes aimed at profit and enrichment.

Some of the specifically troublesome nature of the Kingdom of Naples filtered into European consciousness: by the end of the seventeenth century, it was not simply the Italian bandit that had become famous across Europe but especially the Calabrian bandit. George Sandys travelled by boat along the coast of Calabria, to avoid robbery and murder from the outlaws, sleeping on land below the forts and watch-towers that dotted the coast of the Kingdom of Naples and guarded against Turkish incursions.[8] The Scot William Lithgow (c.1582–c.1645), on the other hand, claimed to have made friends and broken bread with Calabrian bandits.[9]

Violence remained a serious problem in Naples in the second half of the seventeenth century when some other polities managed to tamp down rates of extreme violence reasonably well, whether through the explicit efforts of authorities or other sources of social peace. This is crucial as the deviation between north and south does not appear to be the result of the renaissance but in diverse experiences of the period approximately between 1580 and 1650. When John Evelyn arrived in Genoa in the 1640s he recorded witnessing 'the sudden and devilish passion of a seaman' when another seaman managed to cut in front of the first to collect Evelyn and his colleagues. The first seaman put his finger in his mouth and 'almost bit it off by the joynt, shewing it to his antagonist as an assurance to him of some bloudy revenge if ever he came neere that part of the harbour again'. Whether or not this expressive insult really connected to violence is difficult to assay, but it illustrates Evelyn's expectations, who follows this anecdote with the claim that 'this beautifull City is more stayn'd with horrid acts of revenge and murthers than any one place in Europ, or haply in the world, where there is a political government, which makes it unsafe to strangers'. A few decades later, around 1670, the merchant and politician Slingsby Bethel (1617–97) argued that the stories still circulating about the violence and disorder of the republic of Genoa were false and referred to a time now past. He criticized claims of tens of thousands of outlaws led by aristocrats in the hills of Liguria, arguing that he had travelled extensively and met no such people. Similarly, the streets at night in Genoa itself were always safe: 'nor while I staid in Genoua, which was several Weeks, did I hear of one Murther, nor found cause to forbear in the darkest Nights walking the streets'.[10]

As Bethel reminds us, scholarly questions regarding violence cannot be satisfied solely from the impressions of travellers. From research in criminal archives, we have learnt that high levels of violence did exist but such rates were neither permanent nor the same across the peninsula. For much of the Italian peninsula, the level of fatal violence between males in the second half of the seventeenth century was low in comparison to the preceding decades. This is a lesson, if any were needed, that essentializing stereotypes of Italian character from these centuries do little to explain rates of violence; rather, the quotidian frequency of violence was a historical product.

Factors that historians have identified as contributors to high levels of violence were especially pronounced for the Kingdom of Naples. These include a state with low levels of public legitimacy, especially as regards the judicial officers and tribunals; an aristocracy (or rather a range of overlapping aristocratic elite groups) who reviled submitting themselves to ministerial power and preferred violent self-help; an effectively privatized legal system due to feudal jurisdiction which made enforcing fair standards of justice difficult, as it required huge investments of resources to pursue unjust feudal lords in law courts; a rumbling consistent struggle between ecclesiastical and royal jurisdiction that both caused violence and provided ways for the violent to flee punishment; the military needs of the Spanish crown meant that often impunity was provided in exchange for money or service;

widespread blades and firearms, as well as a notable amount of men who would perform violence for cash. Together these factors produced almost infinite clashes of privilege and jurisdiction as well as the armed men ready to pursue or escalate such strife through violence.

The absence of continuous series of criminal trials for the central tribunals of the Kingdom of Naples means that early modern southern Italian homicide rates are very difficult to quantify. During the Second World War, the collections of the Archivio di Stato di Napoli, evacuated from the centre of the city, were vandalized by Nazi soldiers. A grenade lit a fire that damaged, among other holdings, the collections of the most important central criminal court, the *Vicaria*, leaving only discontinuous records. In the provinces, many tribunals' records do not survive and those that do were drastically reduced by Napoleonic-era purges, when all trials where a death penalty was not issued were destroyed. Therefore, it is very difficult to attain a clear sense of the full business of any tribunal of royal justice in the Kingdom of Naples over any extensive period of time. Moreover, the records of the feudal courts (under which the vast majority of the *regnicoli* lived) have very limited rates of survival, probably due to their relative uselessness to the interests that underpinned familial archives. Most that do survive are to be found as copies sent to other courts or institutions.

Nevertheless, some impressions can be provided. The notary Donato Antonio Cortellisi recorded that Novi suffered 400 homicides in only four years in the 1610s.[11] In 1619 a single man in Trani was said to have committed sixteen homicides in the preceding years.[12] In 1621 accusations reached the tribunal of *real giurisdizione* that one Marino Crapuccio was guilty of: the murder a servant of the court of Aquila; the homicide of a soldier of the *Regia Audienza* of Chieti; the homicide of one Pietro Petrucci with a stiletto; the fatal wounding with an arquebus of Giuseppe Volpetta; stabbing the priest Camillo Cesare six times; the stabbing of the priest Scipione Morello; the beating of a soldier of the *Commissario dei contrabbandi*; escaping from the Bishop's prisons with others; and the rape of a female shopkeeper in Aquila.[13] Murderers could rely on seeking asylum in churches, and evade capture through instrumentalizing the jealousy of ecclesiastical jurisdiction.

The chronicles and governing records of Naples support the notion of a violent society. Civil conflict was multipolar and complex, involving feudal, municipal, ecclesiastical, and royal fields, which created an environment of litigious and highly emotional conflicts ready to shift into violence. Within this jurisdictional environment, strategies for success and enrichment on the behalf of families and individuals also provoked conflict. The extensive presence of bandits, *bravi*, or any other type of armed muscle also increased the violent consequences of dispute, as did the flooding of the

Kingdom with firearms and deadly rapiers particularly from the mid-sixteenth century on.

This chapter takes two paths to trace the contours of violence and enmity in the early modern Kingdom of Naples: the first is to provide a diachronic account of the political factors in the history of enmity up to the eve of 1647, emphasizing the significance of the provisioning of the Thirty Years' War as a factor that exacerbated violence; the second is a synchronic account of the major outlines of forms of violence in the seventeenth century, with a major focus on the role of the aristocracy as a force provoking violence that influenced all levels of society and that was a major target for legislation and other forms of policy.

The Neapolitan history of enmity from the Italian Wars to the eve of the revolt

The history of Naples, for some investigators of history in the sixteenth and seventeenth centuries, provided evidence that the *regnicoli*, the inhabitants of the Kingdom, were by their nature rebellious. A report by a Venetian agent stated that

> between all the varied and marvelous examples of *mutazioni* of state and of governments, that in histories are variously shown, those of the regular and turbulent revolutions of the Kingdom of Naples, seem to me, without compare, and may be the most conspicuous, the most stupendous that are perhaps available to consider.

This was explained by 'the restless nature of these peoples, that also in the most distant times have shown to hunger consistently for the agitation of civil and foreign wars, has given in large part woeful fomentation to many revolutions [*alterazioni*] and disorders'.[14]

One historical explanation for the high rate of violence in early modern Italy is social instability following the Italian Wars (1494–1559) of the late fifteenth and sixteenth centuries. In this interpretation, the military campaigns across the peninsula did not result in a new stable political order. Rather they produced longstanding enmities that smouldered even during periods of truce. Such explanations are well-suited to the Neapolitan case as Spanish rule over Naples emerged out of these bloody conflicts. During the intermittent conflict of the Italian Wars, France and Spain both haggled and fought over the twelve provinces that constituted the Kingdom, even considering a division of the Kingdom, which Machiavelli identified as a ruinous misstep for the French king. While Spain would in fact hold Naples for two centuries, this seemed far from a foregone outcome. Upon Philip II's death in 1599 the persistence of Spanish rule for a further century was not an obvious assumption.

In the wake of the Italian Wars, the establishment and development of the Habsburg viceroyalty led to a number of contests and abandoned reforms that left fertile ground for violence. Most notable was the unfinished, and in fact reversed, war against aristocratic prepotency. Charles V had moved with reasonable vigour against baronial power, particularly through the anti-feudal policy of Pedro Álvarez de Toledo y Zúñiga (1484–1553), viceroy from 1532 until his death in 1553. Toledo was an austere and imposing personage, a fitting figure for the Neapolitan execution of the general policy of states towards harsher justice and firmer rule in the first half of the sixteenth century. He was notably disliked by many of the high Neapolitan baronage for his haughty manner and his disdain towards the sort of familiar intimacy which the nobles believed they deserved.

One of the priorities of Toledo's agenda in the 1530s was to eliminate abuses from the judicial system.[15] In the search after this goal, he issued numerous ordinances. Toledo centralized the tribunals of the Kingdom into the Castel Capuano. Part of the rationale for the judicial reforms was to gain control over the high baronage through severe punishments and to whittle down opportunities for escape through bribery. For instance, he ordered that houses that received bandits and other criminals were to be torn down.

A proportion of the baronage was in a weak position under Charles V and Toledo; Lautrec's ill-fated expedition of 1528, in which he died, had exposed many pro-French barons who had been executed, exiled, or impoverished. A signal example of his severity was the exile and confiscation of lands of the Prince Ferdinando Sanseverino. Confiscated goods and property from rebels as well as sums charged for rehabilitation formed a notable part of the royal income in the 1530s. Yet Toledo's attempts at imperial control met with resistance and some failures. Most notable was the opposition to the introduction of a Spanish Inquisition, that is, one controlled by royal (rather than episcopal) authority. In 1547 riots against such an introduction were one sign of increasing resentment against Don Pedro.

After Toledo the baronage did not suffer in silence: some sought to loosen the strictures they felt had been placed upon them. In 1554, later expanded in 1558, Giulio Cesare Caracciolo's *Discorso sopra il regno di Napoli* presented the grievances of the aristocracy in the aftermath of Toledo's death. Caracciolo lamented that 'there were more nobles tortured in the city of Naples and the whole Kingdom, than for thousands of miles around.' This had led the nobility to 'stay peaceful' because they hoped to regain what they had lost. When the aristocracy 'suffered with displeasure being put down by the hand they hoped would raise them up' dissatisfaction spread and Caracciolo, without explicitly endorsing the claim, wrote that he could understood why someone had spoken of 'bad government'.[16] Caracciolo felt that the Neapolitan baronage was victimized in favour of new classes of men who had been grovelingly loyal to the viceroy. He praised the former viceroys – such as Ramon de Cardona (1505–07) and Charles de Lannoy (1522–27) – who regularly visited the principal nobility and treated them as near equals with 'paternal love'. An unpresumptuous intimacy with the nobility marked good government for him; he drew particular attention to Lannoy's presence at the baptism of Vincenzo Coscia.[17] But in the intervening decades Toledo surrounded himself in pomp and presumed to be above the aristocracy and 'to dress themselves in the garb of supreme lords'.[18]

In part Caracciolo pointed the finger at the rise of the *togati* at this time. The ministerial elite, often from non-noble or minor noble origin and among whom were many Spaniards, came to be crucial tools for the Spanish viceroyalty. The *scientia juris* became a cornerstone of the governance of the Kingdom. The roles of the traditional nobility in the high councils and offices of the Kingdom were marginalized in favour of this rapidly expanding class of experts, some of whom (although by no means all) originated from non-noble or newly noble backgrounds. By 1566 the seven offices of the Kingdom, the traditional offices of authority, could be said to only consist of 'the naked titles', denuded of tangible executive power which now rather lodged with the ministers of the councils and tribunals of the Kingdom.[19] Within the governing councils of the Kingdom, the role for the traditional nobility of the sword was excluded in favour of those with judicial training.

It would be mistaken to characterize the Kingdom of Naples under the authority of Charles V, mediated through Toledo, as a golden age of civil peace. Civil unrest and violence were part of this post-conflict society, as in much of Italy in this time. Nor was Charles V personally as steadfastly opposed to all demands of the aristocracy as could be deduced from Caracciolo's lament. But there was vigorous reform and advocacy for the *popolo* role in civic government of the capital city that would later diminish. The decades after Charles V ceded rule of the Kingdom to his son saw a lack of interest in root-and-branch judicial reform and a subsequent erosion of civil trust among those who felt injustice thereby increased.

An ever-growing source of pressure was the demand that the Kingdom provide financial support for imperial warfare. This created incentives to both sell off the royal demesne and, at the same time, to attempt to win the favour of the traditional aristocracy. The Neapolitan parliament, which voted to approve the crucial special taxes known as *donativi*, was formed by the patrician nobility of Naples in their institutional groupings known as *seggi*. The nobility of the *seggi* thereby retained notable power in issues of the Kingdom's finances that hampered attempts to restrain their excesses, even where there were initiatives to remove the *seggi*'s claimed authority to

Figure 1.1 Portrait of Pedro de Toledo from Domenico Antonio Parrino, *Teatro eroico, e politico de'governi de'vicere del Regno di Napoli* (Naples, 1692). Biblioteca Nacional De España.

be equal to royal power.[20] The patricians of Naples were jealous of their prerogatives and refused most attempts to allow new families to aggregate. However, outside of this patriciate there was a vast transformation of the aristocracy in this period as feudal states were subdivided, and most significantly, royal lands were parcelled off and sold as fiefs.[21] This ballooning of the number of feudal lands also created a challenge for the decorum of justice: hundreds of royal courts became feudal courts.

The turn of the sixteenth to the seventeenth century was a time of considerable upheaval.[22] Fear of Ottoman conquest remained present and raids on coastal settlements continued. The strategic role of Naples in the Spanish Mediterranean theatre in these decades grew as the Ottomans or a Franco-Ottoman alliance threatened the Kingdom. The notable fortification and militarization of the kingdom, the building of forts and billeting of Spanish troops across the provinces, were reactions to these fears over the instability of rule.[23]

The viceroyalty of the Duke of Osuna, Pedro Téllez Girón, from 1617 to 1620 was a striking example of the pitfalls of governing the city and Kingdom of Naples in this period. A veteran of the wars of the Low Countries, Osuna came to Naples in his early forties as a former viceroy of Sicily, already wearing the Golden Fleece. One of the major initiatives that the aristocracy and others objected to most fiercely was the lodging of a huge force of soldiers across the Kingdom as part of the war between Spain and Savoy, part of the struggle with Venice. The Medici agent in Naples reported great suffering across the Kingdom from this large force of over 15,000 infantry who committed 'enormous barbarities'.[24] As well as carrying out unpopular imperial policy, Osuna was accused of having extravagant notions about the reach of his power as viceroy of Naples. It was said that he wanted to transform the capital city and Kingdom into a dynamic imperial base from whence unlikely schemes such as the taking of Constantinople, the invasion of Albania and the conquest of Jerusalem could be achieved. Contemporary accounts also charged Osuna with an obsession for the pursuit of justice following his own mind and not in accordance with the customs and privileges of the Kingdom or the style of their tribunals. Commentators claimed that summary punishments which scandalized the Neapolitans were common as well as huge monetary settlements.[25]

Finally, he was accused of having sought to conquer the Kingdom in his own right and was removed from office. The years of Osuna demonstrated the growing significance of the re-intensifying struggle over the control of Italy in the domestic politics of the Kingdom. In the conspiratorial and paranoid politics of the early seventeenth century, Naples came into focus as a potential leverage point in geopolitical struggle. When the English traveller James Howell arrived to Naples in 1621, the 'hot' nature of the Neapolitans (as well as their dedication to pleasure) was one of the first things he reported upon. It was for this reason that he said the King of Spain spent huge amounts of money on keeping the Kingdom full of both infantry and cavalry. Howell explained that the king did this 'to keep this voluptuous people in aw; for the Story musters up seven and twenty famous Rebellions of the *Neapolitans* in lesse than 300 yeers: But now they pay soundly for it, for one shall hear them groan up and down under the *Spanish* yoak'.[26]

The early years of the 1620s witnessed escalating cycles of violence. Riots over the lack of bread in the capital city occurred in 1622.[27] The worsening situation of the 1620s can be summarized by a single attempt to regulate those seeking revenge against their enemies in a viceregal pragmatic of 1624 under the title of *De offendentibus innoxium pro noxio*.[28] It began by outlining how the Viceroy and Collateral Council had been receiving reports of people 'sometimes avenging offenses, and enmities in the person of the father, son, brother, or relative of their principal enemy'. This was a type of vendetta: 'that lies beyond all human reason and is the action of an infamous and traitorous sort of man'.[29]

Two cross-cutting trends existed in the first half of the seventeenth century. On the one hand, viceroys sought to expand authority in the face of the violence of the capital and the provinces. On the other, any effective dispensation of this task was undercut by growing demands for fiscal contributions. It was only from arranging pacts and compromises with the aristocracy that such contributions could be found. It was Philip IV who, with the exigencies imposed by the Thirty Years' War, allowed any hope of profound reform of the Neapolitan aristocracy to disappear. With the pressing need for funding, Philip IV prioritized the demands of the patrician nobility of Naples over the *popolo civile* for greater representation. Not only was the aristocracy key to providing extraordinary taxation through the parliament of Naples but they were also invaluable in providing the regiments they commanded to serve in the war. Similarly, the ability to purchase a feudal title was an enticing option for anyone who had made a fortune in the Kingdom.

The unprecedented fiscal demands of the 1630s precipitated crisis. A range of new impositions were placed on the Kingdom. The Medici agent resident noted that in 1634 'they study every invention to extract money and men'.[30] The capital city with its privileges was able to escape many of the taxes imposed, inflicting the burden unequally and more on the provinces than the Kingdom which further immiserated them at the same time as various economic activities were declining either relatively or absolutely. For instance, export volumes of important commodities such as Calabrian silk were diminishing.[31] The search for money and manpower stretched all aspects of the Neapolitan state and would continue until the application of a tax on fruit became the final straw and precipitated the riots that would become the rebellions of 1647–48.

One of the most important moments in this history of economic and political discontent was the parliament of 1642, which would be the last general parliament.[32] There had been considerable aristocratic opposition to the 'fiscalism' of the Spanish monarchy in the 1630s, with many important figures opposed to it. Yet by 1642 many had defected to approving the demands of the crown, including Tiberio Carafa, the prince of Bisignano.[33] The viceroy used money and powerful figures to importune wavering aristocrats. The city exploded with *cartelli di sfida*, written challenges, and duels over the issue were threatened.[34]

The viceroys tasked with governing Naples in these years often had a difficult reality to confront. They generally held tenures of only a few years. Pressed from Madrid to provide vast sums of cash and looking in despair at the budgets, they were forced into compromise and hemmed in by restive interest groups. The nobility could protest and trouble a viceroy. In this situation, the pre-eminence of the *togati*, the ministerial elite, was a comforting option to rest upon. Drawing close to ministerial power allowed access to decades of experience, the wisdom and ingenuity proffered by the priests of the law. It, however, could close opportunities to innovate. The typical viceroy was a grandee of Spain who had no experience of the hard facts of Neapolitan politics and little appetite to shipwreck their career on these shoals. Nor did they have official precedence in some matters: the viceroy was not legally able to overrule the *Consiglio Collaterale* in the normal proceedings of justice. The vote of the regents of the *Collaterale* together could overrule that of the viceroy. Although this does not preclude attempts by viceroys to influence the appointment of regents and the pressures felt by regents to have good relations with viceroys.

Viceroys also lacked many of the carrot-and-stick tools common to early modern government. They lacked their own choice in, for instance, which officials to appoint, the administration of sales of offices, ecclesiastical appointments of more than 100 ducats value, and the approval of feudal sales. All these were dispensed from Madrid by the King (in consultation with the Council of Italy).[35] Radical solutions to Naples' political problems, such as the wholescale expropriation or rights-stripping of feudal landowners, were well outside the sphere of action of a viceroy. However, while the statutory reality was stark and hemmed in, in the practical business of intervention, the viceroy maintained options and tools of personal involvement.

Constraints on viceregal power made the politics of grace an even more important tool. While ministerial predominance made the claim of the viceroy to be the *alter ego* of the Spanish sovereign weak beyond the ritual stage, they did retain powers of grace. The viceroy's personal capacity to dispense grace to prisoners was part of a regular round of visitations. The incumbent viceroy would visit the prisons of Naples on Epiphany, Easter, and Pentecost. Equally, a viceroy's arrival and departure provided opportune moments. Like in many other states, Naples demonstrated its loyalty to the Spanish Empire by celebrating royal births, marriages, and deaths. Viceroys expressed frustration at the level of conflict in Neapolitan society. The Count of Medina wrote that 'this Kingdom is so addicted to lawsuits that its inhabitants would rather do without ordinary sustenance than court cases'.[36]

Naples in the period before the rebellion of 1647–48 appeared to many commentators as held in check only by the thousands of Spanish troops that occupied the city. At the same time, the Spanish were extracting vast amounts from the Kingdom. The transformation of the aristocracy was one factor that appeared to well-informed visitors as spreading potential unrest. George Sandys wrote 'townes and cities are subject unto Nobles of sundry titles, ... who as they increase in number, decrease in authority: for that many of them have beene bought by men of base condition; and many of the ancient have exhausted their patrimonies'.[37] From 1590 to 1675 the titled baronage increased from 118 to 434.[38] Sandys argued that 'they have lost their stings: and desperate of their liberty, nourish in their breasts an hatred, which they dare not express, much lesse put into action; having no likelihood of forreine assistance; all the Princes of *Italy* being either in perfect amity with the *Spaniard* or awed by his greatenesse'.[39] The Kingdom of Naples, emerging under Spanish rule from the Italian Wars, shared with the rest of Italy a difficult return to social peace. The 'Spanish yoke', promoted factionalism either intentionally or unintentionally through money-raising endeavours that damaged the institutions of the Kingdom.[40] By the outbreak of the Thirty Years' War, feelings of injustice were spread widely but often difficult to express clearly. The history of homicide teaches us that crises of legitimacy in polities can spread vengeance and other forms of disruptive social conflict.

Contours of vendetta in the Kingdom of Naples

One of the most critical contributing social elements to high levels of violence in the Kingdom of Naples was the aristocracy. Clashes did not only occur between nobles, but also their followers and servants. Moreover, such clashes were, along with banditry, the most significant form of violence in the eyes of the Spanish regime. Therefore, their enmities were of particular significance. The city of Naples particularly saw violence emanating from clashes between aristocrats and their adherents on the streets. Feudal lords increasingly made their residence, at least part of the year, in the capital. The standard view has been that the effect of the 'barons in the city' was not that residence in the city civilized them but rather that they imported destructive aspects of provincial life into the capital. In Angelantonio Spagnoletti's view, the feudal aristocracy, transferred into Naples, did not become courtly nobles but 'often persisted in styles of life and of social relations that expressed all the arrogance and brutality of feudal lords'.[41] The Neapolitan aristocracy never laid down arms in the seventeenth century. But whether this is best understood as an importation of rural violence into the city is less clear; it could have been that the close quarters nature of urban life promoted violence. Seventeenth-century chronicles testify to very high levels of all sorts of violence throughout the seventeenth century. The Collateral Council was very much preoccupied with the best ways to pacify nobles in conflict and whether it was judicious to punish them.

A Tuscan agent wrote to Florence, commenting on how in the restive parliament year of 1642 the viceroy, the Duke of Medina, ordered many aristocrats to remain in their homes, that '[b]ecause here custom holds [*corre usanza*] that relatives to the fourth degree are obliged to defend their relatives; for this, the cavaliers are divided in to many factions, they declare themselves to favour one or the other party, following their kinship'.[42] Injuries done to a single member were held to offend entire kinship assemblages.[43] The obligations of kinship and the complex ties between various aristocratic families led to enmities that became cooperative activities and unfolded over years.[44]

Outside of formal or semi-formal duels, Neapolitan nobles were often ready to draw their swords and fight. When nobles gathered in large numbers the risk of a perceived slight or a shove meant violence or its threat could ensue; there is considerable evidence of others restraining those who drew swords. The numerous theatres, many of which were private performances in noble palaces, were also flashpoints for violence. In 1636 the prince of Forino (a Caracciolo of the *Rossi* branch) was killed just after a performance of a comedy at the palazzo where the viceroy was staying on the riviera of Posillipo.[45]

After the death of the prince of Forino, his widow Marzia Carafa took her sons to live with her father Eligio Carafa as she had 'contracted a serious enmity' with her sister-in-law and her three wild brothers-in-law Tommaso, Giuseppe, and Annibale Caracciolo.[46] The enmity led to the murder of a servant of Tommaso which Capecelatro reported was held to be 'the work of don Ferrante Caracciolo, son of the prince of Santa Buono, and joined by blood with the house of Forino, at the insistence of Marzia Carafa'.[47] This reveals the ways in which bonds of interest and kinship were vital. Enmities could emerge from within the intricacies of making kin and the shared lives which such alliances created for noble families; the various branches of the Caracciolo were not simply on the same side. There were twenty-nine families belonging to the Caracciolo clan.

The next act of violence was the wounding of Giacomo Galeota who, as Capecelatro relates, despite being a close relative of the Caraccioli adhered to Marzia's side in the enmity. Capecelatro's account of the growth of the enmity is useful to cite in full:

> every day the evil hunger amongst them swelled, as often happens between blood kin, there was no lack of wicked people that, spending time with one of those involved, reported back what one had said about the other, continuously sowing new seeds of discord, it happened that, as Tommaso and Annibale returned to their palazzo from the *ostello reale*, where a comedy had been put on, and such spectacles having always been unlucky for this family, around four hours after dark ... they were attacked by some hired thugs called *Taglialatela* of Giugliano.

These hired killers shot at the brothers. Tommaso escaped into the darkness of the night while Annibale was mortally wounded: 'he died wretchedly to the great anguish of his mother, who had loved him tenderly'.[48] Gossip promoted dissension and, when combined with the obligations of the *cavalleresca* way of life, could lead to deaths.

Assassination was a strategy used by some of the aristocracy and others in the pursuit of personal enmity. In 1632, the young Prince of Conca, Matteo di Capua, one of the wealthiest noblemen in the Kingdom was arrested after a Spanish soldier admitted that he had been hired by the prince to shoot a prostitute.[49] His imprisonment in a single room in the Castel'Nuovo with just one servant was viewed as far too harsh by many nobles who begged the viceroy to release him into more fitting surroundings, offering an immense security of 200,000 ducats.[50] Rumour held that the viceroy's choice of incarceration was due to a 'private vendetta, more than for rigour of justice'.[51]

The use of paid assassins was common, one such 'public assassin' was named by Francesco Capecelatro as Tiberio Gallo who had received, so it was said, a lot of money for the murder of Annibale Caracciolo.[52] Francesco d'Aragona, son of the Duke of Terranova, was stabbed to death by an assassin procured by the marchese of Gerace outside the Theatine Church of the Apostles as he stepped down from a carriage.[53] The Duke of Andria was killed in October 1655 'for a certain dispute he had with the nephew of the count of Castriglio [the viceroy]' by a group of Spanish assassins.[54] In the various chronicles of Naples, jealousy lay behind many assassinations.

The noble family known as the house of Conversano, the Acquaviva d'Aragona, can be taken as a case study in the spectrum of aristocratic violence. Across the sixteenth, seventeenth, and eighteenth centuries its members were involved in duels as well as many other forms of violence.[55] A mass battle occurred in October 1630 between some of the Caracciolo and the Acquaviva outside of San Pietro a Majella in the heart of the old city.[56] When the *sbirri* arrived most combatants fled to the Church of Sant'Antonio di Padua.[57] In 1649, outside of the monastery of San Francesco di Paola in Bitonto, Cosimo Acquaviva, the Duke of Noci, duelled with the Duke of Andria. They were accompanied by 'padrini' – duelling assistants – Tommaso and Diego Acquaviva for Noci and the Duke of Gravina and Gisoldo Pappacoda for Andria. Cosimo and Tommaso's father Giangirolamo II (a man with around 80,000 vassals) was exiled in Spain in 1644–45 for violence committed against his vassals and despite a period of bloody fighting for the Spanish during 1647–48 he was again exiled in 1652.[58] In 1665 Cosimo Acquaviva was killed in a duel by the Duke of Martina Petraccone Caracciolo; this was another outbreak of enmity that had spurred the mass brawl thirty-five years earlier.[59] Giangirolamo III took over the feudal possessions until he died in 1681. In 1671 Don Giulio II Acquaviva d'Aragona assaulted the palace of the Duke of Noia don Giovanni Carafa with hundreds of men.[60] After the events of 1671, a deep feud boiled between the Carafa di Noia and the Acquaviva. The viceroy issued a licence for the Countess of Conversano to travel with guardsmen with firearms, directly because of the 'enmity of the Duke of Martina' which had killed her husband six years before, as Petraccone Caracciolo had been acting as the Duke of Martina's stand-in.[61] After some public clashes she was advised to return to her feudal city of Conversano where she could be better guarded from the risks of the enmity. The following year the enmity came to a head with a duel to the death: Giulio Acquaviva duelled Francesco Carafa in Nuremberg, the only place where they could arrange a safe field of battle. After this ended with no clear winner, they reconciled. Giulio would die imprisoned on Nisida in 1691, accused of having tried to bring plague into Puglia.[62]

It is necessary to look beyond the aristocrats themselves to understand their enmities. The locations of noble residence were often in the old centre of the city, where constricted roads full of people and high *palazzi* exacerbated problems of passage. The challenges of such urban movement created occasions for momentary anger to spark noble resentment. In July 1679 a carriage struck a Spanish standard bearer, who proceeded to punch the coachman of a passing marchese. As it was outside the viceregal palace, the marchese was apparently unable to react. But, spying where he lived, the marchese followed him home and hit him with his scabbarded sword. The coachman was of an 'vile spirit' and thus not worthy of an undrawn sword. This was not a costless action for the marchese, who presented himself to be imprisoned in the Castel Nuovo. The standard bearer and his three brothers all lost their rights to continue as standard-bearers.[63] In another instance, a coachman who had fled inside a church to resist arrest was forcibly removed on the orders of the pro-regent of the *Vicaria*, Don Fernando Moscoso, whose guards beat up the coachmen and cut off his hair with knives, then allowed him to return to his asylum.[64]

Coachmen [*cocchieri*], footmen [*staffieri*], standard-bearers [*alfieri*] and other sorts of livery-wearers were regular participants in brawls and altercations that could easily slip into more serious conflicts. Retinues were a major problem both in the capital city and the provinces. It was very common for Neapolitan aristocrats to have scores of liveried men in their service. Clashes between these retinues was a major source of violence. In some cases they were intentionally used as proxy combatants and at other times unintended fights became more serious because they represented the honour of the livery they wore.[65] The diarist Vincenzo d'Onofrio hated coachmen as the source of many conflicts. Discussing one misdemeanour committed by a coachman he wrote:

> [o]ne cannot deny that this doglike race are encouraged and egged-on by their patrons, because he was the coachmen of the duke of Isola Bonita, *avvocato-fiscale* of the Camera, he was very presumptuous, and it's certain that it would take a gallows in every neighbourhood for all the coachmen, since they give off outward luxury for patrons for just 7 ducats a month, dressed in fine cloth, brocaded jackets; and there's more than one of them, that stinks of villainy, and yet they have protection.[66]

This harsh judgement also reminds us that service and connections to *padroni* show how the 'houses' of nobility had influences that reached out much further than their noble members; it was not only wide notions of kinship but clientage that mattered in explaining the extent of violence. These men in the service of nobles – and not only the traditional aristocracy, but also those ministers who enthusiastically adopted the trappings of the nobility – also present two related combinations of place and politics: the first, encounters upon the street, the second, the noble household and its networks. The collection of servants and retinues was a central part of noble life. These sorts of networks are hard to reconstruct but they were one of the most significant aspects of life in the capital. It is precisely the numbers of people involved in noble households that means that studying the nobility is not only the study of a small social elite but also how their systems of protection or solidarity stretched across society. Because of their place as rulers of households, aristocratic violence was rarely individual.

As well as servants who had legitimate occupations the Neapolitan nobility also gathered men of violence into their service precisely for their physical force. Some families were more renowned than others for this practice. As d'Onofrio remarked in June 1660 in response to a murder among the servants of the Caracciolo 'this House has always nourished these sorts of *facinorosi* men'.[67] These men were often very close to outlaws in character, the *bravi* that caused so much violence in many Italian cities. Aurelio Lepre has described the transformation from a 'commercial' and 'artisanal' city in the mid-fifteenth century to one of a more 'residential' character.[68] The search for ties of dependence was one of the main goals of the arriving provincial migrant. In a fragmented society the search for 'aggregation', as Aurelio Lepre described, was the goal: to belong to a guild with social support or to join a lord's service.[69] As the population of Naples boomed, it was increasingly a city full of newcomers from the provinces. The noble households offered a very visible and extensive source of employment and protection in part precisely because of the significance of enmities in noble society.

Vendetta was by no means the sole reserve of the traditional aristocracy, although they were crucial to its widespread significance. There is evidence for violence driven by enmity at all social levels. In 1623 the wool-worker Giulio Volano attacked a colleague named Giovanni Russo. A witness in the trial carried about by the officials of the Wool Guild said that Giovanni's mother had warned him: 'don't go out, because your enemy Giulio is passing by here'.[70] He left anyway and was hit over the head and fell to the ground. They were enemies and 'treated each other as such' because they were involved with the same woman, named Vittoria. Referring to street life in the city of Naples, a law of 1583 noted that during the night, after the bells of San Lorenzo, a church and the seat of the municipal government, had rung, armed men tended to go around singing and playing instruments. From this behaviour 'various brawls, duels and other crimes are caused, but also they create hatreds and enmities; from which other crimes may occur in the future'.[71] While we may doubt the exact truth of the assumptions underpinning such restrictive legislation on merry-making, violence explained by enmity was a common occurrence.

Violence in the provinces

Patricians or other men who sought to extend their authority often used intimidation and physical force to do so. Even some archbishops and bishops used organized gangs to protect their jurisdictions or, perhaps, to extend their power illicitly. For example, in May 1617 the Archbishop of Rossano, led a group of around one hundred armed priests and laymen to respond to an uprising of Albanians in the Calabrian town.[72] In 1628 the Bishop of Isernia, Diego Merino, personally killed a representative of the government of the city of Isernia, Troiano Drago, in the piazza of the city.[73]

The spread of firearms at all social levels meant that confrontations could easily end in death.

Crucial in the history of violence in early modern Naples, at least according to many contemporaries, was the ability for offenders to use the system of pardoning and forgiveness to escape harsh punishments. It was argued that getting away with only monetary penalties for bloody crimes spurred them on. I do not dwell on this vital point here, as this will be explored at length in the next chapter. Another key element in prolonging hostilities was the ability for offenders to seek refuge in churches. Asylum played a key role in how murders played out. After committing an act of violence, an offender could flee into a Church and from there negotiate with various jurisdictional authorities to escape from the rigors of justice. Violence often spread to sacred ground too, even churches were arenas of violent murders.

Violence was profoundly connected to enmity. It was as part of private enmities that a vast range of violence occurred. Moreover, enmity was strongly connected to mobility. People left towns because of the risks of their enmities; in 1666 Giovan Paolo di Giovanpaolo and his uncle Domenico Antonio claimed the hatred that the marchese di Ripa bore them made them abandon Ripalimosani.[74] Enmities were one of the most noteworthy subjects for public gossip and a closely observed part of village and neighbourhood life.

As a variety of historical and anthropological literature teaches us, where feuding exists: peace-making also plays a major role. The judicial investigations into the wounding and subsequent death of Tommaso Naclerio by a man called Baldassare Giannetto in 1608 reveals an unusual perspective on personal peace-making.[75] Tommaso was attacked as he attempted to make peace between two men named Giuseppe Donato and Giovan Battista Florente. The crime occurred in Giuseppe's house and workshop in the centre of Naples. Witnesses did not know precisely why Giuseppe and Giovan Battista were out of friendship; one neighbour talked vaguely of an 'injury' given by Giuseppe to Giovan Battista.[76] The peace-making was not a brief reconciliation but seems to have involved a good deal of negotiation. To solve this dispute Tommaso spent large amounts of time with both of the parties including a day and night inside the house of Giuseppe. Giuseppe offered Giovan Battista one of his daughters to seal the peace. But Giovan Battista was said to be unwilling to accept her because their reputations were marred by the notorious intimacy they held with Baldassare.[77] Baldassare, in turn, was denied his usual access to the household and, observing how Tommaso was welcomed in at all hours, was said to have become deeply jealous.[78] Baldassare was also apparently greatly offended by Giovan Battista's unwillingness to provide him with one of his daughters as a wife. He attacked Tommaso and left him bleeding from his head.

Another act of peace-making that only reaches us due to its failure to go to plan is that between Nicol'Angelo Lucente and Angelo Valentino of the small town of Turi in the Terra di Bari, which was investigated in a trial in 1675.[79] Angelo Valentino came often to discuss magic with Angelo and his wife Veronica. But he spent more time with Veronica, often without her husband present. Soon, Nicol'Angelo said, the talk of the piazza was that these visits 'were without end and offended my honour'.[80] He claimed to have asked Angelo 'civilly' to stop making such visits that harmed both of their reputations.[81] Nicol'Angelo is silent on whether these visits occurred in his absence or if there was any intimacy between his wife and Angelo. But after Angelo's refusal to stop visiting, Nicol'Angelo declared him an enemy and denied him entry. Soon afterwards Veronica fell ill.[82] One of her friends, Vittoria de Tonno, told Nicol'Angelo that Angelo had bewitched Veronica, 'which he's done from hatred'.[83] Nicol'Angelo explained that 'because I wanted to avoid scandal from the people, who had very publicly spread around this enmity of mine' he arranged Angelo to arrive under the cover of darkness, 'to the great harm of my reputation'.[84] By going back on a declaration of hatred he seemed to hint that he was cuckolding himself anew in the eyes of the community. But during this nighttime visit he planned to make peace with Angelo so that he would cure his wife. Nicol'Angelo only denounced Angelo to the episcopal court of Conversano after the reconciliatory visit ended in failure; the risky gambit had failed, Angelo had refused to be pacified, his wife was not cured and his honour freshly damaged.[85] The concern for reputation and privacy in this pacification is notable. As with Tommaso Naclerio's death the issue revolved around access to domestic space. Public peace was a watchword in early modern Italy but many people wished to keep their reconciliations and their enmities away from the talk of the piazza.

In 1704 Andrea Zeolo murdered his brother Giuseppe.[86] He stabbed his sibling to death while they laboured on their land in a place known as the little wood [*la Selvitella*]. This lay just outside their village, Santa Croce di Morcone, which sat on one side of the valley of the river Tamaro, opposite the town of Morcone in northwestern Puglia. Officials sent by the *Regia Audienza* in Lucera interrogated the villagers and they quickly established that there had been a 'past enmity' between the brothers.[87]

The first witness interrogated by the *Audienza* claimed to know many of the details of the internal tensions of the Zeolo family. Andrea and his wife Isabella Capozzo, his mother, his father, his brothers Giuseppe and Francesco and their respective wives Vittoria Damiano and Vittoria Zeolo all lived under the same roof. Households in Santa Croce di Morcone were multigenerational, which was common in certain regions of the Kingdom.[88] The wives of the sons joined the household of the patriarch at marriage. This witness recounted that Andrea's parents showed more affection to the said Isabella than to Vittoria Damiano wife of the said Giuseppe, and to Vittoria Zeolo wife of Francesco Zeolo their other son, and this was because Isabella was the most recent arrival in their home, and she had a large dowry, and also because the same occupied herself with the care of her very elderly mother-in-law, who was almost always on her sick-bed.[89]

Vittoria was 'envious of all of this' and she made it known that she believed the rule of the house should be hers as she had joined it first.[90] In these conversations Vittoria was said to have both belittled her husband for accepting the unequal state of affairs and she was reported to have repeated 'evil things' in his ears.[91]

It was allegedly this offended wife who by constantly uttering such malign words reduced her husband to a state of unnatural hatred for his kin.[92] A relative who laboured with Andrea noted that in the past Andrea had loved Giuseppe 'like a true brother' but 'he gathered such hatred towards him that he no longer wanted to work with me in the vineyard and territories that he had gained through the dowry of his wife, notwithstanding that they lived communally and undivided in a single house'.[93] His brother Giuseppe bore the brunt of his anger. This shattering of a communal life of a household and the upset of natural fidelity was a shocking case. The fraternal bond was supposed to be strong but the practices of working the field together, of sharing various forms of agricultural labour, formed no bulwarks against rivalry and, instead, provoked it further.[94]

In front of representatives of the court, family members and other witnesses recounted details of the aftermath. The father of the brothers, Daniele Zeolo, wept over his son's corpse and walked around shouting: 'Justice, justice!'[95] Other family members who heard the claims that Andrea had murdered his brother said they reacted with disbelief. His uncle, Giulio Zeolo, testified that 'it seems to me a difficult thing to believe, that for such an unimportant reason … one brother would have killed the other'.[96] Other family members were less astounded and they cited longstanding problems with Andrea's temperament. Whereas Giuseppe was a good man, who never said a bad word, Andrea was 'disobedient, and wicked.'[97] Vittoria Zeolo believed the reports straight away because Andrea 'gave himself willingly to such excesses'. Fratricide was the culmination of his misdeeds.

Yet despite his apparently loathsome character and the blood on his hands Andrea Zeolo was forgiven. Through a legal instrument in which his father forgave the homicide they reached an accord. This was redacted with the words that: 'having today resolved to live in a Christian manner and to follow the rules of our sovereign monarch and to do what the Christian law imposes upon us and amongst other things it tells us to pardon offences and so that peace can be embraced … spontaneously and not for force or fear ... I remit, annul and void the aforesaid complaint'.[98] The obligations of kinship were rebuilt and, by consequence, a community's rupture healed.

The contours of violence in early modern Naples were deeply connected to the social role of the aristocracy and the exigencies of the Spanish war machine set many of the rhythms of conflict that would play out in the mid-century crisis. Enmities fed on the wider political situation and the tensions caused by the need to raise money and manpower for the imperial centre. Both aristocratic ways of life and disputes over the political identity of the aristocracy created occasions for conflict which in the 1620s and 1630s seem to have intensified the level of violence in the capital city. In the context of the need for constant flows of profit to the imperial centre, the general prized goal of early modern politics of equilibrium became of even greater import in the Kingdom of Naples. Settlement and re-establishment of equilibrium was the solution for nearly any dispute involving the powerful. One major field for how this developed in practical terms was the law: the next chapter tackles this subject.

Notes

1 John Ray, *Travels Through the Low-Countries, Germany, Italy, France with curious observations natural, topographical, moral, physiological*, vol 1 (London, 1738), p. 342.
2 George Sandys, *A Relation of a Journey Begun Anno Domini 1610* (London, 1615), p. 245.
3 I here intend nation to refer to the contemporary early modern concept, see for instance the preface to Thomas Wright's *Passions of the Minde in Generall* (London, 1604) for discussion of the Italians as a nation with particular emotional tendencies and proficiencies.
4 Giovanni Torriano, *The Italian Reviv'd* (London, 1673), p. 192.
5 Ray, *Travels*, p. 344.
6 Colin Rose, *A Renaissance of Violence: Homicide in Early Modern Italy* (Cambridge: Cambridge University Press, 2019); Stuart Carroll, *Enmity and Violence in Early Modern Europe* (Cambridge: Cambridge University Press, 2023), I note that the present book was in large part completed when this work was published, hence a thoroughgoing engagement with its content has not been possible.
7 Stuart Carrol, 'Revenge and Reconciliation in Early Modern Italy', *Past & Present*, 233.1 (2016), 101–42.
8 Sandys, *A Relation of a Journey*, p. 250.
9 William Lithgow, *Nineteen Years Travels Through the Most Eminent Places in the Habitable World* (London, 1682), pp. 337–38.
10 Slingsby Bethel, *The Interest of the Princes and States of Europe* (London, 1694), p. 237.

11 Pietro Ebner, *Storia di un feudo del Mezzogiorno: La Baronia di Novi* (Rome: Edizioni di Storia e Letteratura, 2004), p. 176: 'poichè da 4 anni in qua solamente sono successi da 400 homicidij commessi con tanto imperio che non vi ha parso segno di giustizia'.
12 ASN, Delegazione della real giurisdizione, Processi, busta 184, fasc. 9, fol. 51^r.
13 Ibid., busta 187, fasc. 13.
14 Published in *Le relazioni degli ambasciatori veneti al senato*, ed. by Eugenio Alberì (Florence: Società editrice fiorentina, 1858), s. II vol. V, p. 449: 'Tra tutti gli esempi delle varie e maravigliose mutazioni di stati e di governi, che dall'istorie ci sono diversamente rappresentati, quelli delle spesse e turbolenti rivoluzioni del regno di Napoli parmi che, senza comparzione alcuna, siano i più cospicui, i più stupendi che si offrano forse a considerare; perciocchè la natura inquieta di questi popoli, che anco ne'tempi più rimoti ha mostrato di appetir sempre l'agitazione delle guerre civili e forestiere, ha dato in gran parte miserabil fomento a tante alterazioni e a tanti disordini, di quanti la maggior parte di Europa, e in particolare la propria Italia, può con le fresche cicatrici ancora far chiaro e lagrimevole testimonio. A questa mala disposizion di natura aggiunti poi gli umori pestilenti che di giorno in giorno si sono andati vie più accumulando in questo corpo sregolato, l'infermità si è fatta di maniera contagiosa che, se non disperata affatto, almeno pericolosa sempre è stata giudicata la cura sua; la quale, dopo tante altre nazioni, essendo oggidì caduta nella spagnuola, si vede chiaramente che con tutto l'aver estenuato e indebolito mostruosamnete questo corpo, ne vive con gelosia e con sospetto tale, che non assicurandosi di veder ogni membro e ogni spirito suo mortificato ed illanguidito, va tuttavia facendo quanto può perchè non riprenda forza, onde avesse a riescir poi, non che difficile, impossibile ogni medicamento.'
15 Guido d'Agostino, *La capitale ambigua: Napoli dal 1458 al 1580* (Naples: Guida, 1979), p. 195.
16 Raffaele Ajello, *Una società anomala: il programma e la sconfitta della nobiltà napoletana in due memoriali cinquecenteschi* (Naples: Edizioni scientifiche italiane, 1996), p. 286: 'sono stati tormentati piú nobili nella città di Napoli et in tutto il Regno, che da mille addietro. Questo ha causato che quelli del Regno che con le nuove signorie hanno speranza di racquistar il perduto, con sdegno se ne ricordano, et quelli che con la presente stanno quieti, e che sono li piú, con impatientia soffrono d'esser abbassati dalla mano onde speravano d'esser inalzati, et cosí, con commune mala sodisfatione, di facile è successo che, dove uno licentiosamente ha parlato del mal reggimento.'
17 Ibid., p. 416.
18 Ibid.: 'a vestirsi gli abiti dei supremi padroni'.
19 Giovanni Tarcagnota, *Del sito, et lodi della città di Napoli con una breve historia de gli re suoi, e delle cose piu degne altrove ne'medesimi tempi avenute di Giovanni Tarchagnota di Gaeta* (Naples, 1566), p. 20.
20 Angelantonio Spagnoletti, 'The Naples Elite Between City and Kingdom', in *A Companion to Early Modern Naples*, ed. by Tommaso Astarita (Leiden: Brill, 2013), p. 205.

21 Rosario Villari, *The Revolt of Naples* (Cambridge: Polity, 1993), ch. 5.
22 For the still majorly important reconstruction of *fin-de-siècle* anarchy see Villari's *The Revolt of Naples*.
23 For the fortification of the Kingdom see Giovanni Muto, 'Strategie e Strutture del Controllo Militare del Territorio nel Regno di Napoli nel Cinquecento', in *Guerra y Sociedad en la monarquía hispánica: política, estrategia y cultura en la Europa moderna (1500–1700)*, ed. by Enrique García Hernán and Davide Maffi (Madrid: Laberinto, 2006), pp. 153–70; Achille Mauro, *Le fortificazioni nel Regno di Napoli* (Naples: Giannini Editore, 1998).
24 Francesco Palermo, ed., *Narrazioni e documenti sulla storia di Napoli dall'anno 1522 al 1667* (Florence: Gio. Pietro Viesseux, 1846), IX, p. 278.
25 Ibid, p. 285.
26 James Howell, *Epistolae Ho-Elianae: Familiar Letters Domestic and Forren; Divided into sundry SECTIONS, Partly Historicall, Politicall, Philosophicall upon Emergent Occasions* (1655), vol. II, p. 65.
27 Palermo, *Narrazioni e documenti*, p. 238.
28 For subsequent discussion of this pragmatic by jurists see Tommaso Briganti, ed., *Pratica criminale raccolta dal dottor Tommaso Briganti* (Naples, 1842), I, p. 275. This pragmatic became the foundation for the later doctrine that one who murdered a relation of someone who had offended them ('trasversale vendetta') was guilty of an aggravated homicide. See Niccola Nicolini, *Quistioni di dritto* (Naples: Tipografia Salita, 1839), IV, p. 315.
29 Lorenzo Giustiniani (ed.), *Nuova collezione delle prammatiche del Regno di Napoli* (Naples, 1803), VIII, p. 145: 'trasversale fuora d'ogni humana ragione, & azzione d'huomo traditore, & infame'.
30 Palermo, *Narrazioni e documenti*, p. 310.
31 Antonio Calabria, *The Cost of Empire: The Finances of the Kingdom of Naples in the Time of Spanish Rule* (Cambridge: Cambridge University Press, 1991), p. 22.
32 See Giuseppe Carignani, 'L'ultimo Parlamento generale del regno di Napoli nel 1642', *ASPN*, 8 (1883), 34–57 and Guido D'Agostino, *L'ultimo parlamento generale del regno di Napoli nell'età spagnolo* (Naples: La Valle del Tempo, 2022).
33 Pier Luigi Rovito, *Il viceregno spagnolo di Napoli: ordinamento, istituzioni, culture di governo* (Naples: Arte Tipografica, 2003), p. 250.
34 Ibid, p. 252.
35 Villari, *The Revolt of Naples*, p. 10.
36 Quoted and translated by Antonio Calabria, 'The South Pays for the North: Financing the Thirty Years' War from Naples, 1622–1644', *Essays in Economic & Business History*, 20 (2002), 1–20 (p. 15).
37 Sandys, *A Relation of a Journey*, p. 201.
38 Villari, *The Revolt of Naples*, p. 119.
39 Sandys, *A Relation of a Journey*, p. 258.
40 On the divide and rule see Rovito, *Il viceregno spagnolo di Napoli*, pp. 144–5.

41 Angelantonio Spagnoletti, 'The Naples Elite Between City and Kingdom', in *A Companion to Early Modern Naples*, ed. by Tommaso Astarita (Leiden: Brill, 2013), p. 199.

42 Palermo, *Narrazioni e documenti*, p. 325: 'Perchè qui corre usanza che i parenti sino in quarto grado son obbligati a difendere i parenti; per questo, divisisi questi cavalieri in molte fazioni, si sono dichiarati a favore dell'una e dell'altra parte, secondo la parentela; e S. E. ha fatto fare a tutti mandato di non partirsi di casa. Di Napoli, 7 Ottobre 1642'.

43 See Marco Antonio Savelli, *Pratica universale del Dottor Marc'Antonio Savelli* (Parma, 1633), p. 179: 'Ingiuria fatta ad uno de'parenti, si reputa fatta a tutta la parentela, da che ne nasce presunta inimicizia'.

44 Stuart Carroll, *Blood and Violence in Early Modern France* (Oxford: Oxford University Press, 2006), p. 10.

45 Francesco Capecelatro, *Degli annali della Città di Napoli* (Naples: Tipografia di Reale, 1849), p. 47.

46 Ibid.: 'contratta grave nemistà'.

47 Ibid.: 'per opera di don Ferrante Caracciolo, figliuolo del principe di Santa Buono e congiunto di sangue con la casa di Forino, ad instanzia di Marzia Carafa'.

48 Ibid.: 'crescendo ciascun giorno il mal talento fra costoro [the three Caracciolo brothers], come suole sovente avvenire fra i congiunti di sangue, non mancando malvage persone che, usando con amendue le parti, riducono quel che l'un dell'altro dice, porgendo tal via sempre nuovi semi di discordia, avvene che, ritornando al lor palagio Tommaso ed Annibale dall'ostello reale, ove si era recito una commedia, essendo stati cotali spettacoli infausti a questa famiglia, verso le quattro ore della notte … loro fur tratte da alcuni scherani detti Taglialatela della villa di Giugliano … miseramente morì con grave dolor della madre, da cui era teneramente amato'.

49 Ibid., p. 95: 'una donnicciuola, pubblica meritrice, di umilissimo stato'.

50 Ibid. The soldier was hanged two days after his arrest.

51 Ibid., p. 96.

52 Ibid., p. 48.

53 Vincenzo d'Onofrio, *Giornali di Napoli dal MDCLX al MDCLXXX*, ed. by Franco Schlitzer, Antonio Padula, and Vittoria Omodeo, 3 vols. (Naples: Società napoletana di storia patria, 1934–39), II, p. 43.

54 Paolo Mattia Doria, *Massime del governo spagnolo a Napoli* (Naples: Guida, 1973), p. 28: 'per certa differenza avuta col nepote del conte di Castriglio'.

55 For the Acquaviva d'Aragona see Roberto Ricci, ed., *Lo stato degli Acquaviva d'Aragona, duchi di Atri: atti di convegno* (L'Aquila: Colacchi, 2012); Maria Sirago, 'Il Feudo Acquaviviano in Puglia (1575–1665)', *Archivio Storico Pugliese*, 37 (1984), 73–122; Maria Sirago, 'Il Feudo Acquaviviano in Puglia (1665–1710)', *Archivio Storico Pugliese*, 39 (1986) 215–54.

56 Antonio Bulifon, *Giornali di Napoli dal MDXLVII al MDCCVI*, ed. by Nino Cortese (Naples: Società napoletana di storia patria, 1932), II, p. 147; Alfred Reumont, *Naples Under Spanish Dominion: The Carafas of Maddaloni and*

Masaniello (London: George Bell & Sons, 1853), p. 206; Benedetto Croce, 'Duelli nel seicento', *ASPN*, 20 (1895), 543–58 (pp. 544–5).
57 Reumont, *Naples under Spanish Dominion*, p. 206.
58 Maria Sirago, 'Due esempi di ascensione signorile: i Vaaz conti di Mola e gli Acquaviva conti di Conversano tra '500 e '600 (Terra di Bari)', *Studi storici*, 36 (1986), 169–213 (pp. 174–5). See also the recent dissertation of Aurora Martino, 'Giovan Girolamo II Acquaviva d'Aragona (1604–c.1665). Signore feudale del Mezzogiorno spagnolo' (unpublished PhD thesis, Universidad de Valladolid, 2012).
59 On Petraccone Caracciolo see Elena Papagna, *Sogni e bisogni di una famiglia aristocratica: i Caracciolo di Martina* (Milan: FrancoAngeli, 2002), p. 125.
60 D'Onofrio, *Giornali di Napoli*, I, pp. 193–6.
61 Ibid.
62 See also Sirago, 'Il Feudo Acquaviviano in Puglia'.
63 D'Onofrio, *Giornali di Napoli*, II, p. 16.
64 Ibid., p. 91.
65 Ibid., p. 80. For the various problems caused by coachmen see the series of pragmatics under the title *Interdictum in Aurigas*. Giustiniani, Nuova collezione delle prammatiche, pp. 239–54.
66 D'Onofrio, *Giornali di Napoli*, II, p. 91: 'Non si può negare che questa razza di canaglia pigliano fomento ed ardire dalli padroni, essendo, questo, cocchiero del duca dell'Isola Bonita, avvocato fiscale della Camera, presumito assai, ed è certo che ci vorrebbe una forca per ogni quartiero per li cocchieri, attesochè fanno un lusso a fronte delli padroni con sette docati il mese, vestendo panno fino, gipponi di broccato; e ci sono più d'uno di essi, che muffa di latrocinio, e pure hanno protezione.'
67 Ibid., p. 29: 'Sempre questa casa ha nutrito queste sorte d'uomini facinorosi'.
68 Aurelio Lepre, *Storia del mezzogiorno d'Italia: la lunga durata e la crisis (1500–1656)* (Naples: Liguori, 1986), p. 107.
69 Ibid.
70 ASN, Consolato dell'Arte della Lana, Processi Criminali, vol. 4, fasc. 90, fol. 32[r]: 'non uscire, che da cqua passar Julio tuo inimico'.
71 'De Excubiis nocturnis', in *Pragmaticae, edicta, decreta, interdicta, regiaeque sanctiones Regni Neapolitani,*, ed. by Domenico Alfenus Varius (Naples, 1772), p. 499: 'sono nate diverse risse, questioni, & altri delitti, ma ancora sono nate occasioni d'odii, e d'inimicizie; dalle quali in altri tempi sono dopo succeduti altri delitti'.
72 ASN, Delegazione della real giurisdizione, Processi, busta 183, fasc. 96, fol. 1[r].
73 Ibid., busta 185, fasc. 37; busta 192, fasc. 1. On Merino see also Giovanni Brancaccio, *Il Molise medievale e moderno: storia di uno spazio regionale* (Naples: Edizioni scientifiche italiane, 2005), p. 237.
74 ASL, Regia Udienza, Processi Penali, busta 3, fasc. 45, fol. 556[r].
75 ASN, Processi Antichi, Pandetta Nuovissima, busta 1884, fasc. 51936.
76 Ibid., fol. 12[r].
77 Ibid., fol 10[v].

78 Ibid., fol. 9ᵛ.
79 Archivio Diocesano di Conversano, Turi, Atti Civili e Criminali, fasc. 209.
80 Ibid., fol. 9ʳ.
81 Ibid.: 'che quella prattica n'era senza fine, e offesa del mio honore'.
82 Ibid.: 'civilmente che li fusse raccomandato la mia, et sua riputatione'.
83 Ibid., fol. 9ᵛ.
84 Ibid., fol. 10ʳ: 'mentre volevo Io evitare lo scandalo delle genti, chi havevamo cossi spartito pubblicamente di detta mia inimicitia, le venuta in casa mia di D. Angelo in gran'danno della mia riputatione'.
85 Ibid., fol. 10ᵛ.
86 Lucera, Archivio di Stato di Lucera, Regia Udienza Provinciale di Capitanata, Processi Penali, busta 14, fasc. 152.
87 ASL, Regia Udienza, Processi Penali, busta 14, fasc. 152, fol. 45ʳ: 'passata inimicizia'.
88 On this see William Douglass, 'The Joint Family Household in Eighteenth Century Southern Italian Society (Molise)', in *The Family in Italy from Antiquity to the Present*, ed. by David Kertzer and Richard Saller (New Haven: Yale University Press, 1991), pp. 286–303.
89 ASL, Regia Udienza, Processi Penali, busta 14, fasc. 152, fol. 40ʳ: 'accasato da circa tre anni l'istesso Giuseppe con Isabella Capozzo, li medesimi mostrorno di portare maggiore affetto a detta Isabella che a Vittoria Damiano moglie di detto Andrea, ed a Vittoria Zeolo moglie di Francesco Zeolo altro loro figlio, e questo si perche la detta Isabella Capozzo era l'ultima venuta in loro casa, e con buona dote si anco perche la medesima si faceva conoscere interessata alla cura di detta sua socera molto avanzata in età, e quasi sempre convalescente'.
90 Ibid., fol. 40ᵛ.
91 Ibid., fol. 45ᵛ: 'si pose ancora ad insultare ed a suggerire cose di male alle orecchie di detto Andrea suo marito'.
92 Ibid., fol. 45ᵛ: 'in maniera che lo ridusse ad odiare detto Giuseppe suo fratello'.
93 Ibid., fol. 46ʳ: 'esso Andrea lo aveva amato da vero fratello e per tal causa accrebbe tanto odio verso di quello che non volse più andare con me a fatigare nella Vigna, e territorij che quello aveva avuto in dote da detta Isabella sua moglie, non ostante che vivevano comunemente ad indivisi in una sola casa'.
94 Indeed, it is not surprising that later in the same century 'fraternity' became the predominant metaphor for supportive, egalitarian association. The sibling bond for a variety of material and social reasons was one of the most important kinship links in early modern Europe. See Christopher H. Johnson and David Warren Sabean, 'From Siblingship to Siblinghood: Kinship and the Shaping of European Society (1300–1900)', in *Sibling Relations and the Transformations of European Kinship, 1300–1900*, ed. by Christopher H. Johnson and David Warren Sabean (New York: Berghahn, 2011), pp. 1–30.
95 ASL, Processi Penali, busta 14, fasc. 152, fol. 77ᵛ.
96 Ibid. fol. 62ʳ: 'parve a me una cosa difficile a credere, che per una causa così leggiera come … che uno fratello havesse ammazzato l'altro'.
97 Ibid., fol. 59ʳ: 'discola, et facinorosa'.

98 ASL, Regia Udienza, Processi Penali, busta 14, fasc. 152, fol. 230^{r-v}: 'havendo oggi risoluto di vivere cristianamente et seguitare l'orme del nostro sovrano monarco e fare quanto dalla Cristiana legge ci vien imposto e fra l'altre ella che dice perdonar l'offese et accio possa essere abbracciata la pace, oggi predetto giorno spontaneamente e non per forza ne per timore ... rimette annulla et irrita la predetta querela'.

2

The 'abominable traffic': negotiating justice, money, and blood

In 1726, during the Austrian rule of Naples, a legal decree titled *De homocidiis puniendis* was issued that indicted the lamentable state of justice in the Kingdom of Naples across the Spanish period.[1] The regents of the Collateral Council recounted how with numerous decrees they and their predecessors had attempted to reduce crime in the kingdom. Such as the eighty-ninth version of *de Armis*, which aimed to 'take away weapons from those avid for human blood'. But looking back over, they reckoned that such energetic legislation had failed to alleviate the problem: these 'perverse men', murderers, were still able to hope for impunity for their crimes. Therefore, the regents wished to 'investigate all the means by which these men are accustomed to fraudulently delude the severity of justice'. Reflecting on these means, they found that it was the ease by which offenders moved to monetary transaction of crimes committed that was the mainstay of such evasion.

The regents identified a widespread trend that characterized the legal culture of early modern Naples (and Italy generally): the potential to negotiate justice through monetary payments, legally notarized acts of forgiveness, and other modes of grace. This chapter turns to the century before this legal pronouncement and explores how justice in the Kingdom of Naples was connected to the murky worlds of peace-making, the composition and transaction of crimes. It first opens with a survey of the institutions of justice in the Kingdom before turning to examine the place of negotiated settlement for violent crimes in the Kingdom.

Topographies of justice in the Kingdom of Naples

Figure 2.1 depicts a piazza, over which a palazzo looms. This is the Castel Capuano, since centuries a seat of regal authority, built first under the Norman Hauteville kings. As part of the imperial reform of justice, the viceroy Toledo had gathered the major legal organs of the Kingdom into this building, the *Gran Corte della Vicaria*. The scene is one of motion and

Figure 2.1 The Castel Capuano, Carlo Capuano/Ascanio Luciani, Museo di San Martino, Naples. Bridgeman Images.

business. Groups of lawyers mill around the approach to the palace and they are approached, cap in hand, by petitioners greeting them with the due obsequies. In the foreground a trumpeter announces proclamations of the tribunal. Crowding the sides are the carriages and sedan chairs which ferried the judges and lawyers and noble or well-to-do litigants to the tribunal. But not only the genteel parts of the rich legal profession in Naples are shown: the violence of justice is represented. In the centre of the composition a man is drawn up metres into the air by a pulley-drawn rope, the *strappado* torture, while a group of legal officials look on. Being marched away from the tribunal is a chain-gang of prisoners, likely being taken to the galleys after sentence. They walk past a column at the base of which rests a decapitated head in a paper crown. This is the column of infamy where the Kingdom displayed heads of bandits and other notorious criminals. The Habsburg crest marks out the scene as a site of imperial rule.

This vivid depiction of the business of justice in Naples is an instructive beginning to introduce the networks of justice in the Kingdom. It captures numerous aspects of justice on the move: the movement of convicts, the business of lawyers, and the inflicting of punishment. Inside the palazzo, the *Vicaria* was the central criminal court of the Kingdom and the head tribunal of provincial justice. Its decisions could be appealed to the *Sacro Regio Consiglio*.[2] The *Vicaria* was a mammoth institution, including both criminal and civil courts. It traced its origin to the *Magna Curia* founded under the Norman king Ruggiero II. The vastness of this institution was famed across Italy in the early modern period, with Traiano Boccalini arguing that the *Vicaria* was a fundamental part of the Spanish rule over Naples, which through the never-ending litigation that it involved the subjects in, acted as a 'brake, saddle, and packsaddle' for the 'Parthenopean steed', and therefore 'maintaining discord between barons and vassals' who both submitted voluntarily to this yoke through litigation.[3]

In the Kingdom of Naples, the geographies of justice and feudalism overlapped: a *feudo* in the Neapolitan context meant precisely a settlement over which jurisdiction in criminal and civil matters was exercised indirectly by an individual invested with such authority.[4] The vast majority of settlements were *feudi* and therefore the first encounter with justice for most of the inhabitants of the Kingdom was the courts of their feudal lord. Most lords possessed both first and second instance jurisdiction, with some possessing third instance as well. Royal justice for the majority of subjects lay past the often-difficult barrier of multiple trials in feudal courts. For those subjects of the crown who did not live in royal lands, demesnial courts were the first instance jurisdiction.

The *Regie Audienze* were royal provincial courts for the provinces of the Kingdom of Naples. They functioned as seats of royal authority in the provinces, which were largely under baronial jurisdiction. For the majority of those who lived within their jurisdiction the *Audienze* functioned as possible courts of appeal (although barons held the right to conduct the first, second, and often third appeals themselves), which could be swifter than appealing to the central court of Naples, the *Vicaria*. Yet for certain special categories of people – widows and unmarried young women – the *Audienze* could be courts of first instance for serious crimes. Due to their function as appeal courts, their documentation often includes originals or copies of courts held in feudal courts. Such evidence of how feudal courts operated is invaluable, considering the lack of criminal justice documentation in surviving private archives.[5]

The personnel of the *Audienze* included a nobleman, of military experience, as the *Preside*, who was appointed by the viceroy. From the mid-seventeenth century, there were also three *Uditori*. Alongside them there was the *Avvocato fiscale*. Other personnel were the *Procuratore fiscale*, the *Avvocato* and *Procuratore dei Poveri*, the secretary and the *Mastrodatti*. The *Audienze* were hybrid institutions: legal, administrative, and military. Along with their judicial staff, the *Audienze* were seats of a squadron of soldiers known as the *Compagnia di campagna* under the military command of the *Preside*. Such soldiers were used most often in forays and manoeuvres against the militarized bandits that were an endemic problem of the rural parts of the Kingdom. They were also put to use against rebels during the 1647–48 rebellions.

The *Audienze* had functions concerned with public administration and sustaining public order. They were under legal obligation to send six-monthly reports to the viceroy concerning the activities of bandits in their territories.[6] The *Audienza*, and especially the *Preside*, were representatives of the 'governo della campagna': the rural government of the provinces that tackled banditry and the connected problems of factional violence in the towns and cities of the provinces.[7] The *governo della campagna* was mainly framed in terms of control of bandit activity. The officials of the Spanish regime often used *campagna* as equivalent to the struggle against banditry in discussions on governance.

The placement of a *Regia Audienza* in a certain town was seen as a form of control over rebellious subjects. For instance, in 1645 there was discussion over the installation of an independent *Regia Audienza* for the province of Basilicata, hitherto the tribunal based in Salerno had responsibility for Principato Citra and Basilicata which had caused 'inconveniences' due to the distance between Salerno and Basilicata.[8] A document listing the virtues of various options noted that the town of Tramutela had inhabitants 'of a very free life, and disturbers [*inquietatori*] of the province, and continually they take to the countryside [meaning they committed acts of banditry]' so 'the brake of the *Regia Audienza* is necessary'.[9]

It would be wrong to assume that because of their status as direct royal institutions that *audienze* were thereby always organs of impartial justice; they were often to be found embroiled in local disputes and subject to corruption. In 1629–31, before the surviving collection begins, there was a trial of every magistrate of the *Regia Audienza*. The cause was the summary execution of a seventeen-year-old boy who carried no weapons, a scandalous occurrence even in the context of the arbitrary tendencies of justice. Despite the obvious injustice of the case, the magistrates involved were acquitted. Most of the judges who considered the crime argued that punishing magistrates for bad decisions was an untenable precedent.[10] In the cities the *Audienze* resided in, they could become involved in local disputes. For instance, in 1636 the *Vicario* of Lucera was accused of roaming the city at night with two clerics all armed with firearms and shooting at the *Auditor* Vaz of the *Regia Audienza*.[11]

The *Audienze* were major institutional interlocutors for the viceroy with the provinces. It was through these institutions that, for the most part, royal authority was extended. They were essential parts of the geography of power in the Kingdom. The records of the *Audienza* of Lucera, then, shed light upon a range of interconnected aspects of life in the Kingdom. They provide numerous perspectives on noble power and its social effects. The complex world of banditry was both in part formed and shaped by royal justice. The movement of rural people, travelling across the roads of the Kingdom moving livestock or taking goods to markets are also highlighted.

In close connection with the *Regie Audienze* were also the *Tribunali di Campagna*, which were tribunals with special responsibility in the 'things of the countryside', that is, banditry.[12] These reported to the regent of the Collateral Council who held the post of 'superintendent of the things of the countryside'.[13] The *Tribunali* exercised justice *ad modum belli*, in the manner of war, with the summary imposition of penalties including death. This was an attempt to accelerate justice in the constant struggle against banditry. The *Tribunali della Campagna* were also peripatetic, they moved often around both to better dispense justice and to avoid burdening a particular locality with their presence. The boundary between a *Tribunale di Campagna* and a *Regia Audienza* should also not be drawn too sharply: the fundamental part of such a tribunal was a single *commissario*, sent around the *Audienze* in order to act with the direct authority of the *Vicaria* against outlaws.[14]

Another common site of jurisdiction were ecclesiastical courts.[15] If a victim or perpetrator of a crime was a cleric then they had the right to pursue their trial in an ecclesiastical court. Such courts were often identified as undermining the decorum of royal justice. As well as this network of ecclesiastical courts, there were certain tribunals for professions. For instance, the guilds of silk and wool in Naples held criminal and civil jurisdiction over their members for many crimes and instances. The arsenal, customshouses and royal mint of Naples also had their own tribunals.

The experience of justice and the consequences of violence

One of the main characteristics of justice could be its slowness. This often resulted in lengthy imprisonments, which could be brutal to the bodies and minds of those awaiting resolutions. A petitionary letter of one Raimondo

Croso, who had been imprisoned in the Castel Nuovo, complained of having been 'left there dying of hunger and poverty [*miseria*] for the space of eight months'. He was a sailor in the Papal fleet, who, while unclear on the exact reasons for his imprisonment, had expected his captain to arrange his release with the viceroy. But the captain was obliged to leave for Genova before being able to complete negotiations. His description of the wheels of justice in Naples was agonizing. He had reached out before to the viceroy, and had even received ten or twelve written dispatches from the office of the viceroy which assured him of moving through justice quickly.[16] Yet even these interventions of the viceroy had not been enough to relieve what Croso described as 'so strange an oppression and calamity'.

After a violent crime had been committed, the absence of policing and the likelihood that a judicial procedure would take some days to be launched, meant that an offender could flee. Such a flight would lead them to be declared, first, in contumacy and subsequently declared an outlaw.

Giambattista Basile, in his collection of outlandish tales *Lo cunto deli cunti* (1634), told the tale of one Cienzo, a son of a wealthy merchant who during a game of stone-throwing injured the King's son. His father became enraged, fearing that the accident would be interpreted as treason. Cienzo dismissed his father's fears, saying: 'we're boys, we ended up in a brawl, it's my first crime, the king is a sensible man'. Cienzo asks: what's the worst he can do? This sanguine attitude provoked his father to spell out the consequences:

> He can banish you from this world, send you off for a change of air; he can treat you like a schoolmaster, with a stick twenty-four spans long that'll have you racking the fish until they learn to speak; he can send you off, with a soap-starched collar three spans high, to take your pleasure with the widow, where instead of touching your bride's hand you'll be touching the hangman's feet.

This catalogue of punishment was meant to stress the obvious wisdom of flight:

> so don't just stand there with your hide paying rent to both the cloth and the shearer, but start marching this instant, and may none of your business, neither old nor new, be known unless you want to get caught by the foot: better to be a country bird than a caged one ... better to kick up your heels than to have someone dogging your every step; better to throw your legs over your neck than to have your neck hanging between your legs; better, ultimately, to walk a thousand feet than to end up with three feet of rope around you. If you don't pack your bags, neither Baldus nor Bartolus will be able to help you.[17]

In these convincing reasons for flight, rather than waiting and hoping for mercy, Basile laid out the predicament common to those who got involved in violent affray.

Nonetheless, it was not necessary for some to leave their communities after committing crimes. Petitions often note that someone had been committing acts of violence for years without needing to move or flee justice. But when the scales were tipped, perhaps by rousing the attentions of a higher institutional authority, flight became an attractive option. In cases where a provincial tribunal's attentions were garnered, escape was easily achieved as news of a scribe from a provincial *Audienza* travelling to a town often arrived in advance. Forewarning allowed for escape. Successful capture, instead, relied upon the authorities being able to use the troops of the *Audienza* to surprise and overpower the offender. Flight from the location of a crime provided juridical grounds for torture.[18]

One possibility from fleeing and being declared outlawed was to form or join a gang of peripatetic bandits who lived from crime. The significance of banditry will be explored in Chapter 4 of this book. Yet far from all fugitives underwent such a transformation. The quixotic peregrinations of Silvestro Bagnuolo in 1672 show how it could be difficult to make a success of fleeing. A resident of the small village of Calcabottaccio in the Molise, he had murdered Angela Colella after she had visited his wife Cattolica and demanded the return of a sum of money lent to Cattolica by a priest.[19] He testified that he had ordered Angela to never bother his wife again, Angela's reply, in Silvestro's telling of the tale, was 'dear Silvestro, if I ever come here again, I want you to kill me with your own hands'.[20] His sister-in-law mocked his inadequate response, 'are you not man enough to rid yourself of the horns?'[21] This questioning of his honour and manhood meant he made a resolution to kill Angela.[22]

Silvestro's confessions reveal a considerable amount of detail about his plans and choices. He spread a rumour that he was going to make the trip to Foggia to labour for a few days. He then hid himself in a place outside of the town where he knew Angela often came to gather firewood.[23] When she came down the road he took a knife out from a bag and stabbed Angela in the throat.

He left her where she fell and, covertly, he travelled to Lucera. Here he entered the service of one Giovanni Battista Farina but soon after word came to the *Audienza* of the killing and he was cited to appear before them.[24] Having heard of this accusation before he was forcibly captured he was able to flee. He went to some pasture land near his hometown where he found a packhorse or mule that he recognized as belonging to one of his townsmen. He stole the animal and took it to Sant'Elia, around thirty kilometres to the south-east, to sell. He found a buyer, a tailor of the Duke of Sant'Elia, who paid 6 ducats for it. But it was discovered that the packhorse was stolen and men of the town's governor came to imprison him. He refused to give his real surname for fear of his murder being discovered. He managed to escape his captors while they took him to the prison and he ducked into a nearby Church, and claimed asylum.[25]

He was clearly not watched closely, as he managed to slip away without being arrested. From here he went to Torre Maggiore and bought a pistol. Now armed, Silvestro went to a wood he knew, next to where his brother harvested grain. The guardians of the farmland came to arrest him. He sought to resist arrest but his pistol misfired and his flight came to an end.[26]

When crimes of inimical violence entered the legal system such causes became potential battlegrounds for rivalries between those who held jurisdictions: feudal lords, bishops, and the courts themselves. For example in Nocera in 1623 one Marzio Baldino shot an arquebus at one of his enemies.[27] As Nocera lay just outside the city of Naples he was imprisoned in the prison of the *Vicaria*. But the Bishop of Nocera managed to get him transferred out with the claim that Baldino was a cleric. The Duke of Nocera complained to the Collateral Council that his clerical status was feigned.[28] Here a revenge killing had an afterlife as jurisdictional conflict. Acts explained by enmity could quickly have a broader significance than the initial circumstances gave them.

Escape could also come after arrest. Often the prisons of towns, villages and cities were insufficiently secure. They were rarely purpose-built and many were in a woeful condition.[29] In 1660, Daniele Calabrese, Libetore Troiano, and Giuseppe Melone escaped from the prison of Rionigro. The prison of Rionigro was the 'old cistern' of the Baronial castle, not a purpose-built holding area.[30] They had beaten open the irons on their limbs and then piled sacks of hay to climb over the courtyard wall of the castle.[31]

Even the prisons of the *Regia Audienza* in Lucera were not immune and two trials for escapes remain extant.[32] Almost no early modern prison was sealed from the outside world. Underinvestment in buildings and underpaid jailors were common, even in central prisons. Apart from neglect, one of the main reasons for the permeability of the prison was that inmates relied on kin, friends, or paid servants to provide them with food and other forms of support.[33] However, the imprisoned often paid high costs for access to the outside world, as bribing jailors was often an important step in enabling access.[34]

Remission, composition, and transaction

Pecuniary composition was underpinned by the idea that the offended parties possessed an interest in the prosecution of their offender which they could renounce. In the case of violent crime or offences to honour, this interest was described as a *vendetta* caused by the spilling of blood or the injury to reputation. Across the provinces the aftermath of violence was shaped by the pressures created by their right to pursue this legal *vendetta*. These particular endowments shaped the experiences of people as they attempted to cope with the loss of a close relative or, on the other side, sought to avoid punishment. The institutional frameworks of remission and composition created difficulties for the government of Naples throughout the early modern period.

Composition was retained in Naples in part due to baronial pressure in the early sixteenth century. Pietro de Toledo, viceroy from 1532 to 1559, attempted to gain control over Neapolitan society through interventionist legislation. One strategy was to abolish every sort of composition in the case of crimes warranting the death penalty or the severing of limbs, except for perpetual services on the galleys; this would have been a radically different course for criminal justice than the one actually taken. In response to this attempt the parliament of Naples requested that the viceroys maintain the power of being able to compose all sorts of crimes.[35] The result of this change in law would have led to many more executions and mutilations, including nobles. In the same parliament a large number of petitions were made of graces to be given to those who had gained the remission of the offended party for the crime they had committed, such as Ferrante Cziczo who had wounded Joan Baptista de Marini and been sentenced to the removal of his right hand.[36]

The right to lodge an accusation – a complaint [*querela*] – was held by the victim of a crime or their close kin.[37] This was one aspect of the survival of 'accusatory' procedure in legal systems.[38] The complainer [*querelante*] was a directly affected party who had the right to complain. In the case of a homicide the widow, parents, or spouse normally lodged the complaint. The wife of Pietro Lotta, murdered in 1657, lodged a *querela* with the *Regia Audienza* of Lucera.[39] These accusations initiated proceedings in many tribunals of criminal justice in the Kingdom. In the episcopal tribunal of Conversano, the widow of the murdered Pietro Montone lodged an accusation against his murderer, a cleric. The wording of this *querela* said that 'until he is punished as the laws, and justice, happen to command, he should not be freed without my knowledge and remission'.[40] The *querelante* required satisfaction.

This, however, was the ideal. In practice, the *querela* was open to abuses. The ability to hold someone accountable for a crime and press for action empowered but also exposed the *querelante* to pressure from offenders and their allies. In April 1620 the count of Conza, and son of Carlo Gesualdo, Don Emanuele, was accused of having wrongly imprisoned a cleric who had refused to withdraw a *querela* lodged against the murderers of the priest's cousins.[41] In 1718 in Conversano the Deacon Giuseppe Troviso was assaulted by one Domenico Lopriore. Giuseppe's brother Stefano had lodged a *querela* against Pasquale di Vagno, which Domenico took objection to and the argument that led to the assault started with Lopriore's attempt to persuade Giuseppe to convince his brother to retract the quarrel.[42]

The maintenance of the ability to withdraw *querele* was defended as a cornerstone of liberty. One of the privileges requested from both Emperor Ferdinand and Emperor Charles V was that in all the tribunals within the city of Naples a *querela* or *denuntia* could be retracted within three days.[43] Part of the reason why attempts to introduce a Spanish-style Inquisition (and even rumours of such attempts) led to violent revolt in Naples was due to its power to prosecute without constraint.[44] Periods of time in which settlement could be reached outside of tribunals were prized, especially by the wealthy with the means and clout to induce withdrawals of prosecution. An honest, unforced retraction of a *querela* was framed as an act of peaceful settlement.

Remissions of the offended party

While retraction of a particular quarrel could be idealized as true reconciliation, forgoing the right to seek prosecution in the future required a further settlement, an obliteration of the original injury rather than a potentially temporary cessation of hostilities. This erasure of the original crime was seen as essential for true forgiveness, as the jurist Pietro Follerio worded it: 'reconciliation presupposes remission of injuries'.[45] These acts of forgiveness were institutionalized in the Kingdom of Naples in the form of the *remissione della parte offesa*. These remissions were seen as a necessary precondition to move to the process of composition for homicide and other serious crimes. When crimes were composed without the presence of a remission, as did occur, it was often noted as improper. In trials the offended party was understood to have a stake in the outcome, an 'interest', and this was what required satisfaction. In requests for mercy, the lack of an offended party was often stressed as a strong reason for grace to be dispensed, as there was no one to be offended anew.

The importance of remission before composition was reinforced as proper procedure by various edicts from the viceroys and the Collateral Council. The *Vicaria* was directly ordered by the viceroy in 1559 not to proceed to composition without having the remissions from all of those that had the right to lodge a complaint and accuse the wrongdoer.[46] As the pragmatic *De compositionibus et commutationibus poenarum* clarified in 1567: 'the admission of delinquents to composition is a form of grace; and it is our will not to admit anybody to composition, if the remissions of all of those who can justly lodge *querele* or accusations are not already acquired'.[47] Remissions were affirmed as vital precursors to the composition of crime, although the need to pronounce against the contrary practice demonstrated its existence.

Despite the clear importance of remissions in the case where accusation originally came from a *querela* (which meant that offended parties existed) another question that Neapolitan jurists debated was whether remissions were necessary even when a prosecution had begun solely from the power of prosecution *ex officio* which could be held by barons and *Regie Audienze*, that is, in criminal cases not directly initiated by the complaint of an offended party.[48] Neapolitan jurists regularly argued for the vital importance of remissions. Novario held that they were still necessary even when prosecution was being carried out on the instance of more abstract representatives of justice.[49] The principle of who needed to provide remissions was modelled on that of inheritance. It was those who had rights to inherit that needed to offer remissions.[50]

Remissions were part of justice in all the various forms it took: baronial courts, local courts of towns in the royal demesne, provincial royal courts, ecclesiastical tribunals, various specialized courts in the Kingdom of Naples (such as guild and military courts), and in the Grand Court of the *Vicaria*. How, exactly, the dynamics of remissions played out in local contexts requires careful reconstruction; the goal of this section is to provide an overview of some of the consequences of the endorsement of remissions and the views of contemporaries regarding the process of remitting crimes.[51]

Within the city of Naples the process of composition was part of the weekly schedule of administration. Defendants or prisoners who obtained remissions in writing could present them to the viceroy or to the regents of the Collateral Council. Every Saturday the regents, sometimes accompanied by the viceroy, travelled from the Viceroy's Palace to the *Vicaria* to 'give graces to the accused'.[52] This could be a full removal of a punishment or a lessening of the penalty. For minor crimes without seriously offended parties the offender could compose directly with the *Avvocato fiscale*.[53] Pardoning was a key tool for viceregal authority. The chronicler Zazzera reported that the Duke of Osuña in January 1617, accompanied by the prince of Conca, upon his taking up of his office set off on a journey through Naples to the Vicaria to dispense grace. Zazzera records that crowds thronged the streets and criminals emerged from churches, where they exercised asylum, to throw themselves on his mercy. He then spent hours at the Vicaria dispensing grace, stopping only an hour after the evening *Ave Maria* bell sounded, far later than the working day. The 'most famous bandit' Penzio Cava was the most notable grace given.[54]

Compositions and transactions of penalties created considerable income for the Kingdom. In 1669, out of a general income of 1,919,382 ducats into royal coffers, 60,000 ducats came from transactions and compositions of penalties.[55] At just over 3 per cent of royal incomes this was not a major funding stream but it was far from a negligible amount as the *Dogana*, famed for the wealth it brought the Kingdom, provided just over 9 per cent of incomes.[56]

Remissions were in form and practice religious; the debates over remission and forgiveness mirror discussions of confession.[57] The obvious correspondence was between a person's remittance of an offence given to him or her and the general remittance of the sins of mankind provided by the sacrifice of Jesus.[58] Certain categories of offenders were excluded from the ability to transact their penalties. The particular types that were rejected help illustrate the logic behind composition. This exclusion was an attempt to stop outrageous crimes from escaping penalty. By excluding certain offences from the possibility of composition the tribunals of the Kingdom attempted to deter these offences. Those who 'received' bandits were denied the ability to compose their crimes in August 1560.[59] Such restraints upon the composition of crimes often in practice fell away.

How the legal institutions of remission and transaction were put into practice was fundamentally shaped by power relations operating within Neapolitan society. Supposedly consensual acts of forgiveness were, in many ways, situations that exposed the injured or bereaved to intimidation and provided the powerful with ways to escape penalty. Abuse of the systems of remission was a regular criticism aimed towards corrupt governors and influential nobles.

The diarist Vincenzo d'Onofrio noted the case of the well-connected bishop Bonaventura d'Avalos who, in his account, was avaricious and immoral. Apart from managing a deft smuggling network, he set himself up in a palazzo just outside the Porta di San Gennaro in Naples where, for money, he arranged 'peaces and remissions' in favour of offenders: 'giving himself at full pelt to mercenary judgements'.[60] D'Onofrio provides no details on whether Fra Bonaventura used threats to coerce, or the semblance of piety to convince those who provided remissions, or if he simply forged the instruments. Another account we have from d'Onofrio is that of the Prince of Riccia. He had been outlawed but entered Naples under the cover of darkness with armed men and forced his way into the monastery of Santo Severino. He claimed the right of asylum to avoid being seized straight away and announced that he had remissions from all offended parties. 'God knows how' was d'Onofrio's succinct comment on these events.[61]

Even those without the considerable power of a bishop or baron could attempt to use violent force to obtain remissions. In 1632 Francisco Silvestro and Mario Volpicella confronted Angelillo Basso as he returned from a day's labour. Francesco had killed Angelillo's sister's son and now pointed a firearm at him, saying, 'don't you want to make your sister give me her remission'. Angelillo refused and Francisco shot him and left him wounded.[62]

In 1664 in the town of Morcone in northern Puglia, Diomede Fiorenza disappeared in the middle of the night. As his father Francesco lamented, he 'never appeared again, alive or dead'. Francesco and others suspected that he had been murdered and his body hidden somewhere by two men: Carlo Vasullo and Sebastiano Calabrese. They had committed the murder, so the talk in the town went, in order to sleep with Diomede's wife; they had also been at enmity with Diomede for years.[63] Francesco complained that he had 'seen them walking about, conversing publicly without any impediment or complaint from anybody, they come and go from their houses to their vineyards as if they had committed no crime at all'.[64] They had not left Francesco in peace. They threatened him continually to agree to sign the remission that would allow them to negotiate with and avoid risking the death penalty, if found guilty, or avoiding the trial and being declared outlaws. In this case, Francesco's stern resolve gave him time to summon the *Regia Audienza* of Lucera to investigate and Sebastiano and Carlo fled, becoming outlaws.[65]

Francesco, Diomede's father, had refused to bow to the pressure of Carlo and Sebastiano to sign a remission even when his own friends approached him as he was about to enter church and encouraged him to sign a remission so as to avoid 'greater harm' in the future. The Capuchin friars of Morcone were apparently particularly emphatic in urging remission, pushing him to make peace by giving in to the demands of Carlo and Sebastiano. Vasullo and Calabrese had been outlawed and they had fled from the hilltop town. Francesco testified that he had refused to sign the remission but the exact terms he uses are instructive. He said that he had told Vasullo and Calabrese, 'I will not sell the blood of my son'.[66] This case was a murder committed apparently as part of a formal hatred. It demonstrates the use by Francesco of a central legal system, the pressure for forgiveness from regular clergy and the eventual outlawing of the two accused and, finally, a refusal to bargain over a dead son. In his testimony Francesco Fiorenza cast himself as the steadfast father who refused to deal in blood.

In 1617 a corporal of the *sbirri* ('cops', enforcers for the tribunals) was imprisoned because he had taken the unauthorized step of composing a crime for the low sum of 4 ducats.[67] In 1724 Saverio Vitiello claimed he suffered an abuse of the process of remission of another sort. He was imprisoned in Torre del Greco for the murder of Antonio Villano for the second time. In the original trial he had received a remission from Villano's kin. Now he claimed that he was re-imprisoned because the Mastro d'Atti in Torre del Greco Giambattista de Marino had removed the documentation of the remission and subsequent grace from the proceedings of the original trial.[68] This example reminds us that we cannot ignore the material aspects of peace-making and the legal systems; the redaction and archiving of physical records mattered.

Another form of disorder, present even in the highest tribunals of the state, was that correct procedure in the exercise of composition was often neglected. Despite viceregal pronouncements the *Vicaria* persistently issued compositions without the requisite remissions and also without notifying the Collateral Council that they had done so. Apart from the damage this did to the 'decorum of justice', it risked creating numerous problems for the viceroy. The difficulties arose from the delegation of viceregal authority into the *Vicaria*. The compositions arranged by the judges of the *Vicaria* were done in the name of the viceroy's authority. In practice, the judges sometimes issued such compositions without reference to the Collateral Council. However, the laws of the Kingdom established that the compositions performed by the *Vicaria* should only be finalized by being read and confirmed in the Collateral. In periodic visitations by the Regent of the Collateral the visitor was given the ability to operate the 'libro di Truglio' and provide compositions to the galleys or to another place.[69] Crimes were composed repeatedly without the accused acquiring the requisite remission.

But these were not understood as periodic malfunctions in the justice system. Throughout the early modern period various viceroys, jurists, and others identified the system of remitting and composing offences as a central wellspring of disorder, for a variety of reasons. In 1566 a pragmatic issued in the name of the viceroy Don Perafan, the Duke of Alcalá, claimed that one 'of the reasons, on account of which many dare to commit crimes, is because of the hope that they hold of obtaining remissions of the parties'.[70] In his viceroyalty, it was ordered that remissions should be issued solely in the presence of judges as an attempt to avoid intimidation.[71]

This analysis held its validity in the remainder of the sixteenth and throughout the seventeenth century. However, with delegated jurisdiction and the great territorial expanse of the Kingdom a working control over the process was impossible. The Collateral Council, the judges of the *Vicaria* and the viceroys could only (at best) react to reports of abuses, which were very likely only a small proportion of those that occurred.

The periodic 'visitors' to the Kingdom, who were dispatched by Madrid to investigate particular instances of corruption or maladministration and to uproot bad governance generally often found grave abuses in the process.[72] Francisco Antonio Alarcon was dispatched in 1622 and noted abusive composition as part of a broad spectrum of illicit uses of the legal system to swindle money from various parts of judicial proceedings.[73]

Abuse of the systems of remission was a regular criticism of corrupt governors and influential nobles. Even Capecelatro, an aristocrat and not favourable towards reform more generally, noted that in the 1630s the criminal system was so well-disposed towards the aristocracy, that despite the fact that they may have committed 'strange and enormous misdeeds' they were always able to use their clout and by obtaining the remission of the crimes – by a variety of underhand methods – 'they can easily compose their crimes'.[74]

The worsening of the situation in the 1620s and 1630s was a probable result of the general collapse of state capacity as justice was lowered as priority in favour of revenue extraction. Only months before the rebellion of 1647, the Duke of Arcos, viceroy of the Kingdom, as part of a preamble to a pragmatic wrote that by

> experience it is known, that the principal cause of crimes committed, and that daily are committed in an infinite number within this most Faithful City of Naples ... as in all this present Realm, was, and is the certainty, that delinquents held and still hold, of obtaining remissions from the offended parties, and with these it is made much easier to obtain compositions, graces, accords, and reduction of punishments.[75]

The status given to the 'offended party' in Neapolitan law, endowed with the capacity to forgive, was a resource that could be tapped by the powerful or violent. To viceroys and some jurists, this was a factor that encouraged people to commit crimes and that explained the notoriously high rates of violence in early modern Naples. The legal environment of the Kingdom created the perfect conditions that enabled people to commit heinous crimes and then extort forgiveness.

Feudal power and composition

The ability to compose crimes was delegated to all feudal lords who held criminal jurisdiction. As the Parman jurist Giovanni Battista Baiardi remarked, noting in his survey of Italian norms an exception to the practice of most states in the peninsula, all barons in the Kingdom of Naples had this privilege of 'gratiandi, sive componendi' of the crimes of their vassals before a sentence was issued but only when a remission of the party had been gained.[76] In a European and Italian context the Neapolitan arrangements endowed the feudatories with very extensive powers.[77] Even in Sicily, mostly comparable in feudal arrangements, this power was only offered to the high baronage that possessed *mero e misto imperio*.[78] In Naples, however, all barons possessed this *mero e misto imperio* as well as the 'four arbitrary letters', which had been dispensed to them by Robert of Anjou. In a notarial document of the Mastrogiudice family these powers are defined as in his state and with the Bench of Justice and with jurisdiction and cognition of first and second causes civil, criminal and *mero et misto impero*, delegated powers. The four arbitrary letters and with the power to compose crimes and commute corporal punishments into monetary ones and the powers to remit in total or in part, given the satisfaction of the offended party.[79]

This list underlines how significant feudal lords' powers to do justice were, and the striking prominence of settlement over punishment. There was some debate over precisely from what privilege or precedent the baronial ability to compose crimes was derived. A major strand of juridical thought saw it deriving from the four arbitrary letters rather than as part of their jurisdiction as lord of the fief.[80] Others stressed the contingency of baronial rights upon fidelity and service to the crown.[81] Earlier kings themselves had believed in their power to remove delegated powers.[82] Barons were supposed to uphold the correct procedures of the Kingdom in their administration of justice as royal officials.[83] Compositions could be considerable portions of judicial revenues for the feudal nobility.[84]

This faculty was brought under increased scrutiny in the mid-sixteenth century. In the earlier sixteenth century some barons had the ability to remit crimes even after the end of the proceedings and the publication of a sentence. The twenty-second pragmatic *de Baronibus* restricted the composition or diminution of penalties to the period before a final sentence was announced. Barons were also banned from commuting the penalties of the exiled and those who had been ordered to stay in their *patria*, their hometown, even if they had obtained remissions.[85]

In practice, such decrees were of little use in restraining feudal lords and misuse of these extensive powers was common. It is impossible to track the rates of such abuse as we lack records from nearly all baronial courts and because such manipulations were concealed. Nevertheless, a number of illustrative cases can be placed alongside the many critiques of feudal government that identified misuse of jurisdictional powers. These often gave special emphasis on the field of composition. Vassals did have recourse to oversight and some instances of abuse of authority were tried in the *Regie Audienze*, these appeals often revealed longstanding abuses and, of course, many more were never taken to court.[86] In 1666 Don Giuseppe Castrocucco the Marchese of Ripa, was accused by his vassals of various misdemeanours.[87] He had forced a marriage to take place between a niece of one of his vassals and one of his supporters, his feudal administrators were his personal coterie, and he extorted illicit taxation from the local pig trade. He also imprisoned at will and then charged what he wanted to transact the penalty, without arranging remissions. As one of the complainants testified 'if you want to leave his prisons you have to compose with him at his judgement, without the vote of the *consultore*.[88] Antonio Piano was charged 80 ducats, and Giovanni Angelo di Monaco 40; these were large sums for many rural vassals.[89]

The problems of baronial abuse of systems of composition were identified as one of the recurring problems that vassals faced. The jurist Giovanni Maria Novario discusses this at length in his *Tractatus de vassallorum gravaminibus*. He dealt with the problems caused when 'Barons perform graces, without the parties being reconciled'.[90] His treatment of this subject noted that it was absolutely undeniable that, from their privileges, barons had the ability to give grace for the crimes of their vassals but that this required a concord made with the offended parties to be valid. In legal formulations and the commentary of jurists, the agreement of the victim or their kin was indispensable. In practice, as the viceroy d'Arcos wrote, 'many have sought to avail themselves of outrageous methods, and they have forced the poor *querelanti* and the offended parties to make said remissions' under threat to their life or goods.[91]

The notary Donato Antonio Cortellisi argued that in Novi in the 1610s the abuse of the system caused crimes: 'as the offenders reach accords over huge crimes with tiny sums of money this has given rise to new crimes and sins'.[92] In 1578 the citizens of Montepeloso complained that their duke 'gets involved in making and in obtaining remissions of the parties, and at times he forces them to be given with violence'.[93]

In the early eighteenth century these abuses persisted and criticism became more direct. Paolo Mattia Doria discussed abuses of baronial jurisdiction in his *Relazione dello stato politico, economico e civile del Regno di Napoli nel tempo ch'è stato governato da i Spagnuoli* (1707).[94] The barons, he noted, had the faculty to 'give grace, and to transact penalties' into monetary penalties.[95] He began by describing the use of these options by feudatories as their attempt to avoid being drawn into the long, twisted paths of justice in the Kingdom of Naples. After an initial baronial judgement, the defendant had the right to an appeal within the feudal court; then, after this, to the *Audienza* of their province and then from the *Audienza* to the *Vicaria*. After the *Vicaria*, they could appeal to the *Sacro Consiglio* the only tribunal whose sentences were absolutely final.[96]

In Doria's account, these potentially long judicial roads meant that the finalities of fiscal penalty or mercy were favoured by the feudal aristocracy. But he also identified the obviously exploitative nature of these powers. Barons, with their ability to give graces, could send a man to kill another 'under the appearance of a particular enmity' and then give a grace to the killer removing all danger that the way the homicide had been committed could ever be 'juridically proven'.[97] At the same time they let others get away with the most disruptive and offensive crimes. The delegated ability to compose crimes was one of the most critiqued aspects of feudal governance in the eighteenth century. As this power enabled barons to cover all their misdeeds, it underpinned a whole variety of baronial abuses.

The fiscal and human resources required by the Spanish Crown influenced the policy of the viceroy and the Collateral Council regarding the issue of composition. A major aspect of this was the need for men who would serve on the galleys as a form of composition, thereby escaping the death penalty.

In 1605 a Tuscan agent in Naples noted that the regent de Ponte was deputized to perform the traditional weekly Saturday visits to the prisons of the Vicaria with a particular request to recruit rowers for the galleys.[98] This was due to the order that Naples needed to have thirty galleys. Yet even with all the efforts of recruitment, together with the efforts of the provincial *Audienze*, by 1606 the agent reported that the criminal judge Mascanbruno toured the disreputable *alberghi* of Naples by night to find men he could accuse of being vagabonds and therefore arrest them and send them to the galleys.[99] There was, therefore, great pressure to find prisoners who could be chained and delivered to the capital whether to serve on the galleys, or in projects of construction, or to become soldiers.

Some evidence for the military needs for forgiveness can be found in the collection titled *Diversorum* in the archival holdings of the Collateral Council in the Neapolitan State Archive. These documents trace the granting of patents and approvals by the Collateral Council including requests that certain towns be excluded from billeting soldiers, approval for individuals to represent national communities as consul, approval to seek alms across the kingdom, and for indulgence for grave crimes committed. Until about 1680, there are many patents granted to those guilty of violent crimes. A smaller number of requests ask for punishment to be applied to 'delinquents' who are actively disturbing the peace.[100] The use of forgiveness in attempts to combat banditry was a repeatedly used tool in early modern states. By rewarding outlaws who killed or captured other outlaws with forgiveness, the hope was that solidarity could be smashed. As well as the surviving books of the *Diversorum* collection, the deliberative minutes (*notamenti*) of the Collateral Council, the, now destroyed, trials of the Collateral Council's tribunal also demonstrate their involvement in processes of providing grace.

The sums of money provided by compositions could at times be huge. The opponents of the Duke of Osuña, during his viceroyalty, accused him of conspiring to take over the kingdom for himself. Some of the evidence lodged for this were the scale of some of the compositions he concluded, with the implication being that the funds were being used for his own purposes. The composition of Domenico Antonio de Sanctis, the baron of

Roccacasale and a key figure in the army led against Marco Sciarra, was named as being 50,000 ducats in value.

Managing conflicts in the Kingdom of Naples: aristocrats, the royal word, and sureties

This section explores the attempts at the control of violence and the promotion of reconciliation through the use of the oath *ad invicem parola sub verbo, et fide Regia di non offendersi, o farsi offendere* and forms of pledging to not offend others that did not use oaths. This legal instrument in its broader form, as a surety not to offend, was widely used throughout Italy in the early modern period. But its Neapolitan version has not been explored at length. The use of this was very common in order to attempt to control violence, especially noble violence. The Collateral Council debated how to pacify nobles in conflict and whether it was judicious to punish them. Much of the time of the Council was spent managing 'differences' among the nobility. A seventeenth-century commentator defined the Council as 'dealing with events that touch the quiet and security of the Kingdom'; a large portion of this business was managing the violent or otherwise destructive behaviour of the nobility.[101]

In Neapolitan history such affirmations were used during the accession of Ferdinand in 1504 and also by Charles V during his Italian residence. In this process of conquest, the surrender of some Neapolitan forces who had sided with the French was secured with the 'parola et fede Regia' issued directly by the *Gran Capitan*, Gonzalo de Cordoba.[102] Offering the faith of the monarch was one of the most important ways to establish the legitimacy of the new Spanish regime as part of the systematic agreements and in order to display that consensus and historical precedent would be respected. The reintegration of some of the French supporting nobility relied upon trust that they would not suffer reprisals.[103] The civic celebrations, parliaments and recognition of privileges that occurred in the early sixteenth century were another example of the new monarchs' assurances that their new subjects would have their rights respected.

Apart from its essential place in the constitutional changes of the early sixteenth century, the same language of royal faith and the royal word had wider cultural purchase. According to the preacher Domenico Paolacci: 'who would not trust under the Royal word? The word of the King should be a precious joy bound with the gold of immutability'.[104] It could be an analogy to explain the divine. The King's word – from a good King – had a broad cultural implication as unalterable, a true bond and firm foundation. In this sense, state-based practices of peace-making as well as religious ones also had longstanding moral traditions. Betrayal of the *verbo regio* was seen as particularly offensive.

In an attempt to draw out a confession from Maurizio de Rinaldis, a noble suspected of involvement in the philosopher Tommaso Campanella's attempted rebellion of 1599, royal counsellors purportedly assured him that he would not lose his life, citing a promise 'in verbo regio'. As he feared he would be executed on direct order without due process – *de mandato regio* – because he was guilty of killing one of his cousins and a woman he confessed all his crimes. But then when he sent his jailer to ask to be freed, he was instead prepared for execution, the confessor Gesuino told him that the 'palabra' was not for evildoers.[105] This was presented by Campanella to the authorities as one of the most egregious examples of the lies and betrayals that had coerced untrue confessions out of his co-defendants.

The broader development of oaths as 'sacraments of power' has been traced by Paolo Prodi.[106] He sees the 'web of oaths, which developed from the most elementary relations of fealty, through the ever more complex and articulated conventions of private associations, to the pacts of lordship and international treaties'.[107] For Prodi, the decline in the significance of oath-making came as the state increasingly successfully managed a monopoly of violence. In this story, oaths are useful when constant agreements are needed to regulate power relations whereas when authority is well established such agreements become irrelevant. However, oaths survived with a variety of uses in southern Italy, becoming central to attempts to control the nobility. They remained part of the political fabric.

The usage of peaces, truces, and vows to control violence was widespread in early modern Europe. Promises to end mutual hostility, in a variety of forms, were the subject of Sebastiano Guazzini's *Tractatus de pace, treuga, verbo dato alicui principi, vel alteri persone nobili, & de cautione de non offendendo* (Rome, 1610). Guazzini defines the *tregua* as a 'mutual agreement between enemies to not offend against each other for a certain time'.[108] A peace, in Guazzini's terms, was a more lasting state without the time limit that a truce implied. The notion of the 'caution to not offend' was broadly used; this was far from necessarily a true peace in the sense of reconciliation. Others such as Francesco Ercolani wrote popular treatises on the subject.[109] As well as these dedicated treatises it was a subject discussed by many jurists.[110] Such assurances were part of many lawsuits and other judicial proceedings.

Such agreements 'under the word and faith of the King' should not be examined in isolation. Instead they should be seen as part of the social history of 'fidelity' both as loyalty given to a monarch and the faith he (and the representative institutions of the monarchy) held with his subjects. The polyvalent notion of fidelity was a central site of negotiation between monarch and subjects in Naples. It was an especially contested ground in the Kingdom of Naples between the aristocracy and the viceregal regime. As Giovanni Muto has put it, fidelity 'was a mechanism of continual negotiation between sovereign and subjects who had understood right from the start the spaces that opened up between an absent sovereign and a kingdom'.[111] The sojourn of Charles V in Naples was marked by public demonstrations of the faith given by the nobles and people of Naples. Ephemeral decoration explored the theme of loyalty; a large poster had the words 'The *Popolo* of Naples is bound to imperial fidelity with love, truth, honour'.[112] Promises or proofs of faithfulness were used to work out the nature of the relationship between King and his subjects.[113] The display of 'fidelity', especially by the nobility, insinuated that obedience was a matter of choice and that other options existed.

Yet at the same time as they should be considered in the Neapolitan history of fidelity, they must also be considered as being seen by contemporaries as pragmatic tools for tamping down cycles of violence. The viceroy of Naples, the Count of Lemos issued a law in 1616 that claimed: 'for experience it is known, that no method is easier and more effective to reconcile brawls, and differences that are wont to occur, especially between noble and principal people, as regards pacifying them, than giving *ad invicem parola sub verbo, et fide Regia* of not offending and being so offended'.[114] These vows to flee conflict were regarded by Lemos as the most effective countermeasure to the various problems of noble violence. These oaths drew upon the claim that royal authority should be 'sacrosanct and inviolable'. Loyalty to the Spanish King was understood as endowing direct agreements with assurance of peaceful coexistence. In the Kingdom of Naples, such acts of giving faith were used by the viceroys to manage the forms of hostility between people of considerable social station; they were the main response to duels and threatened combats between the nobility. Outbreaks of violence and rancour could be countered with a plausible agreement under the auspices of the Spanish monarchy that was cemented by drawing upon claims to fidelity.

Lemos promoted their use and ordered that they be integrated into the chancery system of early modern Naples. They should be taken by the Secretary of the Kingdom, or the *scrivani di mandamenti* or the *scrivani di cancellieri* of the Royal Chancery. In Lemos's law, the logic was that the punishment for breaking such faith should be 'infamy as a breaker of word' rather than capital punishment.

In the Kingdom of Naples the administration of oaths 'sub verbo regio' became an integral part of the viceregal system of peace-making. Their full title was 'sub verbo regia di non offendersi, o farsi offendere'. In this sense they were akin to other pledges of truce, without a necessary component of full reconciliation. But the distinction between models should not be made too clear, as they were defined as 'peaces' in the language of administration and they do not seem to have included any time limits as might be expected in truces. Such a time limit would have been odd considering the active pursuit of such enmities through violence was, at any rate, illicit. The oaths *sub verbo regio* became an integrated part of the bureaucratic centre of the kingdom's institutions. A document outlining the duties and offices of the royal chancery from 1645 noted the bureaucratization of the registration of peace-making, that is 'in materia di Pace', in the kingdom.[115] It should be either the royal secretary or the scribal officers, the *scrivani di mandamento* or the *scrivani di cancellieri*, who should oversee the words of peace. This intriguing mention demonstrates that the peace-making functions of royal authority mediated through the Collateral Council and Chancery may have been more widely used than the surviving documents allow for. That is, because it notes that the secretary Salazar, who never otherwise took any money for individual acts of his office, charged around 10 *carlini* for issuing a peace oath 'because otherwise there would have been many people'. A small charge was a form of administrative management.[116]

The Collateral Council used its authority to pressure parties to accept the settlement of giving the royal word. At times parties attempted to resist such obligations to avoid a reconciliation with a hated enemy. In 1658 Annibale Caracciolo and Ettore Capecelatro (the Duke of Siano) were ordered to reconcile after 'some differences'. Annibale refused claiming that he was a cleric. The ministers of the Consiglio Collaterale decided that he was a 'clerico notorio' (one who invalidated their claims to clerical privileges through immoral behaviour and neglect of duties) and as such should be forced to participate in the peace.[117]

In some cases of enforced peace-making, in which a violent crime had occurred, the authorities were presented with a choice between arranging oaths or passing the case to a law court. In general, handing the case over to criminal or civil judges was seen as antithetical to the quick resolution of the dispute and, in criminal cases, damaging to the reputation and honour of the houses involved. In 1658 the *Collaterale* debated what to do in the aftermath of a 'briga' between the Prince of Cursi and the sons of the Baron of Faicchio; while the details of the case are not present in the records, the word *briga* implies a physical brawl of some sort, possibly a duel. Differences of opinion existed within the council. The regent Burgos voted for the case to be handled by the *Vicaria*, whereas the regents Muscettola and Uyloya came down on the side of handing the case to a trusted cavalier who would arrange the terms of giving the word.[118]

The *parola* was a more respectable and hopefully calmer outcome. They were seen as face-saving agreements that could stop the cycle of offence and possible violence from growing. In 1665 there were 'differences' between the uncle and nephew Francesco Gambacorta and the Prince of Macchia. The origin was a lawsuit that had descended into 'indecent words and behaviours in detriment to their reputation'.[119] The thorny issue for the mediators was how to reach an agreement over rancour that emerged from a lawsuit without prejudicing either side or leaving one of their reputations wounded. When enmities opened up between or within noble clans the government often intervened but they could not ignore honour codes or the sensibilities of noble masculinity.

The authority of the viceregal administration could be used by aristocrats as a resource. Such agreements were sometimes made outside of the chamber and then the *Collaterale* was contacted to assist in the arrangements. Oliveto and Brancaccio wrote to the council to discuss the problems arising in the reconciliation of the prince of Macchia and Francesco Gambacorta. They were writing to alert the Council that in their view the Marchese of Brianza (*cognate* of the Prince) and Giovan Battista Spinello (relations of Francesco) had stakes in the arguments and should also give their words under the faith of the King. The sprawl of dispute across kin and clan allegiances meant that such mass promises were common.[120]

Oaths on the King's word were a malleable tool of policy. They were not only used in cases of intra-noble conflicts but also in attempts to protect those who brought lawsuits or other forms of judicial action against nobles. In 1665 Fabrizio Spinello and his wife Giovanna di Rossi argued that they should not be subject to a *pleggieria* but instead they could give their word under a massive 20,000 ducat penalty to not offend those who accused them.[121] Clearly this was an attempt to reach a more favourable position for themselves that would also be acceptable to the authorities.

The royal word and faith was also used to put indulgences into practice. Giuseppe Ceraso complained of having been imprisoned when he had already stood 'sub verbo et fide Regis'.[122] This was a legal status important to navigate out of punishment or outlaw status.

The use of sureties and oaths to tame the violent aristocracy of Naples in the latter half of the seventeenth century increased. In March 1681 the viceroy imprisoned multiple high-ranking aristocrats in the castles of Naples, including the Prince of Riccia, the Marquis of Fuscaldo, the Prince of Torella, and the Duke of Atri. This was a forced imprisonment in order to make them provide the royal word of not offending against the Marchese of San Giorgio who had killed the Marchese of Arena. These noblemen were deeply unhappy, writing to Madrid to complain that because the homicide had been done with the quality of an assassination they should not be forced to make such a surety.[123] In the end, they managed to leave Castel Nuovo and Castel Sant'Elmo by making a simple pledge to not offend without swearing an oath. The amounts involved reached very high levels. An attempt was made to inflict a 50,000 ducat pledge on Giulio Acquaviva.[124]

The formula of the 'royal word' was also used to assure bandits of their indulgence as it could provide a wide-ranging safe conduct in advance of full forgiveness. It was a promise of protection. The usage of royal authority in such agreements was also explained by the desire to draw upon the direct resources of monarchical authority, with the act of oath-giving removing their mediation through ministers and orders. 'Immediate royal authority imprints in the souls of vassals a greater respect, than that of the Royal Magistrates', therefore 'the crime is more serious when it is disobedience to orders given in the name of the Prince, than to that of the Magistrate'.[125] It is likely the respectful and egalitarian nature of such vows that explains their attractiveness to the nobility. They implicitly made peace a matter of consensus; even when ordered on pains of money, in form they were a respectful promise which had an elective character.

Despite the multiple ways in which they drew upon monarchical authority we should not mistake all instances of such oaths as highly controlled instruments of royal peace-making. On first glance they seem to be an example of the increased control of practices of peace-making on behalf of central authorities. But two previously mentioned characteristics of these peaces disturb this simple picture. First, like many aspects of power relations in the Kingdom of Naples they were delegated and administered by other officials, distant not only from the King but also from the viceroy. Second, they could be arranged privately in the first instance. Criticism of how they were issued places into question how to conceive of their status as tools of government. In 1693 the viceroy, the Count of Santo Stefano, was frustrated with the dispatch of agreements under the royal word to be certified by the central administration. He argued that it caused 'abuses and inconveniences' when oaths upon the royal word were administered without regard to the specific circumstances and, especially, when they were given to 'every sort of person'.[126]

For Santo Stefano, what was at stake was that the 'cautela' of the *regia parola* should only have been given in the most extreme cases and it was only suitable for those of a significant social standing. This latter point is not given a full explanation within the pragmatic, but he notes the damage when those who have given the word were not of adequate status to worry about keeping it or if they had nothing to lose.[127] For those who were not rich or noble, the stakes were too low. He then ordered that in future no oaths should be given or registered without a full account of the parties and issues at stake being presented to him. The attempt to bring provincial peace-making under closer control underscores the potential innovations of regional government and the ways in which the sorts of procedures developed at the margins. With the loss of this sort of everyday administrative paperwork from the *Regie Audienze* we have little hope of understanding the specifics of the structure of most of these sorts of dispensations. The main purpose of such vows was to stop enmities devolving into violence or to pull back from cycles of attacks already begun. This was one of the primary ways that the viceregal administration attempted to insert itself into the kinship politics of the nobilities of the Kingdom.

Enlightenment criticisms of baroque justice do not only present condemnations but vivid depictions of early modern moral situations. One such enlightened jurist, Alberto de Simoni in his commentary on theft includes a discourse on the problems of remission. He argues that in the crime of homicide the remission of the offended party

> is almost never given for nothing, spontaneously, and sincerely, often it is taken with illicit means, violence and for self-protection, extorted with threatening words, and notwithstanding this it has such power that often due to having it, the murderer is exempted not only from the normal penalty of death which he deserves, not only for the offence done to the party, but for the nature of the crime itself, but also from any other extraordinary punishment of the body, in such a way that with horror one can see a homicide satisfied with even a small amount of money, and with this the murderer can buy his own life.[128]

The problems of forgiveness and the logic of exchange have been the topic of this chapter. But de Simoni's comments remind us of the visceral nature of these problems. Only by juxtaposing such critiques with evidence from the judicial archives can we see the potential for a study of the emotional and social effects of the judicial systems reformers criticized.

Above we have read the story of the murder of Diomede Fiorenza by Carlo Vasullo and Sebastiano Calabrese. A murder committed apparently as part of a formal hatred; the use by Francesco of a central legal system; the pressure for forgiveness and the eventual outlawing of the two accused; and, finally, a refusal to bargain over a dead son. Francesco Fiorenza cast himself as the steadfast father who refused to deal in blood. These are examples of the juridical norms and practices explored above, but in this instance in direct contact with one man's emotional world sited in the politicking of a small-town. Such perspectives from towns and villages on the nature of settlement, the selling of blood, and the consequences of violence must be seen as the direct effects of a complicated legal system that was a contested field of authority and not under the simple control of an undivided state. This chapter demonstrates the plural and complex practices that lay behind what was seen in retrospect as the 'abominable traffic' in blood money. The management of crimes committed through various sorts of transactions was crucial in early modern Naples, as well as throughout early modern

Italy and beyond, and the usage of such techniques was widely dispersed throughout different levels of the polity. The *remissione della parte offesa* provided every murder committed with a wide socio-legal meaning, opening up questions of extortion. The *parola regia* was widely used and this chapter has only sketched the surface of the extensive ways this was used in the Kingdom of Naples. The next chapter moves to consider the provincial power relations such legal instruments unfolded within.

Notes

1. An earlier, shorter version of this chapter was published as 'Forgiving Crimes in Early Modern Naples' in *Cultures of Conflict Resolution in Early Modern Europe*, ed. by Stephen Cummins and Laura Kounine (Basingstoke: Ashgate, 2016).
2. Nicolò Toppi, *De origine ominium tribunalium nunc in Castro Capuano fidelissimae civitatis Neapolis existentitum* (Naples, 1655–1666).
3. Traiano Boccalini, *La bilancia politica di tutte le opera di Traiano Boccalini parte prima dove si tratta delle osservazioni politiche sopra I sei Libri degli Annali di Cornelio Tacito* (Castellana, 1678), p. 179 and p. 487.
4. Tommaso Astarita, *The Continuity of Feudal Power: the Carocciolo di Brienza in Spanish Naples* (Cambridge: Cambridge University Press, 1992), p. 38.
5. For an example of the lack of baronial court documentation see Tommaso Astarita, *Village Justice: Community, Family, and Popular Culture in Early Modern Italy* (Baltimore: Johns Hopkins University Press, 1999), p. xv: where he notes that apart from the trial on which the book is based 'I found almost no other examples for the period preceding the end of the eighteenth century'.
6. See the royal pragmatic: *De officio judicium et aliorum officialium*, IV.
7. Francesco Campennì, *La patria e il sangue: Città, patriziati e potere nella Calabria moderna* (Manduria: Lacaita, 2004), pp. 244–5.
8. ASN, Consiglio Collaterale, Affari Diversi, I, busta 1, f. 408r.
9. Ibid, f. 407r.
10. Pier Luigi Rovito, *Respublica dei togati: giuristi e società nella Napoli del Seicento* (Naples: Jovene, 1982), p 68.
11. ASN, Consiglio Collaterale, Notamenti, 33, 15v.
12. Marco Corcione, *Modelli processuali nell'antico regime. La giustizia penale nel Tribunale di Campagna di Nevano* (Frattamaggiore: Istituto di Studi Atellani, 2002).
13. *De officio Iudicis Generalis delinquentes.*
14. Marco Nicola Miletti, 'Strade di banditi, banditi di strada. Criminalità e comunicazioni nel Mezzogiorno del Cinquecento', *Frontiera d'Europa*, 6 (2000), 49–114.
15. See for instance M. Mancino, 'Ecclesiastical Justice and the Counter-Reformation: Notes on the Diocesan Court of Naples', in Eric A. Johnson and Eric H. Monkkonen (eds) *Civilization of Crime: Violence in Town and Country Since the Middle Ages* (Urbana: University of Illinois Press, 1996) and

David Gentilcore, *From Bishop to Witch: The System of the Sacred in the Early Modern Terra d'Otranto* (Manchester: Manchester University Press, 1992).
16 ASN, Segreterie Vicerè, busta 124, nn.
17 Giambattista Basile, *Giambattista Basile's The Tale of Tales, or Entertainment for Little Ones*, ed. and trans. by Nancy L. Canepa (Detroit: Wayne State University Press, 2007), pp. 91–2.
18 Angelo Scialoya, *Praxis Foriudicatoria, seu de modo procedendi in Regno Neapolitano ad sententiam foriudicationis contra reum absentum in eius contumacia vigore Constitutionis Regni poenam eorum* (Naples, 1645), p. 39: 'Fuga delinquentis post delictum sequutum facit indicium ad torturam contra ipsum fugientum'.
19 Calcabottaccio is known today as Castelbottaccio. It was taxed for sixty-one hearths in 1669 and had around 1200 inhabitants at the end of the eighteenth century. Lorenzo Giustiniani, *Dizionario Geografico-ragionato del Regno Di Napoli* (Naples, 1797), pp. 30–1.
20 ASL, Regia Udienza, Processi Penali, busta 4, fasc. 54bis, fol. 640[r].
21 Ibid.: 'tu non sei huomo da levarti le Corne?'
22 Ibid.
23 Ibid.
24 Ibid., fol. 60[v].
25 Ibid.
26 Ibid., fol. 61[v].
27 ASN, Delegazione della Real Giurisdizione, Processi, busta 189, fasc. 49, fol. 2[r]: 'contro un suo nemico'.
28 Ibid., fol. 1[r].
29 ASL, Regia Udienza, Processi Penali, busta 1, fasc. 17, fols. 780[v]–781[r]: 'cisterna vecchia'.
30 Ibid., fols. 783[r].
31 Ibid., fol. 781[r].
32 Ibid., busta 1, fasc. 13 and busta 2b, fasc. 30; there are also two trials for attempted escapes: busta 8 fasc. 84 and busta 7, fasc. 71.
33 For prisons in the Kingdom of Naples, see Mario Scaduto, 'Le carceri della Vicaria di Napoli agli inizi del Seicento', *Redenzione umana*, 6 (1968), 393–412 and Daniela Ambron, 'Le carceri regie del Regno di Napoli tra capitale e province (XVII–XVIII secolo)', in *Carceri, carcerieri, carcerati. Dall'antico regime all'Ottocento*, ed. by Livio Antonielli (Soveria Mannell: Rubbettino, 2006), pp. 145–164. More generally, the historiography on early modern prisons is extensive. See Romano Canosa and Isabella Colonnello, *Storia del carcere in Italia dalla fine del Cinquecento all'Unità* (Rome: Sapere 2000, 1984) and Pieter Spierenburg, *The Prison Experience: Disciplinary Institutions and their Inmates in Early Modern Europe* (New Brunswick: Rutgers University Press, 1991).
34 See the repeated criticisms of the 'extortions' of the jailors of the Vicaria who, at times, established illicit economies around the provision of beds, food and water. Those 'miserable prisoners' [*carcerati miserabili*] were found without

beds or even makeshift beds of hay or textiles instead sleeping upon 'la nuda terra, umida, fangosa, e alle volte anche puzzolente'. Noted in the pragmatic 'De Carcerariis', in *Nuova collezione delle prammatiche del Regno di Napoli*, ed. by Lorenzo Giustiniani (Naples, 1804), I, p. 164.

35 *Privilegii et capitoli con altre gratie concesse alla fidelissima Città di Napoli, & Regno per li Serenissimi Rì di Casa de Aragona. Confirmati, & di nuovo concessi per la Maestà Cesarea dell'Imperator Carlo V et Re Filippo Nostro Signore. Con tutte le altre Gratie concesse per tutto questo presente Anno MDLXXXVII. Con nuove addizioni, & la tavola delle cose notabili e di nuovo ristampati con le nuove Gratie, e Privilegii conceduti e confirmati dalla Sacra Cesarea et Cattolica Maesta di Carlo VI Imperadore sino all'anno 1720* (Milan, 1720), p. 207.

36 Ibid.

37 *Bulletino delle leggi del Regno di Napoli* (Naples, 1813), pp. 255–6.

38 On the now standard account of 'vestiges' or 'remnants' of the older system of *accusatio* remaining in later inquisitorial procedure see Mario Sbriccoli, 'Legislation, Justice and Political Power in Italian Cities, 1200–1400' in *Legislation and Justice*, ed. by Antonio Padoa-Schioppa (Oxford: Clarendon, 1997), p. 48.

39 ASL, Regia Udienza, Processi Penali, busta 1 fasc. 10.

40 Archivio diocesano di Conversano, Conversano, Acta Criminalia, fasc. 29, fol. 1[r]: 'che dò querela criminale control il detto Chierico Renna, acciò sia castigato s'income comandano le leggi, e la giustizia, e non si liberi senza la mia intelligenza, e remissione'.

41 ASN, Delegazione della real giurisdizione, Processi, busta 178, fols. 7[r–v].

42 ADC, Conversano, Acta Criminalia, 13, fol. 1[r].

43 *Privilegii et capitoli con altre gratie concesse alla Fidelissima Città di Napoli, & Regno per li Serenissimi Rì di Casa de Aragona. Confirmati, & di nuovo concessi per la Maestà Cesarea dell'Imperator Carlo V et Re Filippo Nostro Signore con tutte le altre gratie concesse per tutto questo presente Anno MDLXXXVII* (Venice, 1588), p. 47.

44 Peter Mazur, *The New Christians of Spanish Naples 1528–1671: A Fragile Elite* (Basingstoke: Palgrave Macmillan, 2013), pp. 31–2.

45 Pietro Follerio, *Canonica criminalis praxis* (Venice, 1583), p. viii: 'Reconciliatio presupponit iniuriae remissionem'

46 Ibid.: 'a i quali di giustizia compete ragione di querelare, e di accusare i delinquenti'.

47 Varius, Pragmaticae, edicta, decreta, interdicta, regiaeque sanctiones Regni Neapolitani, I, p. 426: 'l'ammettere i delinquenti à composizione è grazia; e la volontà nostra non è d'ammettere alcuno à composizione, se non precede la remissione di tutti coloro, i quali di giustizia possono querelare, & accusare'.

48 Giovanni Maria Novario, *Novissimae decisiones civiles, criminales & canonicae: tam regii tribunalis audientiae provinciarum Capitantae, Apuleae, & Comitatus Mollisij Regni Neapolis, quam causarum delegatrum* (Geneva, 1637), pp. 78–9.

49 Ibid.
50 'De compositionibus, et commutationibus poenarum' (1567) in Giustiniani, *Nuova Collezione delle prammatiche*, I, p. 253.
51 The language can be confusing but Francesco de Jorio's comment clarifies the Neapolitan situation: 'In our legal system [*Foro*] however we use the name *remissioni*, for what are in civil law [*diritto comune*] are called *transazioni*, and according to the language of Civil Lawyers mean the commutation of penalties made by judges, we also call *composizioni*'. Francesco de Jorio, *Introduzione allo studio delle prammatiche del regno di Napoli* (Naples, 1777), I, p. 190.
52 Gregorio Grimaldi, *Istoria delle leggi e magistrati del Regno di Napoli* (Naples, 1749), II, p. 185: 'far le grazie a'rei'.
53 Ibid: 'poichè possono bene i rei concordarsi cogli accusatori, e averne la remissione, e presentandola o al Vicerè, o a' Reggenti del Collaterale, qualora nel sabato vanno nella Gran Corte della Vicaria a far le grazie a' rei; ottener quella della pena, o pure il di lei alleviamento; ma inteso l'Avvocato fiscale, di cui si posson le pene comporre ancora in danajo, secondo la qualità e gravezza del delitto; il che non però non ha luogo in tutt'i reati'.
54 Francesco Palermo, ed., *Narrazioni e documenti sulla storia di Napoli dall'anno 1522 al 1667* (Florence: Gio. Pietro Vieusseux, 1846), p. 499
55 *Nova situatione de pagamenti fiscali de carlini 42 à foco delle Provincie del Regno di Napoli, & Adohi de Baroni, e Feudatarij dal primo di Gennaro 1669 avanti* (Naples, 1670), pp. 465–6.
56 In the same period the Dogana of Foggia brought 177,296 ducats to the treasury. For compositions as a source of royal income see also the 1597 report of the Venetian ambassador, Girolamo Ramusio, Eugenio Albèri (ed.), *Le relazioni degli ambasciatori veneti al senato* (Florence, 1863), p. 348.
57 On these connections see Ottavia Niccoli, 'Rinuncia, pace, perdono. Rituali di pacificazione nella prima età moderna', *Studi storici*, 40 (1999), 219–61.
58 Anna Osbat, ' "E il perdonar magnanima vendetta": i pacificatori tra bene comune e amor di Dio', *Ricerche di storia sociale e religiosa*, 53 (1998), 121–46.
59 'De receptatoribus delinquentium, seu malefactorum' (1560) in Giustiniani, *Nuova collezione del prammatiche*, XIII, pp. 6–7.
60 Vincenzo d'Onofrio, *Giornali di Napoli dal MDCLX al MDCLXXX* (Naples: Società napoletana di storia patria, 1934), I, p. 68: 'trattava paci e remissioni delle parti offese a favore dell'offensori per avarizia, dandosi in potere a tutta briglia all'arbitri da sgherro'.
61 Ibid., p. 210.
62 ASL, Regia Udienza, Processi Penali, busta 3, fasc. 34, fol. 63^v.
63 Ibid., fols. 4^{r-v}.
64 Ibid., fol. 8^r.
65 Ibid., fol. 353^v.
66 Ibid., fols. 4^{r-v}.
67 Palermo, *Narrazioni e documenti*, p. 523.
68 ASN, Consiglio Collaterale, Notamenti, n.s., busta 1, fol 518^r.

69 Grimaldi, *Istoria*, X, p. 541. The *truglio*, another name for a form of pecuniary composition for crimes would come to be a widespread practice in the eighteenth century. On this see Donato Palazzo, 'Del "truglio" e delle sue applicazioni in Puglia', in *Studi di storia pugliese in onore di Giuseppe Chiarelli*, ed. by Michele Paone (Galatina: Congedo Editore, 1977), VI, pp. 59–113.

70 'De compositionibus, et commutationibus poenarum', in Giustiniani, *Nuova collezione delle prammatiche*, III, p. 252: 'una de las causas, por que muchos se atreven á cometer delitos, es por la speranza, que tienen de otener remission de las partes'.

71 Giustiniani, *Nuova collezione delle prammatiche*, I, p. 474.

72 On the visitors see Mireille Peytavin, *Visite et gouvernement dans le royaume de Naples (XVIe–XVIIe siècles)* (Madrid: Casa de Velázquez, 2003).

73 See the discussion of the visit of Alarcon in Peytavin, *Visite et gouvernement*, pp. 81–6. Alarcon named the abuses as: 'hanno fatto alcuno aggravio o ingiustizia per denari o altra qualsivoglia indebita causa, o se hanno commesso frodi, subornazioni, estorsioni, composizioni, occultazioni, negligenze o altri illeciti, per se o per interposita persona, [...] o se hanno occultati beni; stabili o mobili sotto nome altrui [...] per fare con essi mercanzie o altra negoziazione proibita'. For this quotation see *Pragmaticae, edicta, decreta*, IV, p. 298.

74 Francesco Capecelatro, *Degli annali della Città di Napoli (1631–1640)* (Naples: Tipografia di Reale, 1849), p. 2: 'nei delitti criminali si avea molto rispetto ai cavalieri, di modo tale che pareva strana cosa far morire alcun di loro, lo che di rado avveniva, non ostante che commettessero sovente strani ed enormi misfatti, i quali non guari tempo passava che, ottenuta la remissione della parte offesa, agevolmente si componevano'.

75 Giustiniani, *Nuova collezione della prammatiche*, II, p. 271: 'Per esperienza s'è veduto, che la principal causa de' delitti comessi, e che giornalmente si commettono in infinito numero, tanto dentro questa Fedelissima Città di Napoli, suoi Borghi, e Casali, come in tutto il presente Regno, è stata ed è la certezza, che hanno tenuta, e tengono i delinquenti d'ottenere le remissioni delle parti offese, e con quelle poi si rende loro più facile ottenere composizioni, grazie, accordi, o commutazioni delle pene.'

76 Giovanni Battista Baiardi, *Praticam criminalem* (Frankfurt, 1622), p. 214: 'omnes fere Barones habent privilegia gratiandi, sive componendi delicta vasallorum ante sententiam, quando adest partis remissio'.

77 On the comparatively extensive powers of feudal lords in the Kingdom of Naples see Astarita, *The Continuity of Feudal Power*, pp. 40–41, especially footnote no. 10.

78 On Sicilian barons remitting and composing crime see Rossella Cancila, ' "Per la retta amministratione della giustitia": la giustizia dei baroni nella Sicilia moderna', *Mediterranea Ricerche storiche*, 16 (2009), 315–52 (p. 332). See also Giovanni Muto, 'Pouvoirs et territoires dans l'Italie espagnole', *Revue d'histoire moderne et contemporaine* 45 (1998), 42–65 (pp. 57–8).

79 Quoted in Sonia Fiorilli, 'Poteri, economia e stili di vita di una famiglia feudale. Il caso di Sinforosa Mastrogiudice marchesa di Pietracatella (1675–1743)'

(unpublished doctoral thesis, Università degli Studi del Molise, 2010), pp. 46–7: 'ragioni di presentare in quelle e coll'intiero suo stato e signianter col Banco della Giustizia e con ognimoda Giurisdizione e cognitione delle prime e seconde cause civile, criminale, e miste, mero et misto impero, potestà delegati. Quattro lettere arbitrarie e con la podestà di compro delitti e di comutar di corporali in pecuniarie e quelle rimettere in tutto o in parte, soddisfatta per la parte lesa'.

80 This debate led to the distinction between the nature of baronial authority: between that given *in feudum* (their rights to jurisdictional powers intrinsic to them as owners of the feudal land) and *in officium* (that they exercised such rights on behalf of the sovereign, exercising a role). The second was a far less extensive right and one much more subjected to oversight and limitation. Pietro Giannone's discussion of the four arbitrary letters shows the effects of such debates, noting that King Robert intended to give powers only to barons in their role as his 'Ufficiali'. Pietro Giannone, *Istoria Civile del Regno di Napoli* (Haya, 1753), III, p. 186.

81 Giovanni Maria Novario, *Tractatus de vassallorum gravaminibus* (Geneva, 1686), p. 241.

82 King Ferrante of Aragon wrote in 1492 that jurisdictions 'derive from us like streams and water that run swiftly and, nevertheless, always go back to the sea whence they originated'. For this quotation and related discussion see Francesco Senatore, 'The Kingdom of Naples', in *The Italian Renaissance State*, ed. by Andrea Gamberini and Isabella Lazzarini (Cambridge: Cambridge University Press, 2012), p. 38.

83 For barons as royal officials see Aurelio Cernigliaro, *Sovranità e feudo nel Regno di Napoli, 1505–1557* (Naples: Jovene, 1983), II, p. 482.

84 In the state of Piedimonte, a fief of the Gaetani d'Aragona, 205 ducats were raised from compositions for criminal crimes out of a total revenue of 426.73 ducats during the period September–November 1737. See Luca Covino, 'Le carceri baronali del Regno di Napoli nel Settecento' in *Carceri, carcerieri, carcerati. Dall'antico regime all'Ottocento*, ed. by Livio Antonielli (Soveria Mannell: Rubbettino, 2006), p. 188.

85 Ibid., p. 200.

86 On widespread feudal abuses see Rosario Villari, *The Revolt of Naples* (Cambridge: Polity, 1993), esp. pp. 135–43.

87 ASL, Regia Udienza, Processi Penali, busta 3, fasc. 45.

88 Ibid., fols., 561^v–562^r: 'se vuoi uscire da carceri con componersi in pena a suo arbitrio senza voto di consultore'.

89 Ibid.

90 Novario, *Tractatus de vassallorum gravaminibus*, p. 172: 'Barones faciunt gratias, partibus non concordatis'.

91 'De Exulibus XXIX', in Giustiniani, *Nuova collezione delle prammatiche*, IV, p. 274.

92 Pietro Ebner, *Storia di un feudo del Mezzogiorno: La Baronia di Novi* (Rome: Edizioni di Storia e Letteratura, 2004), p. 176: 'mentre con essersi accordati li delinquenti di eccessi enormi con pochissima somma di denaro hanno dato causa di nuovi errori e delitti'.

93 Michele Janora, *Memorie storiche, critiche e diplomatiche della Città di Montepeloso (oggi Irsina)* (Matera: F. P. Conti, 1901): p. 260: 'Item decta Università s'aggrava, qualmente decto Illustre Duca per componere li delitti, et fare proventi, s'interpone, e s'intromette in far fare ed ottenere le remissioni delle parti, ed alle volte per forza di violenza costrenge ad farle ottenere, si poete quod abstineat, quoad vigesimum, quia negatur factum'.

94 Paolo Mattia Doria, *Relazione dello stato politico, economico e civile del Regno di Napoli nel tempo ch'è stato governato da i Spagnuoli* (Naples, 1707).

95 Ibid., pp. 118–19: 'far la grazia, e di transigere le pene'.

96 Ibid.

97 Ibid.: 'puole il Barone far'uccidere uno sotto l'apparenza di particolare inimicizia con quello, e poi far la grazia all'uccisore senza pericolo che un sí fatto omicidio si possa mai giuridicamente provare'.

98 *Omissis aliis.* S.E. ha destinato il Reggente de Ponte, a fare la visita ogni sabato alli carcerati, e vedere di componere li delitti in remieri; poichè S.M. ha bisogno di essi a tempo buono. Remieri si fanno assai, e la Vicaria si smorba; et ogni cosa si compone in remieri. Perchè vi è ordine di corte, che Napoli debba tener trenta galere armate, per tutto quell oche può accadere. Di Napoli, 20 Dicembre 1605.

99 Ibid., p. 265.

100 ASN, Consiglio Collaterale, Cancelleria, Diversorum, b. 2, ff. 49r–53r.

101 Madrid, Biblioteca Nacional de España, MS 6722, 'Relatione del Governo del Regno di Napoli', fol. 15r: 'se tratta delle cose occorrenti per quiete, et sicurezza del Regno'.

102 Bartolomeo Ravenna, *Memorie istoriche della città di Gallipoli* (Naples, 1836), p. 263.

103 On the establishing of the regime see Carlos José Hernando Sánchez, *El Reino de Nápoles en el Imperio de Carlos V: la consolidación de la conquista* (Madrid: Sociedad Estatal para la Commemoración de los Centenarios de Felipe II y Carlos V, 2001).

104 Domenico Paolacci, *Pensieri Predicabili sopra tutti gl'evangelii* (Venice, 1641), p. 311: 'chi non si dee fidare sotto la parola Regia? La parola del Rè deve esser gioia pretiosa legata nell'oro dell'immutabilità'.

105 Luigi Firpo, *Il supplizio di Tommaso Campanella* (Rome: Salerno Editrice, 1985), p. 277.

106 Paolo Prodi, *Il sacramento del potere: il giuramento politico nella storia costituzionale dell'Occidente* (Bologna: Il Mulino, 1992).

107 Ibid., p. 161.

108 Sebastiano Guazzini, *Tractatus de pace, treuga, verbo dato alicui principi, vel alteri persone nobili, & de cautione de non offendendo* (Rome, 1610), p. 235: 'mutua conventio de se non offendendo inter inimicos pro certo tempore'.

109 Francesco Ercolani's *De cautione de non offendendo* (Venice, 1569) was republished for over a century from its first publication, gaining a European readership.

110 Prospero Farinacci, *Praxis et theoricae criminalis* (Leiden, 1635), III, p. 432.
111 Giovanni Muto, 'Fedeltà e patria nel lessico politico napoletano della prima età modernà', in *Storia sociale e politica: omaggio a Rosario Vilari*, ed. by Alberto Merola, Giovanni Muto, Elena Valeri, and Maria Antonietta (Milan: FrancoAngeli, 2006), pp. 495–522: 'era un meccanismo di continua negoziazione tra il sovrano e i regnicoli che intuirono sin dall'inizio gli spazi che si aprivano nei rapporti tra un sovrano assente ed un regno'.
112 Giovanni Antonio Summonte, *Dell'historia della citta, e regno di Napoli* (Naples, 1675), p. 115: 'Il Popolo di Napoli alla fedeltà cesarea è legato con amore, verità, onore'.
113 On 'fidelity as a category of political discourse and as a practice of negotiation' see Giovanni Muto, 'Fidelidad, política y conflictos urbanos en el Reino de Nápoles (siglos XVI–XVII)', in *Ciudades en conflicto. Siglos XVI–XVIII*, ed. by José Ignacio Fortea Perez and Juan Eloy Gelabert González (Madrid: Marcial Pons Historia, 2008). Other relevant contributions to the debate on 'fidelity' in Neapolitan history include Rosario Villari, *Per il re o per la patria: la fedeltà nel Seicento con "Il Cittadino Fedele" e altri scritti politici* (Rome: Laterza, 1994) and Giuseppe Galasso, 'Da "Napoli gentile" a "Napoli fedelissima"', in his *Napoli capitale: identità politica e identità cittadina* (Naples, Electa Napoli: 2003), pp. 61–110.
114 'De pace sub verbo regio inita; et rupta' (1616), in Giustiniani, *Nuova collezione delle prammatiche*, XII, p. 177: 'Essendosi per esperienza conosciuto, che niun modo è più facile, ed efficacie per comporre le risse, e le differenze, che sogliono occorrere, massime fra genti nobili, e principali, quanto il farle pacificare, con darsi *ad invicem* parola *sub verbo*, *et fide Regia*, di non offendersi, e farsi offendere'.
115 ASN, Consiglio Collaterale, Affari Diversi, I, f. 352r.
116 Ibid, ff. 355v–356r.
117 ASN, *Consiglio Collaterale*, Notamenti, busta 62, fol. 1v.
118 Ibid., fol. 159r.
119 Ibid., busta 67, fol. 37r.
120 Ibid, fols. 37^{r-v}.
121 Ibid., fol. 34^r.
122 ASN, *Consiglio Collaterale*, Affari Diversi, I, busta 1, fol. 536^r.
123 Domenico Confuorto, *Giornali di Napoli dal MDCLXXIX al MDCIC*, 2 vols. (Naples: Società napoletana di storia patria, 1930–31), I, p. 62.
124 Ibid., 103.
125 De Jorio, *Introduzione allo studio delle prammatiche del Regno di Napoli*, III, pp. 59–60: 'più grave è il delitto quando si disobbedisce agli ordini fatti in nome del Principe, che a quei del Magistrato'.
126 Diego Gatta, *Regali Dispacci nelli quali si contengono le Sovrane Determinazioni de'Punti Generali o che servono di norma ad altri simili casi nel Regno di Napoli* (Naples, 1776), p. 474: 'Considerando gli abusi, e inconvenienti, li quali si esperimentano dal darsi con tanta facilità, e per ogni sorte di persone, la parola regia'.

127 Ibid.: 'perchè non sieno del grado, che dee attendersi, o perchè non hanno cosa alcuna da perdere'.
128 Alberto de Simoni, *Del furto e sua pena* (Florence, 1813), pp. 104–5: 'Ora se questa remissione della parte lesa nel delitto d'omicidio, in cui non è quasi mai gratuita, spontanea, e sincera, e spesso con mezzi illeciti, e violenti di protezioni autorevoli, e di blandizie minacciose estorta, opera nondimeno, ad ha tanta forza, che spesso per essa l'omicida si esime non solo dalla pena ordinaria di morte da lui meritata, non per l'offesa sola recata alla parte, ma per la natura stessa del delitto commesso, ma anche da ogni altra straordinaria afflitiva del corpo, in modo che con orrore vedesi soddisfare con una somma anche leggera di danaro all'omicidio commesso, e con essa ricomprasi quella vita, che in virtù delle leggi naturali, divine, ed umane aveva l'omicida irreparabilmente perduta'.

3

The politics of enmity in the provinces

When early modern Italians considered the well-springs of the hatreds that haunted communities, it was most often the institutions of communal government to which they turned. Further, they saw the rivalries between nobles and non-nobles as a source of inimical energy that disrupted civil life. Machiavelli, in his Florentine histories, noted the 'grave and natural enmities' between the nobles and the *popolari* as 'the cause of all the evils that arise in cities'.[1] Many other examples of reflections on enmities as the curse of urban life can be cited: Geronimo Marciano, in writing the history of the Neapolitan Oratorians, wrote of 'longstanding [*invecchiate*] enmities, which are the plagues of towns'.[2] The division of a town into factions held together by inherited hatreds, was a common reality and often the primary system of power relations that inhabitants of these towns and the representative of early modern states had to confront. Enmities between powerful families and allegiance of others to them created a large portion of the conditions of public life. Control over the public purse was a much sought-after goal for patrician families, who wanted to reward their supporters and punish their enemies.

The enterprise of politics therefore entailed the craft of managing friends and enemies. This involved the pursuit of enmities but also the judicious use of settlement. The work of Osvaldo Raggio on the Genoese hinterland is foundational for understanding the relevance of enmity and peace-making to local political action in early modern Italy. According to Raggio, the 'political unity of the group of kinsmen was built ... above all on enmities, their settlements'.[3] The overarching significance of enmity was both a language of political formation and as a set of practices that through their exercise defined the field of politics. Enmity had its everyday form as avoidance or the failure to display due politeness or fealty. Violence, both physical and symbolic, was ubiquitous in the strivings over the control of local communities in the kingdom. Municipal life was intertwined with violence.

Andrea Zorzi, in a survey of social conflict in late medieval Italy, has pointed towards the importance of focusing on the emotional and the subjective in accounts of social conflicts, factionalism, and revenge killing.[4] He stresses how relations of friendship and enmity as well as values of individual and familial honour were the foundations of these practices.[5] He has signalled that one direction of study of such conflicts should take inspiration from the history of the emotions: 'the control and management of the passions, of fears, of hatreds and the variety of states of mind and emotions that conflicts catalysed in individuals and in strategies of alliances'.[6] Taking inspiration from research beyond Italy, he underlines that the overlapping practices of insult, offence, vengeance, and reconciliation had emotional economies. For the case of the early modern Kingdom of Naples, the work of Gérard Delille on the Puglian town of Altamura – building on the work of Giovanni Masi – provides some of the most careful reconstruction of the involvement of kinship in local enmities.[7]

From this viewpoint the practices and texture of social conflicts combine social and political structures of various kinds with subjective states of mind and affective dispositions. The emotions are inseparable from experiences of community and local politics.[8] In the provinces that composed the Kingdom of Naples a wide variety of constellations of local power-holders existed: civil conflict was formed out of complex mixtures. Yet within these complexities, enmity was the force that contemporaries identified as animating discord. This chapter surveys the political anatomy of the provinces as it bears upon histories of conflict, arguing for the relevance of enmity as a relational idiom.

What this chapter will demonstrate is the connection between enmities and issues of public life in the towns of the Kingdom of Naples. A set of factors influenced the enmity-prone condition of communities in the Kingdom of Naples. This chapter focuses on violent conflicts over the control of communities, the often-negative impact of long-running litigation, and the complex constellations of authorities that clashed over public affairs. The chapter focuses more on larger communities than the smaller villages of the Kingdom of Naples but, where possible, I seek to illustrate the similarities and differences in these communities.

It was the governments of the municipalities of the Kingdom, the *università*, that were the main focus of inimical divisions.[9] The Cardinal Giovan Battista de Luca observed that:

> experience teaches that with regard to factions and enmities that for the, most part, fight like cats and dogs, are wont to arise from the reason of the public government of communities; they give many a livelihood and a way to enrich themselves from the commune, and from the blood of the poor.[10]

This observation makes the important connection between enmity and enrichment. Towns and cities were often divided between lineages that understood their opposition through the language of enmity. *Università* was the term that 'designates the political and administrative identity' of a settlement.[11] Their institutions and composition varied. Generally, their institutional identity was a *governo* composed by officials called *sindici* and *eletti* (although other terms were used in some places).[12] The *sindici* and *eletti* of a town could be constituted fully by patrician nobles, by a mixture of representatives of the nobles and the *popolo* (often only the well-to-do citizens, those who lived 'civilly'), or – in settlements without much social differentiation – by any well-regarded citizen, who could include the poor and illiterate.[13] The patrician *seggio* (the 'seat' or place which nobles had membership of) of a town could be 'open' or 'closed'. In practice this meant that in open seats, wealthy citizen families could be aggregated to the nobility based on the assent of the existing nobility. Over time, and especially in large towns, it was more common for the nobility to be closed, with entrance being far more difficult to those outside the well-established noble families.[14]

These posts of government were prizes around which factions often competed. Due to this, communes were often mired in seemingly interminable enmities. The Spanish regularly revised administrative practices of town government in an attempt to stop violence between leading families.[15] Regional governors spent much of their time mediating between these clans and gathering reports of recent developments in longstanding feuds.[16] Gérard Delille's research is very important for this history. He has traced this story in a number of contexts and shown how the progressive restriction of access to offices of municipal government was often a scheme aimed at pacifying the worst excesses of factions through institutionalization. He highlighted the regulation of access to the offices of local government and the mechanisms of how such officials were chosen and, fundamentally, the balance between 'noble' and 'popular' representatives as 'a fundamental mechanism of the organization of local power not only in southern Italy but also in other Mediterranean countries'.[17]

A *università* received income from indirect and direct taxes, feudal rights that they had rented from their lord, from access charges to communally owned lands, and from properties owned by them.[18] They controlled public goods and delegated the administration of publicly owned property, such as public bakeries and taverns. They also directly hired 'public' staff such as doctors, physicians, and sometimes the Lenten preacher. Most importantly they oversaw the extraction of direct taxes and also the indirect taxes applied to many goods known as *gabelle*.[19] They often rented out the right to collect indirect taxes. They had a hand in nearly all economic activity in their communities. Material reasons for why these posts generated struggles were abundant. They also formed the main institutional bodies through which communities engaged with the viceregal regime.[20] Even very marginal and distant places were in dialogue with the centre.[21] The *università* were the most significant focal point for inimical conflict in the kingdom.

Scenarios of power in the provinces

In the Kingdom of Naples there were a variety of different assemblages of institutions, personages, and relationships that created the forms of power that can be labelled local politics. In the first place, the geography of human settlement varied considerably across the provinces of the kingdom. For instance, Terra di Lavoro had numerous smaller settlements and could count the royal city of Capua and Gaeta as its most prominent urban settlements, which had functions more as garrison cities than as commercial centres. Principato Citra had the city of Salerno, with a claim to being the oldest university in Europe as well as other settlements of the Amalfi Coast. Some provinces had very sparse urban settlements. Among the communities of Molise, for instance, at the start of the seventeenth century, only Isernia had more than 2000 inhabitants, followed by Morcone with 1615, and Campobasso with 1370.[22] Principato Ultra also had few cities, although ones with strategic importance such as Ariano. Capitanata, the site of the fertile plains of the *Tavoliere*, had the customs town of Foggia, the seat of the *Dogana*, and Lucera, seat of the *Regia Audienza*, as well as coastal towns such as Manfredonia. In the Terra di Bari, there were large urban settlements of considerable nobility such as Bari. The economic differentiation between different settlements also changed the stakes of inimical division. We could take as an example of a major urban settlement, Cosenza which, as a dry port for the Calabrian silk trade, offered opportunities for serious wealth (and thereby serious enmities), despite the calamitous drop in the scale of the trade after the end of the sixteenth century.[23]

Larger urban settlements had more advanced litigious and archival practices, mostly due to the larger number of notaries and lawyers to draw upon and being the seat of more institutions, as well as more money to launch legal campaigns in the capital or even to fund resident agents in Naples. Yet despite having less archival practice, evidence from smaller settlements can be found in collections of criminal trials and other source bodies. The exact situation of land ownership was one of the major variables that determined the local political players. One division was between feudal lands and lands in the royal demesne. A *feudo* was a community in which first-instance jurisdiction over criminal and civil matters, and perhaps also appeals, was controlled not by the Crown directly but by a feudatory invested with this power.[24] The vast majority of villages, towns and cities, around 95 per cent, were feudal.[25]

But this division does not tell us everything about variety within and between the categories *feudi* and royal lands. A feudal lord could be resident, partially resident, or non-resident. Some non-resident feudal lords were Italian princes, such as the Farnese rulers of Altamura, others were members of storied aristocratic lineages, many others were absolute or relative newcomers to feudal authority, due to the relative openness of the land market. Women could also exercise feudal rule. There were also ecclesiastical institutions that owned feudal lands. For instance, the hospital of Naples, the *Incurabili*, possessed feudal holdings.

The existence of a feudal lord did not entail the absence of communally governed institutions that could struggle against or cooperate with the lord. Another major variable for a feudal land was how long it had been governed by a feudal lord. Many towns which had been alienated in the already mentioned sell-off, bitterly resented their new rulers and violently opposed them. Although it is wrong to attribute political unity to vassals, as there were always those who sought power through alliance with feudal lords, even in places that generally prized their liberty. The indignity of being governed by a feudal lord recently risen from neighbouring kin networks, could form a reason for hatred to set on against them. It is important to not regard the division between feudatory and vassals as mapping on to a discrete and permanently fixed situation of power, but rather as an ongoing process influenced by relations with other institutions and with neighbouring feudal lords. Similarly, a royal town near a powerful feudal lord's territory could thereby be involved in litigation and violence concerning the borders between territories or other forms of rivalry.

One important variable, with important connections to size and urban functions, was the presence or absence of a patriciate nobility. From around the mid-sixteenth century, patrician nobilities created 'great books', 'red books', or 'books of gold' in which they defined the lineages with a right to be considered noble and with very high or non-existent routes for successful families to being included. This process did not happen at the same time or to the same extent everywhere. The majority of communities in the kingdom did not possess separate classes of citizens and the *università* of these were governed, at least in theory, by representatives chosen from all male inhabitants. Patrician nobilities, with their jostling between each other concerning status, were a major cause of violence.

Cities in the royal demesne also governed hinterlands of varying size; the relation of the city to its *casali* could vary and often was extractive domination. One of the main prizes for patrician nobilities of towns was the revenues that came directly and indirectly from the agricultural products produced in these hinterlands. There was also not a definite separation between 'central' and 'local' politics as office-holders in royal institutions such as the *Audienze* and other provincial representatives of royal authority could play significant roles in local hatreds. In the same way, those who had purchased the right to collect taxes thereby gained roles that could attract hostility or offer an opportunity to extend it.

'Fervid municipal passions'

The connection between the offices of local government and hatred was idiomatic in early modern Italy. Knowing how to profit from local offices was tightly linked to the skill in handling enmities and the manly governance of offices and patrimony that the patrician noble or ambitious citizen was required to show.[26] Giovanni Battista Labini, a patrician of Bitonto in the Terra di Bari, gave an account of a 'great enmity' in early sixteenth-century Bitonto in the chronicle he composed in 1656, over a century later.[27] In particular Labini remembered an ancestor, who had become *credenziero* of the city, as an outstanding patrician; he 'had many hands in the public things: he settled and made tranquil differences'.[28] This skill at peace-making was particularly obvious in settling an argument over expenses which had led to a division between the city and the bishop along with the clergy. This dispute was 'pursued in diverse tribunals both Royal and Ecclesiastic'.[29] It led to the birth of an accord or 'Capitolatione' in 1530 that in Giovanni Battista's lifetime, over a century later, still resulted in the clergy and citizens living together 'with much quiet'. He discusses the *Cautela* that was written by the Notary Sarro Vacca with a preamble composed by the famous preacher Cornelio Musso.[30]

Further evidence can be found in a handbook aimed at feudatories the *Utili instruttioni et documenti per qualsivoglia persona che ha da eligere officiali circa il regimento de populi* first published in 1530 but reprinted in 1590 and 1600.[31] The guidelines given in this testify to the risks of hatred and enmity that were vested in local politics. The repeated admonitions not to show signs of hatred towards any individual testify, most likely, to such rules being broken. Further, the captain was advised to not give reason for the women of the town to fall into dishonour. The book was aimed at the 'good lord' (*buon Signore*) who would seek to arrange the institutions of his *feudo* with such fairness as to produce union among its inhabitants, rather than division. There should be a form of unity in the *reggimento* elected, because from 'plural *regimento* are born dissensions in cities which heave [*fluttuano*] without peace, following the saying of our Lord, Many shepherds have destroyed my vineyard. And for the *unico regimento* we see Provinces and Cities enjoying peace, flowering with justice, and being full of every good.'[32] Such idealized visions of municipal unity were far from the common reality.

In larger urban settlements of the kingdom extensive factionalism could be found which in the first half of the seventeenth century had degenerated into a situation of violence as a ready resource for the pursuit of enemies. Altamura, for example, was divided between the factions of the families of de Angelis and the Viti 'from which there were and are the most capital enmities'.[33] Bari, with the rich prize of San Nicola di Bari at stake, was ripped apart by factions. Nardò saw considerable violence between the Falconi and the Carignano families, including multiple homicides with firearms.[34]

The public finances were both a major cause and impact site of municipal enmities. The Farnese agent in Altamura, Sempronio Scacchini, wrote to the Duke of Parma in 1598 saying: 'the city is very troubled by debts, and full of infinite discords because everyone wants to manage the public finances in their own way, causing all of their enmities'.[35] Catanzaro in Calabria suffered from a financial disaster at the start of the seventeenth century due to the failure of municipal government. The financial crisis towards the end of the sixteenth century was an accelerating situation that caused serious problems in communities around the Kingdom of Naples. Ignazio Ricciuti described the *governo* of Cosenza as following 'their passions of love or hatred' and 'sustaining a despotic dominion'.[36]

Reform of town councils was a place where attempts were made to tamp down violent excesses. The government of Foggia was subject to repeated reform across the seventeenth century to tackle disorder.[37] In 1697 the governor of the *Dogana*, Andrea Guerrero de Torres, accused the *decurioni* of governing solely to their own benefit. The reform attempts of this period were opposed in 1724 by a group of citizens composed a proposal, writing that:

> Experience having shown that the present system of government of this Public, which was provisionally introduced, instead of ending and destroying the hatreds and rancour amongst the citizens of this City of Foggia, caused by the well-known lawsuit, has had totally opposite effects.[38]

They proposed reforms that they claimed would instead create a durable, and sincere concord in the city and that this would constitute the 'happiness of the citizens'.[39] They cited divine support, particularly from the patron saints of Foggia. Statutes and other regulations mattered as they framed the interactions of communal life.[40]

Beyond the town councils, a variety of different rights and privileges formed causes for conflict. The complexity of authorities and jurisdictions even in small settlements can be seen in an example from the murder in 1651 of Francesco Varaniello in Boiano.[41] Varaniello was a soldier in the *Battaglione*, the part-time state militia whose soldiers gained exemptions from various taxes and duties in exchange for participating in regular exercises and going to war if necessary.[42] He clashed with two men, Carlo Tabegnia and Barbato, who were the *gabelloti* of flour in Boiano. They had purchased the right to extract payment for the flour used in bakeries to provide the town's bread. This could be one of the most significant sources of income for town councils and for the *gabelloti* themselves.[43]

One evening, according to witnesses, they convinced themselves that no more delay in payment would be allowed. They confronted Francesco Varaniello, who replied that he was a soldier and, moreover, a sergeant. Carlo replied: 'you've never been an honoured soldier, you're a cuckold'.[44] Francesco declared that this was a lie and Carlo drew his sword, attacking Carlo.[45] They were separated, but later that night Carlo returned and shot Francesco with an arquebus. Francesco died from his wound. After shots were fired, the governor of the town met with the *mastro giurato* and despatched him to the sacristan of the church, to order him to ring the bells that called the citizens to arms.[46]

However, as the *mastro giurato* was attempting to follow these orders, Carlo Tabegnia arrived in the piazza leading an armed gang. Carlo challenged the governor, telling him, 'you're nothing here'. Carlo claimed that the governor held no jurisdiction. As it was a market day, the *mastro mercato* was the only one with such authority.[47] The governor then returned to his house. As the widow of Francesco cried, fear of these violent men led to no action being taken against them.[48] The plural institutional sources of authority leading to debates over jurisdiction, as well as the overarching authority of force, are well-depicted in this case.

The accusation of enmity in public administration was lodged on many occasions. The 'sindicato' (a review of the actions of a judge or official holding jurisdiction at the end of their tenure) was an important process for considering what had occurred under the governance of certain officials and perhaps overturning their actions if it was proven that they had persecuted their enemies rather than dealt in justice.[49] The motivations behind officials' conduct were examined in these reviews.[50] Hundreds of people could be interviewed as part of syndications.[51] The notion of enmity also affected how they were to be carried out. In 1656, because the *Auditore* Buragna and the *università* of Catanzaro 'hate each other so much and so publically', the Collateral Council noted that 'it doesn't seem that this *sindicato* can be performed'.[52] Don Emanuel de la Escalera was sent to perform the *sindicato* as a neutral alternative.

The enemies of feudatories and the feudatory as enemy

The ubiquity of feudal rule combined with the wide ambit of powers granted feudatories made it a defining political force in the provinces of the kingdom. The enmities of particular municipalities very often occurred in relation to feudal politics. Local communities could be subject to persecution from their feudal lord. Some powerful lords waged what amounts to wars on the neighbouring feudal states or to demesnial cities deemed resistant to feudal power. The antagonistic internal politics of feudal lands could clearly be a provocative and disturbing reality for a feudal lord. It was also difficult for their agents, who attempted to survive resident in towns riven by factions, and communicating feudal desires, without being assassinated.

Rivalry between feudal lords themselves was a highly significant form of conflict which often impacted vassals. A document written in 1706 by Giuseppe Serra, Marchese di Strevi and Duke of Cassano, to instruct his agent Lelio Dominicis in the governance of his feudal lands helps us understand the range of sorts of relationships of hatred that feudal lords had and how fundamental the categories of amity and enmity were to the way they regarded their peers.[53] He wrote that they can be divided 'into three classes: friends, enemies and the indifferent'.[54] He begins be discussing the 'many and powerful' barons in his province.[55] The most trustworthy were the Corigliano and the Oriolo who he orders his agents should have correspondence with 'in every reasonable occasion'.[56]

His enemies instead are the four houses of the Spinelli who were bound together by both kinship and interest and were in opposition to his family's interests. Another relationship of enmity was the Foscaldo. But with this house they shared no borders, so he advised his agents to avoid any engagement with them not necessary to procure 'buona pace'. Borders meant unavoidable entanglement. The policy he advises is that of 'closing all the paths that might open up, to not give to his vassals any grounds to complain but neither to concede to him any prize no matter how minor'.[57] Dealing with the Scalea was less avoidable because while they shared no borders their proximity meant their vassals traded with each other. Finally, there is the case of the Prince of Tarsia, with whom inevitable conflicts arose following their interactions. This was because of the legal wrangling – 'civil and criminal and mixed' – that the Prince of Tarsia was involved in with the Duke of Corigliano, and so as the level of antagonism with each other increased he advised his agent to break off as much communication as possible.[58]

Leading figures on town councils could be exposed to violent reprisals. One of the most notable examples of which is when the Count of Conversano assassinated the *sindico* Manieri of Nardò, part of his own feudal lands. The use of violence by feudal lords to deal with rebellious or otherwise unpleasing vassals could be a conscious strategy. In a relation written to the Duke of Parma, Alberto di Via recommended a possible use of violence to restore the vassals to peace following the example of the major barons like the Duke of Andria and the Duke of Atri (the holder of these titles at the time of writing were Antonio Carafa, c. 1583–1621, and Giosia d'Acquaviva c. 1574–1620, respectively).[59]

Adversarial relations with feudal lords could lead to violence towards the lords themselves. The case of the assassination of Bartilotti which opened this book can also be returned to. These acts of violence were most common in the crisis years after 1647–48. Another case of attacks by vassals on feudal lords is that of Ottavio Vitigliano, Baron of Santa Croce di Morcone, who was shot at after having left his town one Saturday morning in September 1688 and crossing a bridge outside of his territory.[60] He fled on horseback and had only seen the cloud of gunpowder-smoke rise from a bush.

Complaints from vassals to central tribunals and councils of the kingdom was one major form that conflict could take. The Marchese of Casabona was accused of exercising his 'Terribilità' against his vassals through imprisonments, forced purchases of the products of their industries at low prices, and other forms of 'travails and molestations' that had led them to desperation and even thoughts of 'fleeing even to the Turks'.[61] People left towns because of the risks of their enmities; in 1666 Giovan Paolo di Giovanpaolo and his uncle Domenico Antonio claimed the hatred that the Marchese di Ripa bore them made them abandon Ripalimosani.[62]

Ecclesiastical jurisdiction as a locus for enmity

One of the major sources of violence in the provinces of the Kingdom was the clashing between secular and ecclesiastical jurisdictions. Such jurisdictional separations, with their close alliance with privileges including taxation and jurisdictional exemptions as well as control of positive income streams, were natural producers of violent opposition.

The presence of a bishop or archbishop could create bitter divisions and conflicts over control over certain benefices or forms of revenue extraction, as could monasteries. Especially rich ecclesiastical institutions could cause longstanding enmities. Most notable in this light is the church of San Nicolò of Bari, which was the focal point for interminable arguments and enmities divided between parties that coalesced around the figures of the prior and the treasurer.

Giovanni Jacobo della Mura had failed to write a will while living and, now dead intestate, his corpse had begun to stink. In 1619 he had been left unburied as the *Vicario* of Gragnano had ordered that he would not be buried until his family agreed to forge a will to the direct benefit of the bishop.[63] As Giovanni began to rot the *Vicario* dropped his demands, from a posthumous legacy of 150 ducats to 70 and eventually just 30. Some men of Gragnano took his body and buried it in the Augustinians' church without a priest present. The Augustinians feared the anger of the bishop and refused to assist in the burial. Yet the *Vicario* still ordered that the friars should exhume Giovanni from the sepulchre. They refused and the *Vicario* banned all of the clergy except his curates from giving confession.

Francesco Bruschi was the minister of the Conventuals Franciscans' Roman province, professor of theology in the *sapienza* since 1593 and, from 1599, the Bishop of Lettere.[64] The version of the events of 1619 recounted above, however, is that of the *università* of Gragnano, as described in the writings they delivered to the tribunal of *Real Giurisdizione*. They claimed in a petition against him that 'they can no longer bear the extortions, that up to now they have endured with great patience, and hope of emendation' but 'as the case is desperate' they had 'resolved in public parliament to have recourse to His Holiness' and the viceroy.[65] Their petitioning reached the commission of *Real Giurisdizione*, which was established to protect the proper spheres of royal and ecclesiastical jurisdictions and deal with abuses.

The government of the *università* claimed that the bishop's style of rule had resulted in 'unending discords' and had placed dissent between powerful laymen and priests. This 'caused most grave hatreds and enmities which are not without the danger of damaging honour and reputation through diverse unmentionable words'.[66] The bishop patronized men of ill-living, especially young men, giving them offices and thereby making them obedient. Abetted by these men, he oppressed the peaceful. A key player in this was the *Vicario*, the bishop's 23-year-old nephew. This young man was, in the acerbic summary of the writers of the petition, 'of little experience, of lascivious lifestyle, and has committed adulteries and rapes in the diocese'.[67] It was not only run-of-the-mill dissolute men that the bishop used. He had also contacted bandits and registered some into his service. His clergy were given every liberty and many went around armed 'in the style of outlaws'.[68] Under his nephew he had marshalled an armed youth wing of clerics, bandits, and their accomplices.

Bishop Bruschi was described as having no respect for secular authority. He persecuted with 'great hatred' anyone who appealed to superior authorities and excommunicated people for the smallest matter.[69] The *sindico* of Gragnano was excommunicated just for having petitioned the Marchese of Corleto. He summarily released all prisoners from the Royal Governor's prison. The bishop was reported to have said, crushing this plea for justice, 'I hold Gragnano and all of its government under my feet'.[70]

The events in Gragnano, then, perhaps are most easily read as an example of severe abuse of episcopal authority, evidence perhaps for the poor quality of the Neapolitan clergy and the local ambitions of bishops that were made feasible by the fierce opposition between jurisdictions.[71] According to the set of writings sent to Naples, Bruschi had constructed a network of clientage that far exceeded what was appropriate for a bishop, operated extortion through the threat of violence, made illegitimate use of his powers to retract the sacraments, to excommunicate and by arming priests and recruiting outlaws. He stood in profound enmity with the community.

But this account was contested in the response of the bishop. In October, he responded to the tribunal and complained about men from Gragnano who opposed him so fiercely that he could no longer govern his diocese. They threatened and injured his ministers and refused to follow the orders from his court. This rebellion against due obedience was explained by the control over the *governo* of the town by a small group who 'always hold it in their hands'. This rump administration

> spend the money [of the *università*] at their caprice and the accounts do not stand as they should, because the poor and other less powerful citizens cannot speak against it because as soon as they do they are threatened and mistreated and, in sum, they live as if they did not recognize a lord.[72]

Here the tables are turned and the bishop stands up for the victims of factionalism and corruption.

In 1627 the *università* of Rutigliano wrote that the Archpriest of Conversano taking over the jurisdiction over the divine cult had given birth to 'almost the total ruin of this town, being that he has only pursued his own passions, to execute vendettas owing to the hatreds he has conceived against diverse citizens'.[73] With ties to valuable benefices and jealous of protecting jurisdiction, ecclesiastic office-holders were often just as involved in bloody disputes over property as laymen. As institutions with often significant mobile and immobile property, the ability to deny the care due to the living and the dead, and the faculty to excommunicate, local churches and their priests were central to violently contested power relations.

Enmity and central authorities

The widespread use of violence to attempt to make money out of municipal or ecclesiastical authority relied on a notion that royal justice would either not punish or its punishments would be negotiable or at least preferable to the dishonour of inaction. Those who continued to plot murder and to carry it out had at least taken a fair reading of the general tendencies of royal officials and the viceregal regime in the face of the homicidal disorder of enmity. Nonetheless, although settlement was a path often taken, this did not imply inaction.

The correspondence which the governor-general of Calabria, Don Garcia de Toledo, received reveals how significant addressing enmities was for the administration of the provinces.[74] A letter sent to Don Garcia in 1602 by the *Regia Audienza* of Calabria Ultra explained that it was the 'enmities, and conflicts' within the prominent city of Catanzaro that had led the *università* to have contracted 80,000 ducats worth of debt.[75] Public spirit was not to be found, according to the letter writer. The citizens of the city, according to the letter, 'do not busy themselves with anything, unless it's one of them undoing what any other one does'.[76] The economic problems of this large town were explained by the unproductive arguments of the inhabitants. These conflicts of the citizens were causing the town 'to go to ruin'. In any case, the *Audienza* was particularly concerned not to let the conflict result in litigation in the city of Naples, as the costs of this would lead 'to the further harm, and ruin of the said City'. The solution proposed was an inquiry into the public accounts of the last twelve years. Administrative reform could be a mode of peace-making.

Another issue facing Toledo were the problems of the *enemistades* between the Mossolini and the Fossi and Belisarri in Reggio Calabria. The viceroy wrote to him to encourage his involvement. By 1602 these enmities had been running for a number of years and had caused the city to suffer 'many crimes and great harm'.[77] The viceroy advised that dealing with these feuding families required 'a light touch'.[78] The first option for dealing with these was 'with tenderness'.[79] But if this soft-pedalling approach failed, then the *Audienza* had the power to use its 'extraordinary authority' to incarcerate all the offenders. Even when violence had occurred, balance was often counselled over oppression.

One example of how local politics of enmity could be translated through the justice system can be found in the case of the salt mines of Altomonte, where, in 1604 a scandal broke out. The steward [*credenziero*] of the mines, Giovan Battista Mangone, was accused of having procured the theft of salt on a grand scale. The mines lay in the mountainous interior of Calabria and were a prized source of salt for the Kingdom of Naples.[80] Rock salt was hewn from the ground by Albanian labourers, inhabitants of the nearby village of Lungro. This was one of the Albanian (*Arbëreshë*) communities scattered throughout the Kingdom of Naples, many of whom had come to Italy in a set of large migrations, sparked by Ottoman expansion into the Balkans, at the turn of the sixteenth century.[81] The men of Lungro mined the salt and the women then transported it on their backs, a division of labour that continued into the nineteenth century.

Reports of the scandal led to a trial in the provincial royal appeal court, the *Regia Audienza* of the province of Calabria Citra. This province lay in the northern part of Calabria, and Altomonte was a journey of around a week on horseback from the capital Naples. Other officials of the mine alleged that he had been complicit in a panoply of frauds. A judge of the *Audienza* had been informed of the crimes as early as January 1603 but due to a 'long, and tiresome indisposition', he claimed he had not been able to travel to the mines to collect depositions until January the following year.[82]

Giuseppe Ferdinando, a customs official of the mine, testified early in the investigation to account for how he discovered the thefts. In his telling, he found the gates of the mine broken and the chains that should have sealed them lying on the floor. Giuseppe said he had written repeatedly to the highest fiscal tribunal of the Kingdom, the *Sommaria*, to complain about the break-ins, which happened frequently.[83] Giuseppe and other witnesses claimed the Albanian workers at Lungro, the *salinari*, must have played a major role as they were the people 'who knew how to, and were able to' to enter the mine and collect the salt.[84] Later in the trial the suspicion and prejudices the Italians held against the Albanians came into sharp focus. A number of Italian witnesses testified to regarding this separate ethnic group, with their own language and customs, as mistrustful, conspiratorial, and hateful towards Italians. For instance, they were 'a nation of such nature and quality that when they gather together, they cover each other's crimes and sins', moreover, they were accused of being 'the hidden enemies and haters of Italians generally'.[85] These attitudes reflected a widespread prejudice against Albanians in early modern Italy.[86] The participation of the inhabitants of Lungro in a secret plot that damaged the Crown's coffers was thus presented as an unsurprising turn of events.

Other office-holders accused Mangone of forging records to cover the stolen salt. Pietro Antonio di Fravio claimed to have encountered Mangone using two mules to transport some salt together with forged records. In di Fravio's account, Mangone attempted to keep possession of the contraband, telling him that it was none of his business and that he should stay out of the affair.[87] It was alleged that Mangone had persuaded Albanian women to transport blocks of salt by paying them off with a portion of the contraband; one 'rock' of salt was given to anyone who carried 500 *rotole* of salt.[88] A range of testimony was gathered against him that depicted an elaborate system of theft, contraband, and forgery.

Mangone did not concede that the accusations were true. Instead, he claimed that they were the product of the 'instigation of many of his enemies and haters'.[89] He argued that this was an unjust trial given a plausible veneer by false witnesses who bore enmity against him. In Mangone's defence, an advocate of the court proposed a set of counter-allegations that detailed these enmities and the falsehoods produced in their name. This document held that many pieces of apparently damning evidence were, instead, his understandable reactions to the hatred arrayed against him. It was noted how he had been attacked by Lelio's brother Giovanni Campolongo 'who along with other of their brothers and relatives are enemies [of Mangone]'.[90] Lelio was accused of being the central player in an expansive and powerful kinship network. His four brothers and many nephews and cousins constituted 'a clan [*parentato*] that almost runs the whole land of Altomonte and a good part of the nearby lands and so most of the men are afraid of their power'. Lelio in particular was described as someone whom 'when someone doesn't do what he likes then he remembers it well so he can take revenge against it'.[91] In other words, Lelio was a practised hand in the culture of enmity. Mangone argued that this state of enmity transformed the meaning of his actions, so that this decision to move his home to near the mines was not – as was alleged – in order to manage his supposed embezzling initiative more effectively but 'so as to avoid the danger of the enmity that held between him and the said Lelio and his brothers' if he continued to live near them.[92] The male kin of the Campolongo are presented as a powerful group who used the inverted ethic of enmity, revenge, and threat in order to control symbolic and economic resources.[93] This interpretation was plausible: the Campolongo possessed powerful men among their wider kin. These included feudatories, such as Muzio Campolongo, the Baron of Acquaformosa.[94]

But there was also, apparently, peace in this feud: in the course of the trial it emerged that Mangone and Lelio Campolongo had participated in an act of reconciliation. According to one witness's testimony: 'many times has this witness spoken to the said Lelio and in particular one day inside the houses of the court of Altomonte he came to a truce [quiet] and had made peace together with the said Giovanni Battista with many people around'.[95] Such an act hints, obscurely, at a middle-ground between the two interpretations. The rumour, as reported by the witness, however, was that Lelio had neither true forgiveness nor desire to reconcile; that this was false peace, strategically made. Whatever the truth behind this act of peace-making, anthropology has long taught historians that such acts are intrinsic to cultures of interpersonal hostility, not outside of them.[96]

In sum, this was a series of events, or rather narrations of events, that illustrated how, in early modern Italy, groups of male kin could use violence to further their own interest in enterprises of local domination and money-making; how certain men were known as tough characters willing to use their reputations, kin networks, and propensity to physical violence for entrepreneurial ends both licit and illicit. The trial itself revealed the kinship and alliance networks that surrounded and transformed the economic activity of the mine, demonstrating what is often hidden in documents that testify only to official structures and transactions. Conflicts such as this, then, often illustrate the point made forcefully by Gérard Delille that, for instance, acts of sales never reveals the kinship and alliance ties that bind the seller and the buyer.[97] Disruptions such as criminal trials uncovered the ubiquitous role played by enmities in power relations and economic activity, often hidden by the documents produced during 'business as usual'.

Like many criminal allegations in early modern Italy, the trial also produced two mirror images of events. Each side characterized the other in turn as effective plotters, full of hatred, and bearing false witness against them. The logics of a criminal trial or civil litigation exacerbated such partisan inversions, given that a defendant who proved the enmity of a witness enabled the discounting of that testimony. As the author of a *Vita* of a Neapolitan Jesuit, noted, when someone was 'litigating in the Tribunals for regaining what is theirs' often 'self-interest, that so greatly dominates Man, for the most part degenerates into hatred' and therefore 'enmities are contracted under the semblance of Justice'.[98] Yet it was also the case that recourse to law courts was part of the strategies of interpersonal rivalry, a possible act in the pursuit of enmity, not only a site for the confection of fake enmities for strategic purposes. Naturally there were a host of realities behind such similar appearances in different cases: there were people who were truly victims of one-sided predation, those who lied about the hostility of their rivals for personal gain or desired exculpation, and the many mixed cases which lay between or beyond these poles. For those who sought to exploit opportunities to make money or gain influence, 'lawfare' was very often part of their repertoire of action.[99] Certain relational idioms, particularly friendship, kinship, and enmity, were structuring concepts that provided logics and practices to many and varied undertakings in wealth-building, influence-peddling and the artful navigation of a life-course. These relational idioms also had salience in a different but overlapping form as legal concepts, important in the culture of proof, testimony, and punishment. This (at least) dual social and legal importance often meant that court cases and other judicial procedures such as the Altomonte case became arguments about hatred and love, vendetta and reconciliation.

The mines of Altomonte were, in one, sense a state enterprise, representing a source of taxable income for the crown's coffers. Yet due to being administered by office-holders who purchased their positions out of hope for the licit (and often illicit) profits, as with many enterprises, it was equally embedded in local networks of economic interest and power relations. Conflicts arising out of such contentions over offices and the resources they governed entered the complicated levels and interactions that constituted early modern justice.[100] Within these contexts, personal hostilities were very salient, playing important roles for actors to explain and account for motives, the dynamics of interaction and institutional dysfunction. The case of Altomonte equally demonstrates some of the dynamics of fiscal politics in the Kingdom of Naples: the functions and dysfunctions of the delegated offices, often venal, that the Spanish regime relied upon, albeit with high levels of frustration, to deliver them profit from the Kingdom as well as how the monarchy sought to correct these deviations. Issues such as those of the salt mines at Altomonte were assessed in terms of the decorum of justice but also preoccupations about the proper functioning of local institutions, the flows of tax revenue and the more general notion of 'public quiet'. In the hatreds that swirled around the Altomonte salt mines, then, questions of imperial policy, social relations, and the troubled quest for 'good government' can be perceived.

In the Kingdom of Naples, from the capital to provincial towns and rural areas, violent enmities remained strategies for status, emotional satisfaction, and material advancement throughout the seventeenth century. But this was not due to an absence of civic institutions; local political bodies and the broader legal system affected the choices and actions of women and men in the Kingdom. Feudal lords, bishops, and town councils were part of the same local systems of power relations. In the towns of the kingdom, a vast range of different cross-cutting clashes created an atmosphere of intense conflict. The extraction of tax revenue and the disposal of the public purse were major bones of contention. The historiography at times has focused on a notion of supine communities exploited by feudal lords to such an extent that other configurations of power have been less explored. In fact, conflict was far more complex, involving numerous potential players and factors. Enmity functions as the overarching interpretative category for understanding social conflict in the provinces. One aspect that has not been explored at length is the important connection of municipal enmities with the archetypical phenomenon of the countryside: banditry.

Notes

1 Geronimo Marciano, *Memorie historiche della Congregatione dell'Oratorio* (Naples, 1693), p. 407.
2 Niccolò Machiavelli, *Florentine Histories*, trans. by Laura F. Banfield and Harvey C. Mansfield Jr. (Princeton: Princeton University Press, 1990) p. 105.
3 Osvaldo Raggio, *Faide e Parentele: Lo stato Genovese visto dalla Fontanabuona* (Turin: Einaudi, 1990), p. 176.
4 Andrea Zorzi, 'I conflitti nell'Italia comunale. Riflessioni sullo stato degli studi e sulle prospettive di ricerca' in *Conflitti, paci e e vendette nell'Italia comunale*, ed. by Andrea Zorzi (Florence: Firenze University Press, 2009), pp. 7–43.
5 Ibid., p. 39.
6 Ibid., p. 37: 'Il controllo e la gestione delle passioni, delle paure, degli odi e della varietà di stati d'animo e di emozioni che i conflitti catalizzavano negli individui e nelle strategie degli schieramenti'.
7 Gérard Delille, *Famiglia e potere locale: una prospettiva mediterranea* (Bari: Edipuglia, 2011); Giovanni Masi, *Altamura Farnesiana* (Bari: Cressati, 1959).

8 Zorzi, 'I conflitti nell'Italia comunale', p. 39.
9 For an introduction to the history of the *università* see Angelantonio Spagnoletti, 'Potere amministrativo ed élite nelle "università" del Regno di Napoli (sec. XVI–XVII)', in *Congreso internacional espacios de poder: Cortes, ciudades y villas (s.XVI–XVIII)*, ed. by Jesús Bravo (Madrid: Universidad Autónoma de Madrid, 2002), pp. 69–78; Giovanni Muto, 'Istituzioni dell'universitas e ceti dirigenti locali', in *Storia del Mezzogiorno*, ed. by Giuseppe Galasso and Rosario Romeo (Naples: Edizioni del Sole, 1991), IX, 2, pp. 19–67.
10 Giovanni Battista De Luca, *Il principe cristiano pratico di Gio: Battista de Luca. Abbozzato nell'ozio Tusculano Autunnale del 1675. Accresciuto, e ridotto a diversa forma ne'spazij estivi, avanzati alle occupazioni del Quirinale nel 1679* (Rome, 1680), p. 555: 'l'esperienza insegna quanto alle fazioni & inimicizie, che per la maggior parte, a guisa delle discordie tra cani, e gatti, soglion nascere per la cagione del governo publico delle Comunità; facendosi da molti professione di vivere, e d'arrichirsi con quello del Comune, e col sangue de'poveri'.
11 Giovanni Muto, 'Noble Presence and Stratification in the Territories of Spanish Italy', in *Spain in Italy: Politics, Society, and Religion 1500–1700*, ed. by Thomas James Dandelet and John A. Marino (Leiden: Brill, 2007), p. 265.
12 Apart from these most common terms there were a whole variety of terms for the posts of local governance. One other common vocabulary was that of the 'decurionate' with the post-holders known as *decurioni*.
13 Tommaso Astarita, *Village Justice: Community, Family and Popular Culture in Early Modern Italy* (Baltimore: Johns Hopkins University Press, 1999), p. 35.
14 On the *chiusura oligarcha* see Aurelio Musi, *Mezzogiorno spagnolo: la via napoletana allo stato moderno* (Naples: Guida, 1991), pp. 81–4.
15 Gérard Delille, *Famiglia e potere locale: una prospettiva mediterranea* (Bari: Edipuglia, 2011), esp. ch. 11, 'Fazioni e "segmentazioni" dei lignaggi: l'esempio di Altamura', pp. 217–37.
16 Ibid., pp. 77–9.
17 Ibid., p. 26: 'un meccanismo fondamentale dell'organizzazione del potere locale non solo nell'Italia meridionale ma anche in altri paesi mediterranei'.
18 Astarita, *Village Justice*, p. 30.
19 An *apprezzo* of the city of Gravina in Puglia surveys the 'incomes' of the *università*, noting gabels of the communal oven, the tavern, on oil, carts, markets, grapes, meat, goods, grazing lands, grain, barley, and various other foodstuffs. Virgilio de Marino, *Apprezzo della città di Gravina, trascrizione e note* (Gravina: Fondazione Ettore Pomarici Santomasi, 1979).
20 Astarita, *Village Justice*, p. 34.
21 This is one of the major contributions of Tommaso Astarita's *Village Justice* concerning Pentidattilo, a town of less than a thousand people on the far southern coast of Calabria.
22 Ilaria Zilli, 'Per una storia della città e delle città del Molise', in *Le città del Regno di Napoli nell'età moderna*, ed. by G. Galasso (Naples, 2011), p. 584
23 Antonio Calabria, *The Cost of Empire: The Finances of the Kingdom of Naples in the Time of Spanish Rule* (Cambridge: Cambridge University Press, 1991), p. 32.

24 Tommaso Astarita, *The Continuity of Feudal Power: The Caracciolo di Brienza in Spanish Naples* (Cambridge: Cambridge University Press, 1992), p. 38.
25 Ibid.
26 On office-holding as sources of revenue and enrichment see Mireille Peytavin, 'Naples, 1610: comment peut-on être officier?', *Annales: Histoire, Sciences Sociales* 52.2 (1997), 265–91, esp. pp. 284–7.
27 Donato Antonio De Capua, *Cronaca inedita della famiglia Labini in Bitonto* (Bitonto: Liantonion, 1992), p. 39: 'una grande nemicitia fra duoi principali fameglie'.
28 Ibid., pp. 38–9: 'per esser persona molto molto Patritia, et che havea molte mani nelle cose pubbliche sedò, et tranquillò le differenze, vertevano con dispendio dell'una, et l'altra parte fra la Città, et Monsignor Vescovo di essa, et con il Clero in diversi Tribunali cosi'Regi, come Ecclesiastici, et ne nacque l'accordo, seu Capitolatione trà la Città, et Clero con la quale hoggi si vive con molta quiete, et nella Cautela stipulata da esso in nome del pubblico con detto Monsignor Vescovo, e clero nell'anno 1556, per mano di Notar Sarro Vacca vallata con assenso Apsotolico, et Regio: vi è un preludio inserito in detta Cautela di quel famoso Dicitore di Monsignor Cornelio Musso'.
29 Ibid.
30 Ibid.
31 Geronimo Mancino, *Utili instruttioni et documenti per qualsivoglia persona che ha da eligere officiali circa il regimento de populi et anco per officiali che seranno eletti, et università da quelli gubernate con li Riti della Vicaria, e Pragmatiche Vulgari* (Naples, 1590).
32 Ibid., p. 2.
33 ASN, Farnese, 2016, letter of 3 May 1651.
34 Gio. Battista Biscozzo, 'Libro d'annali de successi accaduti nella Città di Nardò, notati da D. Gio: Battista Biscozzo di detta Città', *Rinascenza salentina*, 4 (1936), 7–44.
35 Masi, *Altamura Farnesiana*, p. 84.
36 Quoted in Raffaele Colapietra, *Vita pubblica e classi politiche del viceregno napoletano (1656–1734)* (Rome: Edizioni di storia e letteratura, 1961), p. 44: 'si sono tassati a loro piacere et hanno seguito gl'altri secondo le proprie passioni d'amore o d'odio, mantenendo quali oppressori tutti gli altri pesi della città; e ne tengono e vogliono sostenere un dominio dispotico'.
37 For the history of these changes see Pasquale di Cicco, *Libro Rosso di Foggia* (Foggia: Amministrazione Provinciale di Capitanata, 1965), pp. 22–32.
38 Ibid., p. 35: 'Avendo l'esperienza dimostrato che il presente sistema del governo di questo pubblico provisionalmente introdotto, invece di togliere e distruggere gl'odi e rancore tra i cittadini di questa Città di Foggia dalla nota lite cagionati, ha partorito effetti totalmente contrari'.
39 Ibid.
40 Edward Muir, 'The Idea of Community in Renaissance Italy', *Renaissance Quarterly*, 55 (2002), 1–18 (p. 9); Astarita, *Village Justice*, p. 5.
41 Archivio di Stato di Lucera, Regia Udienza, Processi Penali, busta 1, fasc. 4.

The politics of enmity in the provinces 113

42 This was founded as part of the 1563 military reforms and 25,586 *Battaglione* soldiers were stationed around the Kingdom in 1602. See John A. Marino, 'The Rural World in Italy under Spanish Rule', in *Spain in Italy: Politics, Society, and Religion 1500–1700*, ed. by Thomas James Dandelet and John A. Marino (Leiden: Brill, 2007), p. 416. The *presidi* of provinces had the duty to oversee their training and potential mobilization. Archivio di Stato di Napoli, Consiglio Collaterale, Notamenti, busta 67, fols. 196^{r-v}.

43 See, for example, the incomes of the town of Lavello who in 1629, from an income of 6760 ducats, received 3920 ducats from flour taxation. In the same town in 1667–68, after a period of declining population, out of an income of 3264 ducats, 2037 came from flour taxation. In smaller settlements, the gabel of flour was regularly by far the largest single source of income. This was the case in Ripacandida, where 700 ducats out of 865 came from the gabel of flour. Marcello Romano, *Gli apprezzi e le plate dell'Archivio Caracciolo di Torella come fonte per la ricostruzione del paesaggio e della 'forma Urbis' medieval degli insediamenti del Vulture* (Potenza: Olita, 2004), p. 277.

44 ASL, Regia Udienza, Processi Penali, busta 1, fasc. 4, fol. 58^v: 'tu non sei mai soldato honorato ma un cornuto'.

45 Ibid.: 'una mentita'.

46 Ibid., fol.: 72^r.

47 Ibid.: 'tu sei niente quà … perche hoggi vi è il mastro mercato'.

48 Ibid., fols. 72^{r-v}.

49 On the legal history of *sindicato* see Ginesio Grimaldi, *Istoria delle leggi e magistrati del Regno di Napoli, continuata da Ginesio Grimaldi* (Naples, 1771), IX, pp. 167–76. See also Pier Luigi Rovito, *Respublica dei togati: giuristi e società nella Napoli del Seicento* (Naples: Jovene, 1981).

50 For the larger Italian context on syndication see Gino Masi, 'Il sindicato delle magistrature comunali nel sec. XIV (con speciale riferimento a Firenze)', *Rivista italiana per le scienze giuridiche*, 5 (1930), 43–115, 331–411.

51 The syndication of Cola Francesco Serrano in 1638 involved 137 people; Archivio diocesano di Conversano, Rutigliano, Atti Criminali, fasc. 6, fol. 3^r.

52 ASN, Consiglio Collaterale, Notamenti, busta 60, fol. 128^{r-v}: 'che stante que l'Auditore et Universita le sono odiosi cossi è notorio non par che possar ricevere questo sindicato'.

53 'Istruzioni di Giuseppe Serra marchese di Strevi e duca di Cassano per il dr. Lelio Dominicis agente generale dello *stato* di Cassano in Calabria Citra', in Luca Covino, *Baroni del 'buon governo': istruzioni della nobiltà feudale nel Mezzogiorno moderno* (Naples: Liguori, 2004).

54 Ibid., p. 131: 'I baroni della nostra provincia sono molti e potenti. Si possono dividere in tre classi: amici, nemici ed indifferenti.'

55 Ibid.

56 Ibid.: 'in ogni raggionevole occasione'.

57 Ibid.: 'chiudendo tutte le vie che se n'aprissero, e non dare à suoi vassalli campo veruno di lamentarsi mà nemeno concedergli arbitrio benche minimo come gettato al vento'.

58 Ibid., p. 132.
59 ASN, Farnese, 2016.
60 ASL, Regia Udienza, Processi Penali, busta 10, fasc. 98, fols. 324^r–325^v.
61 ASN, Delegazione della real giurisdizione, busta 180, fasc. 21, fol. 336^r: 'quanto sono timorizzati dalla Terribilità di detto signor Marchese'; fol. 337^r: 'hanno minacciato fuggirsene insino alli Turchi'.
62 ASL, Regia Udienza, Processi Penali, busta 3, fasc. 45, fol. 556^r.
63 ASN, Delegazione della real giurisdizione, Processi, busta 178, fol. 10^r. The right claimed by bishops to make wills for the intestate was seen by secular authorities as a 'pretension' that they claimed was a 'historic custom' of their dioceses. See 'De'Testamenti, che i Vescovo del Regno, pretendono poter fare per coloro, che muojono ab intestato' in Bartolomeo Chioccarello, *Archivio della Reggia Giurisdizione del Regno di Napoli* (Venice, 1721), pp. 242–44.
64 Gaetano Moroni, *Dizionario di erudizione storico-ecclesiastica da S. Pietro sino ai nostri* (Venice: Tipografia Emiliana, 1854), LXV, p. 63.
65 ASN, Delegazione della real giurisdizione, Processi, busta 178, fol. 2^r.
66 Ibid., fol. 4^t: 'ha examinato di continuo zizzarie et posto dissensioni tra seculari potenti et sacerdoti quale sono causati grandissimi odij et inimicitie non senza periculo di morte a con'macchiar l'honor et reputatione di grave ingiurie con diversi et indicibili parole'.
67 Ibid., fol. 9^r: 'di pocha esperienza, di vita lasciva, che ha commesso nella diocesi adultierij et stupri'.
68 Ibid., fol. 8^v: 'che vadino armati d'arme prohibite et contra pragmattiche a modo di fuorigiudicati'.
69 Ibid., fol. 9^r: 'ha persequitato con odio grande ciascheduno che sentendosi gravato, ha havuto ricorso a superiori, escomunicandoli poi, ogni leggiera causa, et in particolare escomunicò indebitamente il sindico di detta Terra per essersi gravato al Signor Marchese di Corlete'.
70 Ibid., fol. 9^r: 'dicendo, io tengho Gragnano et tutto il Governo sotto li piedi'.
71 On the quality of clergy see David Gentilcore, *From Bishop to Witch: The System of the Sacred in Early Modern Terra d'Otranto* (Manchester: Manchester University Press, 1992), pp. 45–9.
72 ASN, Delegazione della real giurisdizione, Processi, busta 178, fol. 3^r: 'il governo dell'Università stà sempre in mano loro et spendono li denari di quella al loro capriccio et non se li vedeno li conti in quella maniera che si deve, perche li poveri, et altri Cittadini meno potenti non possono parlare perche subito da q.lli sono minnacciati et maltrattati et in somma vivono come non riconoscessero padrone'.
73 ADC, Rutigliano, Atti Criminali, fasc. 6, fol. 1^r: 'nata quasi la total ruina di questa terra, poiche havendo sol mira alle pop.e passioni, et a' sfogar le sue vendette per li conceputi odij ed diversi cittadini, ha persecutato contro quelli vane inquisitioni, e con chiare importune, e suppositioni già notorie a tutto questo Paese, ha ridotto i estremi calamità molte fameglie'.
74 Don Garzia de Toledo was governor-general of Calabria Ultra and possessed extensive authority in overseeing administration in Calabria Ultra. See Giuseppe Galasso, *Economia e società nella Calabria del Cinquecento* (Naples: Guida, 1992), p. 313. Biblioteca Nazionale di Napoli, Fondo San Martino, MS 103.

75 BNN, Fondo San Martino, MS 103, fol. 143ʳ: 'che per le Inimicitie, et gare, che occorrono fra li Cittadini di questa Città'.
76 Ibid.: 'poi che non attendono ad altro, se non l'uno a disfare quello che far l'altro'.
77 BNN, Fondo San Martino, MS 103, fol. 111ʳ: 'mas delictos y mayores danos'.
78 Ibid.: 'la mano luego'.
79 Ibid.: 'con blandura'.
80 For an introduction to the enduring significance of the salt industry and trade and monopolies related to it see Alan Frederick Charles Ryder, *The kingdom of Naples Under Alfonso the Magnanimous: The Making of a Modern State* (Oxford: Clarendon Press, 1976), p. 353; for an introduction to the history of the salt mines of Altomonte see Raffaele Mastrini, *Dizionario geografico-storico-civile del Regno delle Due Sicilie* (Naples, 1838), II, pp. 236–38 and Giovanni Sole, *Breve storia della Reale Salina di Lungro* (Cosenza: Edizioni Brenner, 1981).
81 The history of the Arbëreshë can be introduced through Patrizia Resta, *Parentela ed Identità Etnica: Consanguineità e Scambi Matrimoniali in Una Comunità Italo-Albanese* (Milan: FrancoAngeli, 1991).
82 Archivio di Stato di Napoli [ASN], Processi Antichi, Pandetta Nuovissima, busta 1772, fasc. 49692, fol. 1ʳ: 'Per una lunga, e fastidiosa Indispositione'.
83 Ibid., fol. 6ʳ.
84 Ibid., fol. 63ᵛ.
85 Ibid., fol. 63ᵛ: 'sono natione di qualita, e natura tale che se la tengono insieme, e coprono vicendevolmente gli loro diffeti, e delitti … sono occulti nemici e odiosi d'Italiani generalmente'.
86 For an introduction to these stereotypical attitudes see the discussion and references in Giovanni Brancaccio, *Il Molise medievale e moderno: storia di uno spazio regionale* (Naples: Edizioni scientifiche italiane, 2005) pp. 163–5. Especially relevant is the quotation from the historian Giovanni Antonio Summonte, *Dell'historia della citta e regno di Napoli* (Naples, 1675) who commented: 'ovunque si trovano gli Albanesi niuna cosa vi lasciorno sicura; non v'era armento così distante che per il corso non fusse preso'.
87 ASN, Processi Antichi, Pandetta Nuovissima, busta 1772, fasc. 49692, fol. 8ʳ: 'era negotio suo'.
88 Ibid., fol. 13ʳ: roughly 450 kilograms.
89 Ibid, fol. 32ʳ: 'ad instigatione di molti suoi nemici et odiosi'.
90 Ibid., fol. 94ᵛ: 'assaltato da Giovanni Campolongo fratello carnale de Lelio li quali con altri loro frateli e parenti sono nemici di esso Giovan Battista'.
91 Ibid., fol: 82ʳ⁻ᵛ: 'Lelio Campolongo tiene quattro fratelli carnali et diversi nepoti che quasi tirano lo parentato de tutta la terra d'Altomonte et bona parte delle terre convecine che per la loro potentia la maggior parte delli huomini tutti stando in timore e temeno il detto Lelio et quando non se li compiace acquello che desidera ne tiene particular memoria per posser si vendicare di quelli che non convescendeno alla sua volunta'.
92 Ibid., fol. 62ᵛ: 'per evitare qualche pericolo per la nemicitia ch'era durava fra lui e detto Lelio e fratelli'.

93 The Campolongo remained an important group in Altomonte. In 1727 another Lelio Campolongo was governor of the town, and other Campolongo members held other posts, as can be seen in Franz Von Lobstein, 'La presa di possesso di un territorio da parte del feudatorio', *Rassegna storica dei comuni. Periodico di studi e di ricerche storiche locali*, 1 (1969).
94 Gisela Bock, *Thomas Campanella. Politisches Interesse und philosophische Spekulation* (Tübingen: Niemeyer, 1974), p. 81.
95 ASN, Processi Antichi, Pandetta Nuovissima, busta 1772, fol. 95^r: 'che esso testimonio piu volte ha parlato con il detto Lelio et in particulare uno giorno dentro le case dela corte de Altomonte che si fosse quietato et havesse fatto pace insieme con il detto Giovanni Battista'.
96 The classic text for this argument is Max Gluckman, 'The Peace in the Feud', *Past & Present*, 8 (1955): 1–14.
97 Delille, Famiglia e proprietà nel Regno di Napoli, p. 13: 'un atto di vendita non ci dirà mai che l'acquirente era il cognato del venditore o piú semplicemente che i due protagonisti della transazione sono legati da vincoli da parentela o di alleanza'.
98 Simone Bagnati, *Vita del servo di Dio P. Francesco di Geronimo della Compagnia di Gesu* (Naples, 1705), p. 25: 'Alcune nimicizie si contraggono sotto specie di Giustizia; quando litigandosi ne'Tribunali per riaver il suo, l'interesse, che tanto predomina nell'Uomo, per lo piu traligna in odio'.
99 For an example of the instrumentalization of justice in early modern Italy see Irene Fosi, *Papal Justice: Subjects and Courts in the Papal State, 1500–1750* (Washington, DC: Catholic University of America Press, 2011), p. 36.
100 A detailed study of one major institution is John A. Marino's study of the *dogana* (sheep customshouse) of Puglia: *Pastoral Economics in the Kingdom of Naples* (Baltimore: Johns Hopkins University Press, 1988).

4

Banditry and the culture of enmity

In 1676 an outlaw's corpse was found hanging upside down from a tree outside a small town in northern Puglia. A strip of paper pinned on his chest read:

> This is that traitor Pietro Brancazio, who has betrayed a companion of Matteo Banco and as he fell into my hands, I have given him the punishment that such traitors deserve and so that others will think before they commit any other betrayal – Caporal Donato Demante[1]

The note survives in the archival holdings of the *Regia Audienza* of Capitanata and the Molise in the small state archive in the remote town of Lucera. The note testifies to the atmosphere of violence and intimidation that occurred on the rural byways and royal roads of the Kingdom of Naples: the groups of men who used paramilitary organization and a corresponding code of loyalty and betrayal to pursue their enemies. Contracting the enmity of a bandit was a potentially fatal turn of events. The culture of enmity that permeated Italy had its sharpest edge in banditry.

The territory that made up this kingdom posed challenges for the effective administration of royal justice, allowing for *capibanditi* to exercise potent influence over space; a challenge common to many early modern Eurasian states with low urbanization and extensive hinterlands.[2] A large portion of the twelve provinces of the Kingdom was agrarian, with few large urban settlements, many poor roads, as well as possessing the mountain ranges and foothills which made travel difficult, especially the spine of the Apennines which hew the Kingdom in two and created further difficulties of carrying out the commands of the capital city on the other side of the range. As a measure of the difficulty and insecurity of land transit, boats were often used to travel from Naples to the southernmost region of Calabria rather than roads. Connected with this difficult natural and human geography was the legal topography of the provinces, an overlapping patchwork of feudal, royal, and ecclesiastical jurisdictions. In the Kingdom, royal justice had to make decisions on how to operate in the provinces where its authority waned as distance from the sole major administrative city increased.

This chapter explores the phenomenon of banditry in the Kingdom of Naples. By surveying the behaviours and practices associated with bandits, I demonstrate the fundamental significance of the culture of enmity to their way of life. The politics of enmity in the provinces of the kingdom were inseparable from the reality of banditry, therefore this chapter continues the preceding chapter's analysis.

The definition and self-definition of bandits

Bandit was a term with a set of different possible meanings. In the strict legal sense, it merely identified a person subject to a *bando*, most often enforced when a summons to appear before a court had been blatantly ignored. Lapsing first into contumacy, such people were next declared outlawed. As has already been discussed, this covered large numbers of people in early modern Italy – and especially the Kingdom of Naples – with its severe but easily escapable and widely distrusted organs of justice.

Yet it also denoted, especially from the sixteenth century onwards, a social type: the man who lived as an outlaw, who had taken *alla macchia* or *alla campagna*, to live as a career criminal outside the bounds of respectable society. In the official pronouncements of early modern Italian governors, councils and tribunals – the ever-flowing stream of *prammatiche*, *gride*, *bandi*, *editti*, et cetera, that made such reliable business for town-criers and printers – such 'malfattori' were identifiable and marked out as a different sort of person than the law-abiding.

The reality was more shaded: banditry could be a seasonal occupation and it was always more ambiguous than the starkly black-and-white definitions of sovereign authorities. The overlapping of the two poles – the purely legal descriptive label and the moral-social type – occurred as the medieval notion of the *latro* (the professional criminal of the countryside) and the *foriudicatus* (any man subject to outlawing) blurred into ambiguity and from the growing propulsion of those subject to legal sanction towards the outlaw life.[3]

In the sixteenth and seventeenth centuries this elision of legal status with assumptions of character and behaviour was very strong.[4] The spectrum behind the term bandit has been usefully detailed by Irene Fosi:

> they are *fuorusciti*, that is nobles or citizens ejected in the course of the constant struggles between municipal factions; they are then the thiefs, highway

men, robbers, or unemployed soldiers, but there are also, and I would say, above all the bandit *tout court*, common criminals subject to a sentence of contumacy for crimes committed against property and/or persons and deprived according to local statutory regulation of their goods, if they had them, and exiled for a period of time or their whole life, following the gravity of the offence, from the place where the crime was committed.[5]

One characteristic that emerges from criminal sources is that bandits were distinctive in their clothing and their weaponry.[6] In Naples in the records of court cases and other documentation the phrase 'dressed/armed in the fashion of bandits' was common. When a group of men knocked on the door of the house of Col'Angelo Romano in Acquaviva and robbed him, he recalled that they were armed like bandits with harquebuses and long knives.[7] In 1667 a group of violent men led by Domenico Allegretti from Mirabello in the Molise were identified by a witnessed as armed in the 'modo di banditi'.[8] The Abruzzesi bandits, who in 1686 stayed in a mill near Carovilli, were described by witnesses as 'dressed in the manner of bandits and insurgents [*scorritori*] of the countryside'.[9] The clothing, weaponry, and behaviour of men all identified them as bandits. For the majority of the population it was these qualities, rather than detailed knowledge about their exact position in the eyes of the law, that defined a bandit. This was a legal vision as well: those who acted like bandits were treated as bandits, and could be killed *ad modum belli*.[10]

While we can find views of bandits from the outside, the self-image of bandits is harder to access. One intriguing but ambiguous sort of evidence is the nicknames taken on by bandits. These clues towards outlaw identities hint towards a creative and ludic culture. They often implied ferocity and skill in combat: the Serpent, the Big-Wolf of Caserta, the 100,000 Men, the Old Wolf of Santo Stefano, and the Toothless Maw are just some examples.[11] Others seem to hint towards the comedic such as the Amorous of Guglionisi or the Goblin. Some nicknames portray hyperbolic ferocity such as the Mountain-Breaker or the Despoiler of Christ. The spread of names in one particular gang underscores the variety of such names: Caporale Domenico Monteleone, Campione, Roina, Madonna, Chichirichi, Constanzo, Giuseppe, Spagnuolo, Ricca, and Santuccio.[12]

Given this revelry in savagery, banditry should be connected to the broader culture of violent men in early modern Italy. The men of arms known as *bravi*, *guappi*, or *smargiassi* – who, when not technically outlaws, existed at the blurred edges of banditry – were swaggering men who laid claim to skill in vengeance. The noble poet Del Tufo made fun of these *bravoni* by noting their performed fierceness – the foam in their mouths and the livid colours of their cheeks – and he described them in terms taken from the chivalric universe of *Orlando furioso*. As he wrote:

> *bravoni,*
> *Bravissimi, bravazzi,*
> That we call corner-cutters,
> Iron-breakers and chain-eaters,
> Carrying at their belts,
> With their fearful intoxication,
> With dog-like anger,
> The devil, always, and ready to draw,
> They go catching, as they know how,
> Discords and conflicts with their nets[13]

Although such men cultivated an appearance of fierceness they still caused real problems. As well as a 'broad category' of all sorts of extra-legal activities, banditry should also be considered as a range of masculine identities and practices, formed in part through their own material culture, gendered aspects, and cultural codes which were part of wider culture of enmity in early modern Italy, but with distinctive emphases that drew from the world of soldiery.

When they came together, outlaws used military style organizations to define their groups and hierarchies. While the laws and officials of the Kingdom referred to them as 'bandit chiefs' [*capo de banditi*] the term used most commonly in writings they produced was the longer form 'corporal' [*caporale*]. One Giuseppe Amorese, a muleteer who was kidnapped by an outlaw gang for ransom, recalled that all the bandits called their leader 'corporal' and, later, he found that this man was known as *caporale Disperato*.[14] The members of a bandit gang described each other as 'compagni' most regularly and valued the practice of good sociability; one bandit went by the nickname the Good Companion [*Buon compagno*].[15] The distinction between bandits and bandit-chiefs in jurisprudence was not wholly invention, although the categories were, of course, fluid.[16]

One type of bandit we could identify are the foreign interlopers, groups from the Abruzzi or the Marche that descended onto the *Tavoliere* or into the Molise and were identified by locals due to their distinctive speech and dress. While it was more regularly the case that these men committed crimes with no agenda of vengeance, these men could be co-opted into gangs that participated in local politics. In 1675, thirty 'Marquitos', men from the Marche region, were committing kidnaps in Palata and Ururi.[17] Their origin was identified in witness statements by their clothes and dialects.[18] Of course, this outsider status was contextual and these men may well have been involved in local political strife in their own communities. One of the common themes in bandit careers is the combination of directed vengeance and 'pure' criminality.

Banditry and justice in the provinces

The *Regia Audienza* that was based in the town of Lucera provides the source base for this investigation. Its territory was the provinces of Capitanata (modern-day northern Puglia) and the Molise. This area included the sparsely populated *Tavoliere*, a fertile but semi-arid plain with much land given over to sheep grazing.[19] Flocks of sheep were brought down from the Abruzzi highlands through wide grassy passages known as *tratturi* to pass winter in the milder lowlands. This dedication to the wool industry led to sparse population of the province. The Apennines and its foothills formed the western part of Capitanata and the Molise. The *Audienza*'s jurisdiction spread over lowlands and highlands, with all the difficulties of administration this implied.[20]

By the end of the sixteenth century, as Rosario Villari has vividly reconstructed, financial crisis and bad harvests led to an increase in disorder in the countryside, the practice of violent extraction of resources by bandits, and the formation of large forces of bandits who posed authentic challenges to royal

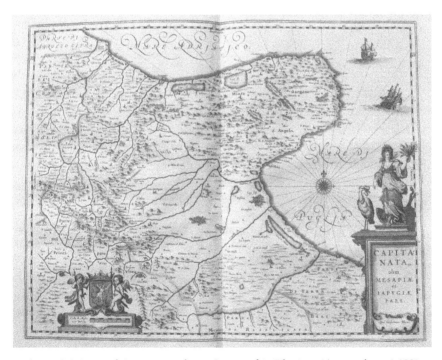

Figure 4.1 Map of Capitanata, from *Geographia Blaviana* (Amsterdam, 1659). Fondo Antiguo, University of Seville.

sovereignty. Most notable among these was the famed Marco Sciarra who led an army that occupied cities, and had the trappings of an upstart ruler or rebel such as standard-bearers and trumpeters. Given such incidents, banditry was central to the idea and practice of provincial justice. The image of public authority was tied to the image of men who committed criminal acts as a part- or full-time way of life. By the sixteenth century bandits had become a clear enough social type in early modern Italy referred to as *fuorusciti* or *banditi*. We shall return to examining such definitions later in this chapter, but for now it is enough to note that they were a clear element in the mapping of the work of justice, a key part of understandings of disorder and criminality.

Such experiences of weakening authority away from administrative centres and the banditry-feudal power nexus were common to early modern Italian states. The borders between the many states that divided the peninsula provided routes of escape and the instrumentalization of jurisdiction. For the Kingdom of Naples, the neighbouring Papal States were obviously the most significant area for flight. The Kingdom also possessed a papal enclave, Benevento, a major node for networks of bandits.

The main organs used to manage rural disorder, apart from periodic special commissions, were the *Presidi* and their allied institutions the *Regie Audienze*, whose functions have previously been discussed in Chapter 2. From 1584 this *Regia Audienza* had its base in a palazzo in the town of Lucera. The town lay on a small hill roughly twenty kilometres to the northwest of the larger urban settlement of Foggia. Its interesting origin as a Saracen settlement, with residents recruited by Federico II, had left little trace by the early modern period. In the numeration of 1631–32, Lucera had 1355 households (*fuochi*) liable for taxation. It was a town where the major economic and political power lay in the hands of the men of the *Popolo* families rather than the patrician nobility.

The two provinces the *Regia Audienza* of Lucera possessed authority over were sparsely urbanized. Communities titled *città* (which should not automatically be assumed to be large urban settlements), numbered twelve in Capitanata and five in the Contado di Molise. The *Tavoliere* was the end of a vast annual process of transhumance. This dedication of portions of land to the wool industry led to sparse population of the province. The Apennines and its foothills formed the western part of Capitanata and the Molise. To the east lay the promontory of the Gargano, the mountainous and forest-covered spur of the Italian boot. The *Audienza*'s jurisdiction spread over these lowlands, highlands, and coastlands, with all the difficulties of administration this implied.

Foggia, as the administrative centre of the sheep-trade, was the most significant urban settlement in Capitanata. This was a centre of trade, capital accumulation, and export. All of this trade was overseen by the sheep customhouse, the *Dogana*. Due to the significance of the customshouse and its need to be able to exercise powers of justice, the tribunal of the *Dogana* held jurisdiction over criminal and civil cases related to the business of the *Dogana*. This explains the location of the *Audienza* in the less jurisdictionally crowded settlement of Lucera. The palace of the *Regia Audienza* in Lucera did not dominate even this small town and was tucked away from the major piazza of the city. Yet despite the humble setting, it played an important role in public life and the viceregal regime's ambitions of control over the provinces.

The surviving archival holdings of the *Audienza* mostly testify to this ongoing battle against banditry. They span 710 trials from 1649 to 1806. The trials of the 'Spanish period' (ending in 1713) includes 141 trials. They deal with woundings, thefts of significant sums of money or livestock, robberies on public roads, homicide, kidnaps for ransom, rape, jailbreaks, and pursuit of notorious bandit gangs. The holdings of the Luceran archive also include civil trials, but these overwhelmingly deal with the eighteenth century on.

The crimes of bandits

Bandits were seen by many inhabitants of the Kingdom as a recurrent disaster. For instance, the notary Cesare Faratro wrote of bandits in the same manner as bad harvests or devastating weather; intermittent tragedies inflicted upon peaceful men. What was different from natural disaster was that he saw bandits as sordid prodigies of fortune, whose wealth would incur punishment from God.[21] Chroniclers or diarists based in the city of Naples such as Vincenzo d'Onofrio, Domenico Confuorto, Antonio Bulifon, and Francesco Capecelatro often recounted especially outrageous crimes of bandits and regularly noted when they were executed in the city or when their corpses were carried to Naples in triumph.[22] For d'Onofrio bandits were monstrous because of their abnormal rise from vile status through vicious crimes. He had a fascination with the physiognomy of these gross prodigies.[23] The remains of bandits were buried near the bridge of the Maddelena outside the city walls to the east.[24]

Banditry was a problem on a large scale, with thousands of bandits normally operating. From Table 4.1 we can get a sense of the scale from the number that met with some form of justice in the years 1675 to 1682.[25]

The activities of bandit were many and varied. Many of their crimes preyed on the mobility necessity in rural life. One of the most characteristic crimes of bandits was the kidnapping of men and women for ransom. It

Table 4.1 Figures of bandits 1675–82 from *Reassunto de servitii ottenuti nel felicissimo Governo dell'Eccellentissimo Sinor Marchese de los Velez* (Naples, 1682).

Bandit chiefs accorded	127
Bandits accorded	1743
Accorded from services	70
Heads of bandit chiefs	105
Heads of bandits	431
Bandit chiefs executed	27
Bandits executed	200
Sent to the galleys	1598
Sent to war	248
Total number	4549

appears that it was mostly bandit gangs who had travelled far from their home regions who performed these crimes. Men and women from all social classes could be taken when travelling or even during raids on towns and villages. There were notorious cases of the kidnap of aristocrats and prominent ecclesiastics.

In reality it was common folk who were most frequently at risk as they were unable to arrange the armed escorts that the wealthier found essential.[26] In 1675 a gang of around thirty bandits from the Marche were kidnapping for ransom in the Molise.[27] Giovanni di Maggio, his father Felice, Mattia Pecoriello, and others were travelling from Carpinone towards the fair of the Maddalena at Castel di Sangro to buy and sell livestock. As they made their way along the road, they were stopped by a group of bandits. They were forced to empty out the coins hidden in their boots. At first, Caporale Ursino – known as *Nerone* – demanded a ransom of 100 ducats for each of their release. But, as the released victims testified, eventually this was driven down to a nearly affordable handful of ducats as they protested that the original sum was impossible even if their families were to sell all their property and goods.[28]

In another incident the bandit chief known as Caporal Disperato accosted the muleteer Giuseppe Amorese in 1679 as he was transporting twenty mules belonging to his employer, Don Giuseppe Stantione.[29] When the bandits stopped him, Amorese first claimed that they were the mules of the local marchese – hoping to dissuade the bandits from offending him with the threat of an aristocrat's retaliation – but after being hit and threatened he admitted the identity of their owner. He was left with a letter to give to his master that unless someone was sent with a ransom to the little convent ('conventuolo piccolo') near Rocchetta he would never see the mules again.[30] Disperato and his gang kidnapped but they also gave ransom notes without possessing the property they threatened to destroy. Disperato's notes are entered into the trial proceedings and they range from courtesy and threat in a discomfiting mixture. Here are two examples:

> As you receive the present your lords will do me the grace of sending me three hundred *scudi* and within two days I'll be waiting where this man will tell you and you'll send it unless you want me and my companions to destroy all of your possessions forever.[31]

> When you receive the present you'll do me the grace of sending me three hundred scudi and within two days I'll be awaiting your reply in the convent of Santa Maria della Rocchetta and you better do it unless you want that I turn my mind to the destruction of all of your goods.[32]

Government policies may have contributed to the attraction of kidnapping as communities were licenced to pay ransoms.[33] The Collateral Council in Naples issued such licences to be paid, unenthusiastically endorsing the practice as inevitable as hunting out the holdfasts of bandits was a lengthy and difficult process.[34]

Other actions committed by bandits included murder, robbery without ransom, and extortion with threat to destroy livestock, crops, or harm people. Arson, uprooting of crops, slaying of livestock, or even more dramatic acts as when, in the summer of 1680, bandits dug under a house, planted gunpowder beneath it and blew it up. This latter act was revenge for the householders informing the court of the bandits' whereabouts; denouncing bandits was a sure way to incur their wrath.

Bandits and enmities

Bandits were an essential part of the culture of enmity in early modern Italy. The crimes that led to exile were most often woundings or murders committed against the person of an enemy. A vicious circle then ensued: enmities made men ready to do violence, the punishment for which pushed them into a marginal life where violence was their stock-in-trade, and they could pursue their enmities with gangs of armed men and be hired to commit violence for other's imbroglios. The cultural image of the bandit (from which bandits themselves drew symbolic resources) was of fierceness, savagery and unwavering pursuit of those who had wronged him. The cheaply printed pamphlet *Lamento, et morte di Benedetto*

Mangone (Florence, 1599), a fictional life in verse of a real *capo di banditi*, revels in the revenge-driven mania of the bandit. In something close to verisimilitude, Mangone becomes a bandit after murdering his 'first enemy', one Mauro Corcione. The narration of his subsequent crimes is an epic of vengeance, including the slaughter of 700 buffalo in pursuit of a 'cruel blood vendetta' against their owners.[35] The scholar Giulio Cesare Capaccio, in a perhaps truer account, identified the reason that Mangone became a bandit as enmities with the nobility of his hometown Eboli.[36] This connection between local enmities, especially between elites such as patrician nobility, and banditry was widespread and profound. Local enmities both created and utilized bandits.

Enmities themselves, especially with bandits, could force mobility. When conflict reached such a pitch that bodily security was imperilled, people often chose or were compelled to displace themselves. The factional conflicts that characterized urban life at times remained at simmering levels, with the odd clash and confrontation, but could boil over into intolerable hostility. An example can come from Domenico Confuorto's *Notizie di alcune famiglie populari della città e regno di Napoli*, in which he records how one Pompilio Gagliano, a lawyer who rather lived off his inheritance than was successful in the practice of law, was forced 'against his will' to move to Naples due to a 'grave enmity' he had with a relative of his Michele Merolla who was a *capo di banditi*.[37] The inseparable phenomena of enmities with banditry – due to the outlawing function of the judicial system – caused dislocation, not only of bandits who took to peripatetic lifestyles but also those who clashed with them, who were forced to move to comparatively safer urban areas.

Rosario Villari claimed that it was pointless to try to identify the political motivations of 'the' bandit due to the general 'illegality' of the bandit's life.[38] While the flexibility of loyalties, the pragmatic quest for survival, and the opportunistic criminality of a bandit definitely contradict attempts to see bandits as embryonic revolutionaries, if we widen our scope of the 'political' to include local power struggles over resources and contests between kin groups, the bandit can be perceived as a political actor. Such involvement in local politics was contextual. The same men could perform random assaults or robberies as well as wield targeted violence in pursuit of their affairs and interests. Their interests could be based in villages, towns, or regions but at times they were also national and even international in scope. The violent tenor of local politics in the Kingdom of Naples was the reason why many men were outlawed. Their violence cannot be separated from the regular practice of local politics. The role of enmity in communities was a crucial factor that explains the individual origins of bandits.

Receiving bandits

Bandits despite their wild self-depiction could be well-integrated into networks of support, succour, and assistance. Some could return to their hometowns to stay with kinfolk. Others were, in the terminology of the criminal law, 'received' by nobles and religious orders who offered them protection or hospitality. The connection between bandits and friaries or monasteries was notorious. A very liberal interpretation of the right of asylum explains part of this connection.

In 1635 Gennaro Adriano Carafa, the Duke of Forlì, was accused of receiving bandits. In the governing council, the Collateral, Regent Munez described it as the 'best proven' case he had ever seen. The bandits Carafa was accused of protecting were suspected of murder, and Carafa had then arranged for remissions (notarized documents of forgiveness) to be collected from the relatives of the victims, probably through bribery or intimidation. Carafa had offered 5000 ducats in recompense, but Munez argued for a minimum of 6000. Another regent, Zufia, argued for the notion of combining an extraordinary grace from the viceroy with exile from Forlì for three years. The regent Januarius suggested taking the 5000 ducats while also sending Carafa to serve as a commander in the Spanish army. The agreement reached was to insist upon the payment of 6000 ducats but to offer a full grace in return.[39] In such policy debates the decorum of justice was balanced with considerations of state finances and the best way to ensure the Kingdom's peace by not outraging the aristocratic elite.

Communication between bandits and resident populations could be fluid and regular. In Bovino, the notary Cesare Faratro recalled (in the chronicles and meditations which he wrote at every year's end in his bound volumes of notarial records) thirty-five bandits who spent months living in the countryside near the town, until the Duke of Alba sent Don Giuseppe Gusman in their pursuit.[40] He remembered times when outlaws came into Bovino well-dressed and spending doubloons with a free hand.[41] The laws of the Kingdom repeatedly identified these sorts of interaction and attempted to prevent them, but without armed forces present such pronouncements had little efficacy. The coercion of kin under threat of punishment was one approach. Courts tried to map out a bandit's networks by ordering lists of their kin to be composed by officials in their hometown, which could then be used both for questioning and for threatening punishment by proxy.[42]

Despite the support provided to bandits, either from choice or coercion, or their involvement in local factional conflict, we should not assume that communities never cooperated in anti-bandit initiatives. Incursions by bandits were indeed a blight on many communities. As the council of Capracotta wrote to the *Regia Audienza* of Lucera: 'this poor land never lacks for hardships, and it seems, that the bandits are no longer happy to take away our goods and now they seek to take away our lives'.[43] Outlaws murdered, kidnapped, robbed, and extorted. They threatened to and did burn crops or buildings down.[44] Towns were supposed to resist bandits through the ringing of the *campana all'arme* and through citizen militias, known as 'frati giurati'.[45] Towns and cities debated how to resist the depredations of bandits in parliamentary assemblies.[46] In September 1672 in Roseto, when the bell rang, the *camerlingo* of the town Sebastiano Romano ran to close the town's gates and then proceeded to the baron's palace to organize civic defence.[47] In September 1686 some men of Carovilli attacked and killed some bandits who had hidden in a stable near their town.[48] There were numerous reasons why bandits would be supported or opposed, which depended on the perceived risk to the community and whether they knew the bandits in question; such support was also likely to be varied along all sorts of internal community divisions.

Soldiers and bandits

Addressing the problem of outlaws was one of the main duties and preoccupations of the 'government of the countryside', a term that was used to designate aspects of policy aimed at ensuring good order in the rural or semi-rural areas of the Kingdom.[49] The institutional structure to address banditry remained relatively constant throughout the early modern period. The system was under the control of a regent of the Collateral Council who held the role of Commissar General of the Countryside (the post was later changed to the Superintendent General of the Countryside). The *Regie Audienze* were the key institutions one in each province.

One of the prominent duties of royal officials was to apprehend, kill, or pacify bandits. Let us take the case of Aniello Porzio's attempt to 'quiet' part of the Abruzzi in July 1660, reported by the diarist Vincenzo d'Onofrio. He was to 'pacify [*quietare*] some leaders of men [*capi di gente*], some due to private enmities, and others that scourged the countryside'.[50] Pausing here, we can see the recurrent division between those motivated by the politics of private enmity – men who took revenge and organized violent gangs to do so – and those who robbed or attacked with no particular personal animus. This may have been more of a jurisprudential frame than a real one. Porzio mediated both formal and informal oaths between bandits. The ability to 'adjust' bandits and to pacify their enmities was key to the skills of the government of the countryside.[51] Many different levels of government had to have familiarity with bandits. From *eletti* in town councils, regional governors, the *auditori*, and commissioners of the countryside, all of these levels could know outlaws personally. There was a disjuncture between official language that talked of them as demons made flesh and the practice of everyday life in which they could be well-known and important actors in local politics. In practice, it was necessary to cultivate a 'buona corrispondenza' with such powerful men if their enmities were to be settled.[52] This pragmatism blurred into corruption. Planned activities of anti-bandit forces were leaked in advance, allowing the wealthy and well-connected to keep in front of the law.

One case from the *Audienza*'s records provides an unusual insight into the relationship between bandits and officials. In Oratino, a group of councilmen, notables and their friends dined together and drank without moderation. The guests included the governor and other members of the government as well as one Salvatore Vito.[53] After too much drink Salvatore apparently kept talking about the notorious bandit-chief Abbate Cesare.[54] The other guests testified that they had told him to be quiet. Apparently this was a dangerous topic of conversation and one that could be perilous. While this could well have been just a convenient excuse to explain why a fight broke out, it is interesting that this carried explanatory power. Discussion of banditry was potentially dangerous and silence was often preferable.

The use of military forces to counter bandits had considerable limitations. Across the early modern period the quality of the forces used was often lacklustre. Many attempts at reform were undermined by insufficient investment or training, such as the anti-banditry militias called the *barricelli* that were established in the early sixteenth century. They were initially funded by extraordinary taxation but then not properly financed after this.[55] Many features were similar between bandits and soldiers. They were both mostly young men, aged from around eighteen to forty, from mixed locations and they travelled well-armed, often far from their hometowns. One case illustrates the connections well.

Caporale or *capitano* was the title used both by bandit chiefs and by commanders of the squadrons of the *Regia Audienza*. The professionalism of anti-bandit forces was often lacking. Underpaid and under disciplined, they were regularly sourced from pardoned bandits themselves. The path to soldiery was open to many bandit groups.[56] The Spanish monarchy was grateful for a source of men who would fight willingly and, if they left the kingdom, it solved the disruption of their presence without military assault and therefore saved money on a number of fronts. It was notoriously difficult to raise volunteer armies, sometimes men had to be led to war in chains, so it was hard to resist eager armed squadrons to bolster the ranks of the armies.[57] The bandit Giulio Pizzola was recruited as a *caporale di campagna*.[58]

From many perspectives, soldiers were unwelcome interlopers. They were not a welcome source of law and order in every land in the Kingdom.

Communities complained about forced billeting, which was a favoured strategy against banditry but a heavy weight on communities. In 1665 the Duke of Oratino chased away *Capitano* Ludovico Pilorei and his soldiers while they were in the process of inventorying the goods of a man who had failed to appear before the court.[59] For many feudal lords, support of the Spanish regime was implicitly offered in exchange for a lack of interference in their affairs. Instead of royal servants performing the justice of the King, the soldiers were interpreted as a group of armed outsiders, coming to insult and injure the vassals of a feudal lord.

Distrust of soldiers could be warranted. The *Regia Audienza* squadron led by Giovanni Pietro Ringolo committed considerable violence in the small town of Monteroduni in the Molise when they came to collect an arrested outlaw in 1678; Gratia Todesca was dragged by her hair and punched to the ground, Laura dello Fiavo was beaten with the butt of a harquebus and many residents had similar stories of abuse.[60] The soldiers of the *Audienze* were not a welcome sight in many towns. Corporals and soldiers could cooperate with bandits.[61] The higher levels of anti-banditry administration were similarly compromised. As Daniela Ambron has noted it was common 'that the *presidi*, uditori, governors and subaltern officers themselves favoured bandits, reinforcing the clientage networks that marked the political and social dialectic of the *ancien régime*'.[62]

Militarized responses to banditry may have caused banditry to organize more effectively as they prepared themselves to resist the squadrons of the state. Insufficient fine-grain management of surges in troops led to the dispersal of firearms and deserting manpower. 'Persecution' was the way in which military anti-bandit campaigns were framed. The notion of banditry as a 'revolt against the establishment of the modern state' is only part of the truth.[63] The reality was far more a case of strange interactions and underground connections between supposedly distinct legal and illegal worlds.

Extirpating bandits: the government of the countryside after 1647

The extirpation of banditry was a major concern for the authorities of the kingdom, and numerous individuals made their careers based on the pursuit of bandits, which involved not only the ability to lead military forces but also often involved cultivating a certain amount of good correspondence with bandit chiefs.

In the 1660s bandit chiefs returned to the top of the power dynamics in the Abruzzi. In 1667, a leading bandit chief, Titta Colraniero, was presumed to be in contact with the French ambassador turning the valence of the disorder from provincial chaos to a potential threat to the Kingdom.[64] By the 1680s the situation had deteriorated further. One violent division was organized around the two most prominent *capobanditi* Titta [Giovanbattista] Colraniero (sometimes recorded as Cola Raniero, or Colaraniero) and Santuccio di Froscia. They had killed each other's kin and were in a state of deep enmity. Livestock were murdered in revenge attacks, farms were burnt to the ground, and mills were stilled by the blocking of their waters.[65] The auditor Tauri tried to convince Santuccio and Colaranieri to make peace.[66] Despite the success of this venture, Titta was said to have feigned peace and violent hostilities soon began again. Francesco Perez Navaretta (or Navarette), the Marquis of Laterza, was dispatched to the Abruzzi in his capacity as *commissario di campagna* to make peace between Titta and Santuccio as well as other bandits involved in the complex rivalries of the region such as those who followed the bandit-chief Bianchini.[67] Francesco Navaretta had proven himself at least an enthusiastic persecutor of bandits in the 1670s, when he was excommunicated for pursuing outlaws into the Papal States.[68]

He promised indulgences in return for some heads of named bandits. Behind such grisly demands it was actually the authority that leading bandit-chiefs had to ensure quiet which was the real power that made pacification feasible. Navaretta spent eight days in the company of Titta Colranieri in the hope to make peace through personal intervention. It was even reported that he took one of Titta's sons, Francescantonio Colranieri, back with him to Naples with the intention of supporting him through legal training.[69] After this, Francesco Navaretta seems to have lived in Camplì along with Santuccio for three years. Santuccio is an intriguing figure who, as Daniela Ambron reconstructs, had a close association with Giovan Francesco Sanfelice, the Duke of Lauriano.[70] For representatives of the *governo della campagna* 'good correspondence' was indispensable to peace-making, especially with such notorious outlaws. But such approaches were at least temporarily replaced in 1684 by a major military campaign against these bandits. The town of Montorio again suffered, being held by Colraniero with 600 men.[71]

In the case of Montorio and surrounding areas we see the fine-grained, personal reality of both banditry and attempts to resolve it. Homicides of particular people sparked feuds and officials were sent to act as both peacemakers and persecutors. Men of influence became bandits when their activities came to the attention of the court. For example, in the mid-1670s in the town of Roseto, the violent Ruggiero brothers Paolo, Antonio, and Michele along with their nephew Gateano Pappano used violence to extort goods and rape women.[72] Eventually, a gang was formed to drive them out of the town and Paolo was killed. The others fled and were outlawed. Five years later one Antonio Ruggiero of Roseto was noted as a dead bandit in the *Reassunto de servitii ottenuti*.[73] It was this encounter with the *Regia Audienza* that appears to have pushed them from local troublemakers to travelling bandits.

The case of Domenico Allegretti

One of the common themes in bandit careers is the combination of directed vengeance and 'pure' criminality, not motivated by pre-existing hatreds. If we turn to one particular trial from the *Regia Audienza*, we can see how banditry testifies to a number of themes in the relation between justice and space: especially, first, the productive possibilities that legal exile created for the formation of new social relations and, second, the instrumentalization of such spatial-legal practices as the right of asylum.

In the late 1660s Domenico Allegretti from Mirabello in the Molise was investigated for being a *capo di banditi* and most members of his alleged gang were killed or arrested.[74] The trial for the crimes committed by Domenico Allegretti and his bandit gang illuminates many of the themes about banditry's connections to local conflicts and inimical relationships. It also shows how the social networks and geographical space of the Kingdom shaped how such local conflicts were pursued. The detail of the story reminds us of the complexity of banditry and how its characteristics cannot be placed into overly simple typologies. It depicts the complex relational world of 'service' that spanned illicit and licit systems of clientage in early modern Naples.

It is useful to start investigating Domenico's story by considering the status of the Allegretti family. In 1569 Giovan Lorenzo Allegretti became Lord of Mirabello.[75] While exact links between Domenico and the dukes are unclear, it seems plausible that he was a young member of a minor noble family who lived in his clan's provincial seat or, perhaps, was related to the noble branch of this family.[76]

An account of a skirmish begins the trial from which Allegretti's story emerges. The account is that of Gennaro Mancarella, a captain of the *Regia Audienza*, the twenty-four-year-old who led soldiers of the *Audienza* in pursuit of 'some wrongdoers'.[77] They were to scour and clear areas of the *Val fortore* to the south-east of Lucera from where reports had come that a gang of bandits held a pass and were robbing those that attempted to travel through. Once they reached the area they encountered the armed men, and in a skirmish killed one bandit, while the rest fled.[78] These violent encounters were, due to the right to proceed *ad modum belli* against bandits, part of legal practice and a way in which the countryside as zone of conflict was produced.

After this encounter the *Regia Audienza* began investigations in the surrounding towns with the aim of identifying who had been killed and finding the rest of their companions. The man who had been killed was finally identified as Cesare Cerrone. In Mirabello, they found witnesses who knew about Cesare. Three years ago, he had come to work in the service of Domenico Allegretti. The villagers said they had often seen Cesare carrying a firearm. Cesare had been one of a gang of eleven men that Domenico had recently gathered, all bearing long knives and harquebuses, who had spent some time in Mirabello. Cesare was known as Ciccio, and others referred to him as a Domenico's 'servant'.[79] Pietro Antonio di Luccio recorded how Cesare was Domenico's 'creature' who 'because of some of his enmities he has always had an armed gang of men'.[80] It was the language of patronage and service that expressed the bonds between armed men and their leaders. Domenico apparently had dangerous enemies and, therefore, he went around in a gang for his own protection. Enmities such as this were a reason to hire servants, accomplices, or others to provide protection.

The townspeople noted that these men came and went. 'From time to time', a witness testified, 'I wouldn't see them for about a month' and that 'I do not know where they went'.[81] They appeared, disappeared and reappeared. The group was also violent. They had shot dead Francesco Petillo, an *arciprete* in Mirabello, as he was Domenico's enemy.[82] For this attack Cesare Cerrone, Pietro Antonio Guglielmo, and Giuseppe Sadimarco were all declared outlaws. But they remained able to socialize publicly 'without fear of justice' and intimidated the whole town.[83] Intimidation and fear were often the reasons communities gave for why outlaws had been accommodated. The plausible assertion of fear could also be cover for collusion. A climate of silence, whatever the reasons that lay behind it, and weak enforcement meant that men of homicidal violence could continue to dwell in their own communities.

In the investigations after the skirmish some members of the gang were found in the Chiesa del Santissimo Salvatore by soldiers of the *Regia Audienza*. Allegretti and his companions forestalled their forcible arrest by claiming to be in the service of the Marchese di Baranello, Diomede Carafa. At this time, Diomede was only twenty years old. He was a member of one of the most prestigious aristocratic clans in the Kingdom, yet his branch of the family was neither the most well-positioned nor the richest. Decades later he would be remembered as a 'paradigm of wise shrewdness, and gracefulness'.[84] When the men claimed service to Diomede they cast themselves in the most generous interpretation as legitimate *guardiani* or *sbirri* of a feudal lord and, in the least generous, bandits under powerful protection. This constructive ambiguity was enabled by the vast importance of private armed guards for all sorts of powerful people in the Kingdom.

A witness said that the men of the squadron decided to write to Diomede Carafa.[85] The soldiers, perhaps unwilling to be exposed to Diomede's anger if they turned out to be under his legitimate protection, sent the letter then sat and waited rather than capturing them. But the squadron was very lax in observing the men and the bandits were able to loiter outside the church and they drank and ate together – showing how laws could be bent. A reply eventually arrived from the marchese stating that he 'did not protect cutpurses' and had no idea who they were, washing his hands of them (whether accurately or not).[86]

From the subsequent confession of Nicolo Pirolo it emerged that days before Domenico Allegretti and the marchese made peace together [*pacificato*].[87] This points again to the cross-class nature of provincial alliances, where noble status mattered but relationships spread across local networks in which nobles were embedded. The political worlds that feudal lords operated within were diverse. Before they 'were pacified' Diomede and Domenico apparently were enemies.[88] The texture of this relationship is not clear, but it demonstrates the significance of the relationships between feudal lords and less eminent gentlemen. The realities of provincial life entailed a variety of sorts of relations beyond vertical vassalage. Once they had made peace, Domenico spent time with the marchese, eating, drinking, and sleeping in his palazzo.

The two men in the Church of the Santissimo Salvatore walked out calmly when the marchese's reply arrived; the soldiers had not given away the nature of the response. The men were then arrested with ease. In the subsequent interrogations of Nicolò Pirilo the actions of Domenico's gang came into a far sharper focus than the perspective offered by the vague reports they had received of robbers in a valley pass. They were murderers who had killed several people and they had most recently tried to assassinate Michele Gentile, an enemy of Domenico Allegretti.

But as the *Regia Audienza* took another set of depositions a campaign of attempted misinformation was uncovered that helped to explain the unclear stories they had received before Nicolò had begun to confess. One Donato lo Russo said that he had gone to Lucera to testify but that afterwards a man came to find him and give him wine worth 7 *carlini* on behalf of Papa Allegretti of Mirabello, Domenico's sister-in-law, and was asked to tell him exactly what he had told the *Audienza*. This information gathering revealed a sophisticated understanding of judicial proceedings and a dispersed network of informants. Knowledge about law and jurisdictions was instrumentalized in an attempt to stay one step ahead of the *Audienza*.[89]

Don Gennaro Pirazzo, a priest of the Church of the Santissimo Salvatore, began canvassing the townspeople, offering payment in exchange for sworn accounts that the soldiers had forcibly extracted Nicolò and Francesco from the church. The production of testimony was often a reflection of political force. Such reports successfully brought the Vicar-General of Benevento into the legal fray. The vicar-general alleged that this removal was a violation of ecclesiastical jurisdiction and sought to have the accused handed over to him. However, this appeal was successfully rebuffed by a combination of legal proofs that the men left the church of their own free will and that, furthermore, the vicar-general would not have been the relevant ecclesiastical authority in any case. Instead the holder of such jurisdiction was the Bishop of Boiano who had been informed at every stage and was apparently happy to see such men of evil life captured.[90] The motivation for Gennaro's campaign remains obscure in the records of the trial but it seems very likely that he had been mobilized by relatives or supporters of Domenico as a last-ditch attempt to forestall the trial of the outlaws; although he may have had his own jurisdictional reasons. Such jurisdictional adventures, related to particular spaces, demonstrate the legal practices of bandits could be sophisticated manipulations of laws. Bandits had agency within early modern legal culture, using the countryside and its laws to shape their actions.

Gennaro's campaign demonstrates how the heights of ecclesiastical and state authority could be dragged into marginal events involving people otherwise distant from the elite. The tense relationship between jurisdictions was one of the marked characteristics of the Kingdom of Naples; the resulting sensitivity gave power to those who could cast their particular legal dealings as an offence to one or the other jurisdictions.[91] In this case, two outlaws leaving a church led to letters exchanged between the viceroy, the *Audienza*, the Bishop of Boiano, and the Vicar-General of Benevento. The prickly issue of the jealous protection of jurisdictions could be manipulated for various ends and instantly transform what was at stake in many legal proceedings.

The interrogation, torture, and confession of Nicolò Pirolo in Lucera reveals the activities, itineraries, and sociability of the group identified as Domenico's *comitiva*.[92]

The language of friendship and service are used to explain how they cohered and operated together. Nicolo's interrogation is recorded in penitent and confessional tone. Raised on the cord, he claimed 'I want to tell the truth' and 'I will tell all that I have done'.[93] Turning to their peregrinations across the south of Italy, a clearer picture emerges of issues of solidarity and cohesion among outlaws.

Nicolò started his tale with the events of May 1667. He had stolen two horses from outside Manfredonia and a letter arrived from his friend Scipione Vasullo telling him that the authorities were searching for him for the crime.[94] Scipione advised him to come to Terra della Guardia not only to escape arrest but also so he could talk to him 'di cosa di mio servicio'.[95] Nicol related that between him and Scipione there was a 'stretta amicitia' since they had been imprisoned together in Benevento until the last Sunday of Carnival in February of 1667 when they fled together, perhaps taking advantage of festive distraction.[96]

Nicolò returned to Benevento after his meeting with Scipione in Terra della Guardia. He explained this by citing his friendship with Scipione, who had asked him to go back to the city he had only recently escaped from to find a set of men that Scipione wanted him to gather. He succeeded in gathering Giovanni Giannino from Naples, a man he knew only as Vito from Quarata and one Constantino, a Calabrian. He described this as 'making a union'.[97] Together they went to find Scipione in Terra di Guardia, in the house of Don Filippo Cavilio. Here they found him along with Domenico Allegretti, who Nicol had never met before. The plan introduced by Domenico was to accompany him to the town of Vitulano and from there to Mirabello where they would murder Domenico's enemies.[98] Domenico, Scipione, and Nicol set out with weapons to Vitulano where they met with two more men, Cesare Cerrone and one Aniello Rossillo, originally from Benevento. 'All five of us, united and armed', testified Niccol, went to Vitulano and they stayed in a hermitage called Sant'Angelo above the hamlet of Foglianese. Here the friars provided them with food and drink.[99]

From here they moved to a Benedictine abbey, Santa Maria de Gruptis, on a high hillside above Vitulano.[100] Its altitude made it a good refuge for a gang of armed men. There they met with Carlo Jolle and left. When they arrived in Mirabello they met with eight more men in Domenico's house; now they were a group of thirteen. It was late June, and they went out into the countryside following a woodland path. They stayed the night at a place known as Croce di Cercia. Nearby they encountered another group of armed men. After a brief conversation, they identified the other group as soldiers of the *Regia Audienza* and a skirmish began. This was the encounter that left Cesare Cerrone dead.[101]

After this, they escaped to Mirabello. Nicolò went to the city of Campobasso in Molise along with Constantino Calabrese and Aniello Rossillo, staying there for fifteen days. They waited for a woman called Giulia Annuncia, a friend of Domenico, to arrive from Naples. Then they returned to Mirabello and stayed throughout September when Domenico and Nicolò, along with Francesco Riccio attempted to murder Michele Gentile after having heard that he was trying to give their whereabouts to the *Audienza*.[102] Despite Nicolò's claim to want to discharge his conscience and his subsequent claims to have told the entire truth when he was tortured, his testimony includes no account of the crimes that local residents had reported that the men had been committing. No reductive model of banditry accounts for the multiple sorts of mobility, contacts, and exchange of knowledge that shaped the lives of the men who travelled with Domenico

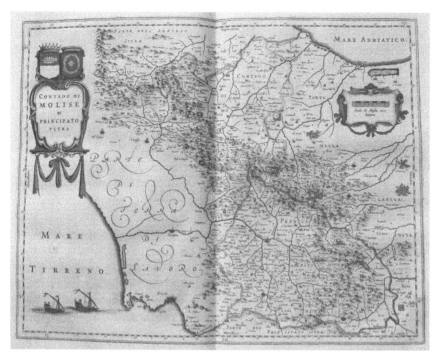

Figure 4.2 Detail of a map of the Molise, Joan Blaeu, (Amsterdam, c. 1640). Norman B. Leventhal Map Center, Boston Public Library.

Allegretti. It is clear that a bandit gang could be formed from a set of alliances, overlapping purposes, and also be a temporary and fluid group. We can note the relative absence of kinship ties; instead, friendship and prior acquaintance explained most of the alliances formed. Nevertheless, it was precisely Allegretti's kin who were mobilized to influence the judicial proceedings. Allegretti's companions can be tied to no one particular locality, they were from a wide range of areas. They cohered around the project of revenge, to assist in the murder of Domenico's enemies.

Specific places mattered too and the location that emerges as most significant is Benevento. An enclave of papal jurisdiction it was an easy place for men of 'evil life' to hide in and to make contacts with patrons and allies. Benevento was for centuries a 'confugium', a place for those fleeing the jurisdictional gaze of the Neapolitan authorities.[103] It is the best example of how the jurisdictional patchwork of the Italian peninsula enabled criminals to successfully avoid justice. But its function was not only as place of escape but also of potential rescue; it was from Benevento that ecclesiastical jurisdictional power reached out in an attempt to protect the captured bandits.

Entrepreneurs of violence, such as Domenico Allegretti, could utilize the rural spaces of banditry and the labour of men ready to do violence in order to attempt to achieve personal goals of triumphing over his enemies. Part of what was required was a widespread set of contacts, knowledge about geography, and methods of recruitment. He was able to build a group to pursue his enemies through letter-writing and personal meetings. One strategy for the ambitious local man who sought to enrich himself, extend his dominion, or protect himself from adversaries was to cultivate personal connections to banditry. These sort of connections probably developed over time, in part by chance, as men he knew took *alla campagna*. The world of banditry informed and impinged upon many of the ways in which people could deal with their enemies and pursue their hatreds, as well as the mobility that was a normal part of labouring practices.

Gathering men was fundamental to banditry. It is important to focus on how bandit groups were formed and remain open to interpreting them as various sorts of assemblages of relationships. The easy creation of solidarity between outlaws was at the core of what made banditry a problem on such a large scale; it survived attempts to shatter trust by rewarding bandits who presented the heads of other bandits with pardons.[104] One other major point, that emerges in the sociability between bandits and soldiers, was the extensive similarity between the two worlds. This goes beyond the surface to a deeper connection. Bandits were offered forgiveness for taking up service in the King's armies. Spanish soldiers sent to Italy had often been bandits themselves in Spain.

Banditry was an essential context for the meanings of enmity and peace in early modern Naples. The political imagination of what it meant to pacify was formed by the realities of banditry. The use of armed men and violence in local battles over authority and jurisdiction provided a large place for banditry. The stability of the Kingdom was connected in manifold ways with the enmities that drove men to gangs. Similarly, gangs of outlaws were resources in the pursuit of local enmities.

Notes

1 Archivio di Stato di Lucera, Regia Udienza Provinciale di Capitanata, Processi Penali, busta 8, fasc. 83, fol. 526ʳ: 'Questo e quello traditore di Pietro Brancazio il Quale a traduto uno compagno di Matteo Banco et avendomi capitato nelle mani li ho dato quello castigo che meritano questi traditori acci ci penzano l' altri a commettere qualche altro mancamento Caporal Donato Demante'.
2 For a synthetic account of these challenges see Charles Tilly, 'Invisible Elbow', *Sociological Forum*, 11 (1996), 589–601.

Banditry and the culture of enmity   139

3 Luigi Lacchè, *Latrocinium: giustizia, scienza penale e repressione del banditismo in antico regime* (Milan: Giuffrè, 1988).
4 Mario Sbriccoli, 'Brigantaggio e ribellismi nella criminalistica dei secoli XVI–XVIII', in *Bande armate, banditi, banditismo e repressione di giustizia negli stati europei di antico regime*, ed. by Gherardo Ortalli (Rome: Jouvence, 1986), pp. 496–7. Also see the discussion in Francesco Gaudioso, *Il potere di punire e perdonare: banditismo e politiche criminali nel Regno di Napoli in età moderna* (Naples: Congedo Editore, 2006), p. 22.
5 Irene Fosi, 'Il banditismo nello Stato Pontificio nella seconda metà del cinquecento', in *Bande armate, banditi, banditismo e repressione di giustizia negli stati europei di antico regime*, ed. by Gherardo Ortalli (Rome: Jouvence, 1986) pp. 70–1: 'sono i fuorusciti, cioè nobili o cittadini cacciati in seguito alle sempre accese lotte fra le fazioni municipali; sono poi i ladroni, grassatori di strada, masnadieri, ossia soldati disoccupati, ma sono anche e, direi, sopratutto, banditi *tout court*, delinquenti comuni colpiti dal bando in contumacia per crimini commessi contro il patrimonio e/o la persona, privati, secondo la normativa statutaria locale, dei beni, se ne avevano, ed allontantati per un periodo di tempo determinato o per tutta la vita, a seconda della gravità dei reati, dal luogo dove era stato commesso il crimine'.
6 On these difficulties see Fosi, 'Il banditismo nello Stato Pontificio', pp. 70–1.
7 ASL, Regia Udienza, Processi Penali, busta 1, fasc. 17, fol. 572^v. [108] ASL, Regia Udienza, Processi Penali, busta 4, fasc. 47, fol. 711^r.
8 Ibid., busta 4, fasc. 47.
9 Ibid., busta 10, fasc. 93bis, fol. 654^r: 'vestiti a banditi e scorritori di Campagna'.
10 For a brief survey of the broader Italian picture on similar powers, also known as 'ex abrupto' in Sicily see Marco Corcione, *Modelli Processuali nell'Antico Regime: La giustizia penale nel tribunale di Campagna di Nevano* (Frattamaggiore: Istituto di Studi Atellani, 2002), p. 11.
11 *Reassunto de servitii ottenuti nel felicissimo Governo dell'Eccellentissimo Sinor Marchese de los Velez* (Naples, 1682).
12 ASL, Regia Udienza, Processi Penali, busta 5, fasc. 62, fols. 579^v–580^r.
13 Ibid., p. 142:

> Già perchè questi tali
> gli traggon le calzette, o le stivali.
>   Conoscon certi, pur certi bravoni,
> Bravissimi, bravazzi,
> Chiamati tra di noi tagliacantoni,
> Fracassa ferri e mangiacatenazzi,
> Portando a la cintura
> Con certa lor tremenda intosicatura,
> Arrabiando da cani,
> Il diavolo sempre et alle mani.
>   Così pescando van come sapete
> Le discordie e le lite con la rete.

On the figure of the *bravo* or the *tagliacantone* see the satirical analysis of such men by Buoso Tomani, *Della Compagnia de'Tagliacantoni, descrittione*

universale. Nella quale à pieno si scuopre l'origine, & progresso della vita loro (Venice, 1601) and Benedetto Croce, 'Il tipo del napoletano nella commedia', in his *Saggi sulla letteratura italiana del seicento* (Bari: Laterza, 1911), pp. 303–5.
14 ASL, Regia Udienza, Processi Penali, busta 7, fasc. 75, fol. 316[r].
15 *Reassunto de servitii*, p. 58.
16 One of the most fundamental jurisprudential guides was Angelo Scialoya, *Praxis forjudicatoria, seu modus procedendi in Regno Neapolitano ad sententiam forjudicationis contra reum absentum in eius contumacia vigore Constitutionis Regni poenam eorum* (Naples, 1645).
17 ASL, Regia Udienza, Processi Penali, busta 5, fasc. 62.
18 Ibid., fol. 580[r].
19 For an introduction in English to the *Tavoliere* and the world of the *Dogana* of Foggia see John A. Marino, *Pastoral Economics in the Kingdom of Naples* (Baltimore: Johns Hopkins University Press, 1988); John A. Marino, 'Wheat and Wool in the Dogana of Foggia: An Equilibrium Model for Early Modern Economic History', *Mélanges de l'École française de Rome. Moyen-Age, Temps modernes*, 100 (1988), p. 876.
20 For an introduction to the mountains as a challenge for Mediterranean states see Fernand Braudel's commentary on the mountains in *The Mediterranean and the Mediterranean World in the Age of Philip II*, 2 vols. (New York: Fontana, 1975).
21 Pasquale di Cicco, 'Una Cronaca Bovinese del Seicento', *La Capitanata* (1986), 53–91.
22 Guido Panico, *Il carnefice e la piazza: crudeltà di stato e violenza popolare a Napoli in età moderna* (Naples: Edizioni scientifiche italiane, 1985), p. 70.
23 Vincenzo d'Onofrio, *Giornali di Napoli dal MDCLX al MDCLXXX*, ed. by Franco Schlitzer, Antonio Padula, and Vittoria Omodeo, 3 vols. (Naples: Società napoletana di storia patria, 1934–39), II, p. 165.
24 Panico, *Il carnefice e la piazza*, pp. 70–1.
25 *Reassunto de servitii ottenuti nel felicissimo Governo dell'Eccellentissimo Sinor Marchese de los Velez* (Naples, 1682).
26 During a parochial visitation the bishop Aniello La Guardia in the 1670s travelled 'associatus a multis armatis personis'; Pietro Ebner, *Chiesa, baroni e popolo nel Cilento* (Rome: Edizioni di storia e letteratura, 1982), I, p. 447.
27 ASL, Regia Udienza, Processi Penali, busta 5, fasc. 63.
28 Ibid., fols. 600[r]–604[r]
29 Ibid., busta 7, fasc. 75.
30 Ibid., fols. 321[r]–322[r].
31 In translating these letters I have sought to retain the syntax of the original Italian. ASL, Regia Udienza, Processi Penali, busta 7, fasc. 75, fol. 323[r]: 'In ricevere la presenta V.S. fora gratia di inviar mi tre centi scudi e fra due giorni mi sta attendendo resposto a q'luogo dove vi diera il presente a voce è mi inviti meno si non voleto spianate da me su[…] tutti li vostri bene e per fine con tutti li miei compagni.'
32 Ibid., fol. 328[r]: ' In ricevere la presente vi mi fora gratia de mandarmi tre centi scudi è fra due giorni mi sto attendere risposta nel convento di Santa Maria

della Roccheta e non mancasi si voleti che io in faccia volere la struttione di tutti li vostre bene'.
33 Ibid, fols. 326^{r-v}.
34 Ibid.
35 Murder of livestock was indeed a realistic charge, bandits killed livestock and burned crops when a farmer was subject to their wrath.
36 Giulio Cesare Capaccio, *Il Forastiero. Dialogi di Giulio Cesare Capaccio* (Naples, 1634), p. 429. Benedetto Mangone continued to be remembered and mythologized for centuries after his death, described in travel accounts and history books as an example of the first generation of brigands and as precursor to nineteenth-century brigandage. In this way, his name mirrors the constant exchange between the reality and myth of banditry through telling and retelling of events. Pietro Giannone recalled him as 'quel famoso bandito …, di cui rimane ancora l'infame memoria per le tante scelleratezze commesse nella campagna d'Eboli', *Istoria Civile del Regno di Napoli* (Haya, 1753), IV, p. 280. A classic example of his fictional transformation is the story: *Benedetto Mangone; or, The Brigand of Eboli* by Charles Macfarlane published in *The Literary Souvenir, or Cabinet of Poetry and Romance* (London, 1832), pp. 253–85.
37 Fortundio Erodoto Montecco [Domenico Confuorto], *Notizie di alcune famiglie popolari della città e regno di Napoli: divenute per ricchezze, e dignitá nobili, e riguardevoli*, Philadelphia, UPenn Ms. Codex 1475, 9v–10r.
38 Rosario Villari, *The Revolt of Naples* (Cambridge: Polity, 1993), p. 48.
39 ASN, Consiglio Collaterale, Notamenti, busta 30, fols. 32^{r-v}.
40 Di Cicco, 'Una Cronaca Bovinese del Seicento', p. 77.
41 Ibid.
42 Rosario Villari, 'Congiura aristocratica e rivoluzione popolare', *Studi Storici*, 8 (1967), 37–112 (p. 87): 'La spietata persecuzione dei parenti dei banditi … non era semplicemente una misura di rappresaglia. Base del prestigio e dell'autorita politica per i feudatari, il *parentado* non era meno importante per i contadini. Era il nucleo fondamentale dell'organizzazione interna del mondo contadino, la base più solida e resistente della difesa delle comunita rurali di fronte a minacce e pericoli provenienti dall'esterno e dell'aiuto reciproco nei bisogni della vita quotidiana; era un vincolo complesso che solo per ragioni interne, e non per la condanna da parte dell'autorita pubblica nei confronti di uno dei membri, poteva essere spezzato.'
43 ASL, Regia Udienza, Processi Penali, busta 1, fasc. 4, fol. 606^{r}: 'Al questa povera terra non mancano mai guai, et pare, che li banditi non sono ancor satij di levarci le robbe et procurer levarci la vita'.
44 Niccola Palma, *Storia ecclesiastica e civile della regione più settentrionale del Regno di Napoli* (Teramo, 1833), III, p. 112.
45 Elena Papagana, 'Ordine pubblico e repressione del banditismo nel Mezzogiorno d'Italia (secoli XVI–XIX)', in *Corpi armati e ordine pubblico in Italia (XVI–XIX sec.)*, ed. by Livio Antonielli and Claudio Donati (Soveria Mannelli: Rubbettino, 2003), p. 56.

142   *States of enmity*

46 The council of Camplì discussed 'super cura adhibenda custodiae hujus Civitatis ab aggressionibus exulum', cited in Palma, *Storia ecclesiastica e civile*, III, p. 146.
47 ASL, Regia Udienza, Processi Penali, busta 6, fasc. 67, fol. 180^r.
48 Ibid., busta 10, fasc. 93bis, fols. 89^v–90^r.
49 This term, *governo della campagna*, was used to define anti-banditry measures such as in the *Governo della Campagna dell'Eccellentissimo Signor Marchese de los Velez* (Naples, 1683) and is matched in the titles of anti-banditry officials such as *commissario della campagna*.
50 D'Onofrio, *Giornali di Napoli*, I, p. 46. See also Domenico Antonio Parrino, *Teatro eroico, e politico de'governi de'vicerè del Regno di Napoli* (Naples, 1694), III, pp. 107–8.
51 Aniello Porzio had experience in these matters. As a judge of the Vicaria he was sent to the Cilento by the viceroy Oñate to punish the protectors of bandits. On this see Ebner, *Chiesa, baroni e popolo*, p. 207. Adjustment was institutionalized as one of the ways to counter banditry. For this see Francesco de Jorio's overview of the anti-banditry pragmatics in his *Introduzione allo studio delle prammatiche del Regno di Napoli* (Naples, 1777), pp. 274–6.
52 Palma, *Storia ecclesiastica e civile*, III, p. 157.
53 ASL, Regia Udienza, Processi Penali, busta 5, fasc. 53, fol. 10^r–12^r.
54 Cesare Riccardi was not only famous during his bandit career but remained alive in the folklore and vernacular topography of the south. Keppel-Craven in the early nineteenth-century noted the 'Grotte dell'Abbate Cesare' which locals associated with Cesare Borgia but Keppel-Craven believed, more soundly in my opinion, was actually owed to Cesare Riccardi, who had hidden himself in the area. Richard Keppel Craven, *Excursions in the Abruzzi and Northern Provinces of Naples* (London, 1838), pp. 304–5.
55 Antonio Calabria, *The Cost of Empire: The Finances of the Kingdom of Naples in the Time of Spanish Rule* (Cambridge: Cambridge University Press, 1991), p. 15.
56 The set of codexes titled 'diversorum' of the Collateral Council record many instances of outlaws being issued licences (*patenti*) in exchange for deals to serve in war. ASN, Consiglio Collaterale, Diversorum.
57 Rosario Villari provides evidence of this, noting a 1639 petition against the levying of troops which argued that it was shameful to take men to the arsenal to send out of the Kingdom in chains and immiserated their families as they were the heads of poor households. Rosario Villari, 'Baronaggio e finanza a Napoli alla viglia della rivoluzione del 1647–8', *Studi Storici*, 3 (1962), 259–305.
58 Parrino, *Teatro eroico, e politico*, III, p. 107.
59 ASL, Regia Udienza, Processi Penali, busta 3, fasc. 39, fol. 94^r.
60 Ibid., busta 7, fasc. 72bis, fols. 233^r–235^v.
61 In 1636 the corporal of the 'Company of Lucera' was investigated for friendship with a bandit chief he was supposed to be opposing. ASN, Consiglio Collaterale, Notamenti, busta. 33, fasc. 5^v–6^r.

Banditry and the culture of enmity 143

62 Daniela, Ambron 'Il banditismo nel Regno di Napoli alla fine del XVII secolo tra istituzioni regie e protezioni baronali', in *Banditismi mediterranei, secoli XVI–XVII*, ed. by Francesco Manconi (Rome: Carocci, 2003), pp. 383–4: 'che proprio presidi, uditori, governatori e subalterni favorissero i banditi, rafforzando le reti clientari che contrassegnavano la dialettica politica e sociale di antico regime'.
63 Fernand Braudel, *The Mediterranean and the Mediterranean World in the Age of Philip II* (New York: Fontana, 1975), p. 39. Here he sees banditry as representing 'social archaisms'.
64 Ibid.
65 Palma, *Storia ecclesiastica e civile*, III, p. 155.
66 Ibid.
67 Francesco Navaretta was the son of Antonio Navaretta who also made his career as a minister in the Spanish tribunals and, among other duties, was governor of Capua during the 1647 revolt.
68 For the story of Francesco's excommunication see Marco Battaglini, *Annali del sacerdozio e dell'imperio intorno all'intero secolo decimosettimo di nostra salute* (Venice, 1701). The version of the story presented there is supported by the 'Instrumenta absolutionis Didaci de Soria Marchionis Crispani et praesidis Montis Fuscoli necnon Francisci Navarretta Commissarii Campaniae in Regno Neap. (per atti contro l'immunità) 1677' in the Fondo Carpegna in the Archivio Segreto Vaticano. See Agostino Lauro, *Il giurisdizionalismo pregiannoniano nel Regno di Napoli: problema e bibliografia (1563–1723)* (Rome: Edizioni di Storia e Letteratura, 1974), p. 280.
69 Palma, *Storia ecclesiastica e civile*, p. 159.
70 Intriguingly these documents show that Santuccio was said to be the great-nephew of Marco Sciarra.
71 John A. Marino described this from documents from Simancas in 'Wheat and Wool in the Dogana of Foggia', p. 887.
72 ASL, Regia Udienza, Processi Penali, busta 6, fasc. 67, fol. 175^v.
73 *Reassunto de servitii*, p. 181.
74 ASL, Regia Udienza, Processi Penali, busta 4, fasc. 47.
75 Ibid.
76 For hints concerning the Allegrettis' connections to Mirabello see: Gaetano Scatigna Minghetti, 'I figli di S. Paolo della Croce a Ceglie Messapica: scansioni socio-storiche di un'esperienza centenaria', in *I Passionisti a Ceglie Messapica: 1897–1997*, ed. by Carmelo Turrisi (Empoli: Barbieri, 2003), p. 41; Domenico Contigliozzi, ed., *Calendario d'Oro* (Rome, 1899), pp. 158–60; Amilcare Foscarini, *Armerista e Notiziario delle famiglie nobili, notabili e feudatarie di Terra d'Otranto* (Lecce: La Modernissima, 1927), p. 27; Gaetano Scatigna Minghetti and Luigi Ricci, 'Ferruzzo nella storia di Casa Allegretti', *Riflessioni: Umanesimo della Pietra* (1986), 113–17; Tobia Aldimari, *Raccolta di varie notitie historiche non meno appartenenti all'historia del Summonte che curiose* (Naples, 1675), p. 31. The historian and philosopher Benedetto Croce was a descendent of the Mirabello Frangipani-Allegretti: Gianfranco Giudice,

Benedetto Croce (Rimini: Luisè, 1994), p. 13. Maria Luisa Frangipane married Benedetto Croce, grandfather of the philosopher. He remembered her as very much connected to the *periodo spagnolo*: 'Aveva in bocca certi curiosi vocaboli e formule, che dovevano essere rimasti sin dal seicento nella nobiltà di provincia, e di cui io appresi il significato solo quando, molti anni dopo, studiai la lingua spagnuola'. Benedetto Croce, *Montenerodomo: storia di un comune e di due famiglie* (Bari: Laterza, 1919), p. 38.

77 ASL, Regia Udienza, Processi Penali, busta 4, fasc. 47, fol. 6[r]: 'gente di mala vita'.
78 Ibid.
79 Ibid., fol. 39[v]: 'garzone'.
80 Ibid., fol. 34[r]: 'per alcune sue Inemecitie have sempre armato in cometiva di gente'.
81 Ibid.
82 Ibid., fol. 39[r].
83 Ibid.: 'senza timor della giustitia'.
84 Domenico Antonio Parrino, *Compendio istorico, o sian memorie delle notizie più vere e cose più notabili, e degne da sapersi, accadute nella felicissima entrata delle sempre gloriose Truppe Cesaree nel Regno, ed in questa Città di Napoli* (Naples, 1708), p. xix: 'prototipo di saggia accortezza, e di grazie'.
85 ASL, Regia Udienza, Processi Penali, busta 4, fasc. 47, fol. 102[v].
86 Ibid., fol. 104[r]: ' che lui non proteggeva marioli'.
87 Ibid., fol. 135[v].
88 Ibid., fol. 135[r]: 'Domenico Allegretti nostro Capo si era pacificato con detto Marchese nell'istessa Terra di Baraniello, mentre per prima stavano Inimici'.
89 For discussion of the 'instrumentalization' of jurisdictions in early modern Naples see Giovanni Romeo, *Aspettando il boia: condannati a morte, confortatori e inquisitori nella Napoli della Controriforma* (Florence: Sansoni, 1993), pp. 53–8.
90 ASL, Regia Udienza, Processi Penali, busta 4, fasc. 47, fols. 97[v]–98[r].
91 Lauro, *Il giurisdizionalismo pregiannoniano nel Regno di Napoli*, pp. 77–80.
92 Could this be the same Nicol Pirolo who had been accused of bestiality ten years earlier? In February 1656 the *Audienza* of Lucera related an investigation into Nicol Pirolo who was accused of having posted an inflammatory *cartello* to the walls of Manfredonia and also of being involved in the 'sin of bestiality'. ASN, Consiglio Collaterale, Notamenti, busta 60, fol. 130[r].
93 ASL, Regia Udienza, Processi Penali, busta 4, fasc. 47, fol. 133[r].
94 Ibid., fol. 133[v].
95 Ibid.
96 Ibid.
97 Ibid., fol. 133[v]: 'fare detto unione'.
98 Ibid., fol. 134[r].
99 Ibid.
100 Ibid., fol. 134[v].
101 Ibid., fols. 135[v]–136[r].

102 Ibid., fol. 104^r.
103 See Alfredo Zazo, 'Bandi e repressioni per i "confugientes" in Benevento nei secoli XIV–XVII', in *Ricerche e studi storici*, ed. by Alfredo Zazo (Naples: Istituto della Stampa, 1961); Aurelio Musi, *Benevento tra Medioevo ed età moderna* (Manduria: Lacaita, 2004), p. 76; Maria Anna Noto, *Viva la Chiesa, mora il tiranno: il sovrano, la legge, la comunità e i ribelli (Benevento 1566)* (Naples: Guida, 2010), p. 163; Gaetana Intorcia, *La comunità beneventana nei secoli XII–XVIII: Aspetti istituzionali. Controversie giurisdizionali* (Naples: Edizioni scientifiche italiane, 1996), pp. 93–114; Irene Fosi, *La società violenta: il banditismo nello Stato pontificio nella seconda metà del Cinquecento* (Rome: Edizioni dell'Ateneo, 1985).
104 For the use of this strategy in fifteenth-century Venice and the Veneto see James S. Grubb, 'Catalysts for Organized Violence in the Early Venetian Territorial State', in *Bande armate, banditi banditismo e repressione di giustizia negli stati europei di antico regime*, ed. by Gherardo Ortalli (Rome: Jouvence, 1986), p. 391; for the strategy in sixteenth- and early seventeenth-century Venice see Peter Laven, 'Banditry and Lawlessness in the Venetian Terraferma', in *Crime, Society and Law in Renaissance Italy*, ed. by Trevor Dean and Kate Lowe (Cambridge: Cambridge University Press, 1994), pp. 221–48.

5

Jesuit missions and the emotional politics of enmity and peace-making

In 1657 the Jesuit Andrea Uccello led a mission in the port town of Trani in Puglia. The year before the town and entire Kingdom had suffered the devastating plague of 1656, following on from the disturbances of the 1647–48 civil wars.[1] The chronicler of the mission, the notary Domenico Beltrano, blamed the illness on 'our grave sins' and the mission was framed as penance for these wrongs and thanksgiving for the passing of the plague.[2] On a Sunday in June people gathered to hear Uccello preach in the chapel of San Nicolò. Spurred by the word of God, many declared how they had wronged their neighbours and threw themselves at their enemies' feet. Many peaces were made as forgiveness was both begged and freely given. The next day a large procession gathered with the *Preside* of the province, the Marchese di Creccia, at its head. He wore white sackcloth and held a skull in his hand. He walked barefoot with forty of the soldiers of the *Regia Audienza* 'chained by the neck, with the chains they use to send wrongdoers in the galleys'.[3] A medal pinned at his breast marked him as a 'slave of the Virgin Mary'.[4] In his 'imitation' all the other office-holders of the city followed hand-in-hand with the town's nobility.

Beltrano recounts that the instruction of the sermons and the example of the procession encouraged many more people to make peace with their enemies. They lamented their old ways of living and wept copiously. This was a period of religious enthusiasm that involved both representatives of royal justice and the elite of the community. Both groups performed bodily and spiritual mortification in front of a public audience. It was, we are told, the Marchese di Creccia who had procured the mission in order to 'extirpate from this City those sins with which it was marked'.[5] This was a mission that took place in the piazzas and churches of the city. Symbols of domination, such as chains, were repurposed for Baroque devotions. All the city was in tears and the people entered into extraordinary devotions; one 'poor peasant' vowed to paint a portrait of Francis Xavier.[6] Domenico Beltrano, who wrote a published account of this mission, was the secretary of the *Regia Audienza* and likely anxious to improve his station.[7] While stressing the involvement of his patron was convenient, the central place for nobles and representatives of the King recurred in many missions.

A crucial part of this mission of 'extirpation' was the confrontation of the moral plague of discord and the violence that resulted from enmities. Settling enmities and making peace was one of the regular activities of Jesuit peace-making and central to their understanding of the sacrament of penance. Jesuit missionaries saw themselves converting the hate-filled to peace. This act of conversion had its effects in the passions, sentiments and flesh: it was an emotional, physical, and spiritual transformation.[8] In all Jesuit missions, such emotional transformations, the physical mortifications, and the acts of peace-making connected to them cannot be set aside from community and authority: the structures, ideology, and practice of government, law, and communal life. To understand the peace-making rituals performed in Jesuit missions it is necessary to turn to both the emotional content of these conversions as well as to the civil context: the laws of the Kingdom and those charged with enforcing them. By exploring these factors, Jesuit peace-making can be better understood and, at the same time, the religious or sacred aspects of governance and community, and the vital place of peace-making in these, in early modern Naples will be established.

Further the vivid and evocative symbols of Jesuit devotion reveal aspects of the emotional politics of enmity. That is, the symbols and discussions of enmity in Jesuit sources, I argue, shed light on the wider significances of enmity in early modern Italy and the post-revolutionary Kingdom of Naples in particular. This may be considered somewhat tendentious, seeing as the goals of the Jesuits were to depict the miraculous effects of their mission, and therefore their documentation of the missions does not provide an unfiltered depiction of the experiences of those who were not Jesuit fathers. However, I make the case that we can indeed find a lot of illuminating evidence when we place the Jesuit missions in the larger context of enmity as depicted in this book. I would argue that it is important to start by at least placing aside the question of their claims for miraculous healing of enmities; it is more probable that we deal with missions that provided truces rather than real cures. But even if we may disagree with their claims for fundamentally solving the problem of enmity, their depictions of the dilemma found in towns and cities matches well with supporting historical documentation, as reconstructed in the rest of this book.

Jesuit peace-making only makes sense in light of their understandings of enmity, understandings which had to have appeal and make sense to those they ministered to. In turn, their notions about enmity do not make sense if divorced from the communities in which they operated.

Scholars have tended to fix much of their attention on the internal history of the society, writing from the perspective of historians of the Jesuits in particular or early modern missions more generally. Much has been gained from these approaches: the detail of the expansion of the Jesuits, their institutional dynamics, and rich accounts of the content and development of their missionary strategies. Elisa Novi Chavarria and Jennifer Selwyn, in particular, have highlighted the ways in which the Jesuits developed techniques of peace-making and made these techniques central to their missionary style. Selwyn frames her work as the exploration of a Kingdom that was characterized as a 'paradise inhabited by devils'.[9] In so doing she explores the ways in which the Jesuits reacted to the proverbial disorder of the city of Naples and the violence found in the entire Kingdom: their peace-making was, in this light, an attempt at promoting social integration, in the aftermath of the recurrent outbreaks of rebellion.[10] David Gentilcore has pointed to the ways in which Jesuits developed a theatrical and, at times, almost Carnivalesque approach that led, in his view, to valuing the aesthetic content of devotion higher than the more mundane work of instilling deep understanding of Christian doctrine.[11] Elisa Novi Chavarria's studies have done much to establish the significance of the 'specific situations' that shaped Jesuit missions. The Jesuits intervened in situations of varying conflict between 'populations and secular and ecclesiastical authorities'.[12] She has also noted the mediatory usages of the Jesuits in the period of revolt and plague of 1647–56 and established how '[t]he need for mediation and the control of the bitter conflicts and the ruptures that had opened between communities, nobles and civil authorities and a work of social and religious re-aggregation determined the direction of the practical interventions of the Company in the capital and neighbouring centres'.[13] This period of unrest and suffering led the Jesuits to reinforce the importance of their peace-making practices and set the tone for the second half of the seventeenth century.

This chapter draws on the varied accounts of Jesuit peace-making missions in the Jesuit archive in Rome. As well as the written reports of missions, I also reference incoming correspondence from town councils and aristocrats in the kingdom. Another significant source for this chapter is Scipione Paolucci's *Missioni de Padri della Compagnia di Giesù nel Regno di Napoli* (Naples, 1651).[14] Paolucci studied a range of internal documents on missions to write an edifying account of what had been done in the Kingdom; categorizing the various achievements of the missions and providing commentary on missionary practice. The abundance of evidence that during scores of missions in the Kingdom in the aftermath of emotive preaching hundreds of men and women embraced others who had killed their relatives and, weeping, begged for reconciliation counterbalances the range of problems of using Jesuit reports, letters, and works of synthesis; all of which were crafted from conventional languages and formed into strategically composed lists of successes. But what did this mean? And how can this inform us about the place of enmity in communities? The Jesuits saw such events as the conversion of sentiments and it is these transformations of hate into love that this chapter considers.

Homicides led to memories that could be material in various ways. The bloody shirt of a murdered son or the bones of another were reminders and symbols of a bitter enmity. It was precisely on these terms that the Jesuits engaged with cultures of enmity. Their obliteration of hatred used exactly the objects and substances that could, in other contexts, serve as instruments that memorialized offences received.

Jesuit missions drew from the penitential method, combining bodily mortification with techniques of spectacle. The violent mortifications that shaped this penitential method were not accepted as legitimate by all Catholic clergy.[15] Scipione Paolucci refers to a bishop who described penitential actions as 'not customs of men, but rather of beasts'.[16] But despite such criticisms they held special appeal in the aftermath of the middle years of the seventeenth century the events of which – open rebellion and devastating plague – seemed to underscore the profound need that Neapolitans had to seek forgiveness through contrition.[17] The bodily signs of penance, instruments used to abrade, cut, or burn skin, the resulting blood, and the funereal dress of penitents had both direct and symbolic links to enmities and violence. What marked Jesuit devotion and missionizing, in contrast to the more common image of Jesuits as cerebral scholar-priests, was bloody public penance through mortification: whippings with leather straps, iron chains, and nails. Blood-splattered walls, dust, and cries of pain were all part of the glory and honour of Jesuit missions. This connection was drawn from a participation in the enmities that were a fact of life in the towns and villages where they preached.

Requests from local governments seem to have been the main reason for their presence in many towns and cities.[18] At least for urban missions there was an active demand-side. In the Foggia mission of 1665, they had been requested by the 'signori del governo'.[19] Beyond generic requests for missions, towns also requested particular missionaries. In Monopoli in 1625 the *governo* wrote to the Jesuits talking of the 'considerable devotion, and great affection, that this City has towards the Company' and requested that Padre Francesco Antonio Russo be sent along with an assistant.[20] In 1713, Padre Francesco di Geronimo was so famous that the *sindico* of Molfetta petitioned for Geronimo to dispense his 'evangelical bread' there.[21] Any internal decision-making is hard to access, but it is clear that preference for the Jesuits varied, in 1669 the first mission in Putignano occurred and this was due to the election to the *governo* of a well-disposed gentleman who convinced the others to ask for a mission. Internal division can also be seen later in Monopoli when two factions seem to have emerged, one hostile towards funding Jesuit missions and their residence and the other positive. Elsewhere a Jesuit foundation could be unifying. In Lecce, as David Gentilcore has noted, the Jesuits' residence marked an act of conciliation between two factions in the town.[22] Both factions contributed 300 ducats towards the foundation of the college. A *sindico* of Salerno in 1630 noted that 'finding ourselves this year as the Government of this city … to show our devotion to the Glorious Saints Ignatius and Francis Xavier'.[23] Devotion, politics, and varying assessments of the efficacy of missionary activity underlay the attitudes of local governments towards Jesuit activity. It is, however, misleading to concentrate solely on missionary activity when considering attitudes of local government towards the Jesuits. Much of the fiercest battles within communities occurred over questions of providing for the establishment of a Jesuit residence in a town; this was due to the amount of money involved in founding a Jesuit college, school, or residence and the fact that factions tended to gravitate around support or opposition towards such expenditure. The provision of education was one attractive prospect. As the government of Salerno noted in 1635, there was no comparison between 'the fine guidance of the Jesuit fathers, and the direction of a simple priest, who is often neither capable nor sufficient to teach everyone'.[24] The exact reasons for particular rural missions are less clear, although even small towns could engage in correspondence with religious orders and express preferences about the devotional lives of their communities.

Peace-making was at the centre of these missions and understood as a fruit of penitence. Lengthy accounts of peaces achieved were regularly included in the annual accounts of activities in the Neapolitan province and other incidental reports that were despatched to the central Jesuit administration.[25] These were often noted in long lists under the rubric 'notable reconciliations'; they were a recognized and discrete category of activity registered with care and attention.[26] An account of all missions in 1640 focused almost exclusively on peaces made in cities across the Kingdom. Reconciliations and 'composition of enmities' were defined as one of the 'principal fruits' of a mission to Foggia in 1665. Jennifer Selwyn has argued for the centrality of these rituals of reconciliation.[27] Scipione Paolucci, in his printed account of all that had been accomplished in the missions of the late sixteenth and early seventeenth centuries, placed peace-making firmly at the centre of his vision of the Jesuit achievement. From a reading of his volume, it would be reasonable to see the Neapolitan Jesuits as overwhelmingly occupied with the business of reconciling those at enmity. One chapter of his published account is dedicated to narrating the 'very difficult peaces' that were carried out in virtue of the missions. Within this chapter, remissions of offended parties feature repeatedly and prominently in accounts of peace-making.

Paolucci provided a synthetic account of what the usual Jesuit peace-making was. A day should be set aside to explore 'the necessity, and most great utility, that is provided by pardoning our enemies, and to invite all the people to practice it', normally this would have been a Friday.[28] The Jesuits made the Christian drama of the sinner as someone who had offended God and the notion of confession as reconciliation with God central to the practice of their missions. Scipione Paolucci encouraged his readers to imagine themselves as observers of these festivals of peace:

> what esteem, what admiration is merited the sight of not one, or two, not even ten or twenty, but more, many hundreds (where the population of the city permits it), of every age, every sex, of every quality, or condition of person exclaiming in loud voices, and with sincerity of heart, that they pardon those every offence, every injury to their enemies.[29]

The notion of the audience lies at the centre of the performance of exercises of mortification: the penitents were both engaged in devotions that exhibited their own contrition but they also created a spectacle that could be observed and absorbed as it touched the hearts of the audience. As I will explore, this 'heart-touching' was not a tired cliché for the Jesuits.

Despite his enthusiasm, Paolucci noted the problems that remained: 'one can affirm with truth, that in many small cities, and very rarely, there remains enmities to be reconciled'.[30] The Jesuits often encountered obstinacy and deeply embedded ethics of vengeance which at times frustrated their tasks, although total failures were admitted rarely. On the other hand, they often highlighted difficulties that were later overcome in triumph. The Jesuits knew what they were confronting: enmities were present everywhere. It was not only the threat of further violence that was problematic but also grief or memories of offences could shatter community and eradicate Christian charity. Peace-making was needed for the sacrament of penance. This emphasis led the Jesuits to deny any right to resentment; unforgiveness was not possible, instead it was diabolic. In most Jesuit sources the arduous and complicated moral task of forgiving an enemy was miraculously simplified. They knew it was hard to forgive but in most of their accounts when pardon was given it emerged from an instantaneous and total spiritual conversion.

Visions of enmity

There was no doubt for these missionaries that enmities harmed communities and endangered souls; the most awful result of division and discord was homicide. In reports of missions, the Jesuits noted the influence of the devil and the diabolic spirit that filled towns and cities. There was a deep belief in actual diabolic presence.[31] They used the term enmity as their most predominant lens of interpretation for problems within cities. Inimical relations were a composite of injuries and offences as well as the hatred and *dolore* caused by these. Offences received created resentment that then spread through towns and had poisoned the civil life of towns and cities in the Kingdom.[32] Clearly, as other chapters of this book have shown, these terms had specific legal meanings as well as representing emotional states.

What did the Jesuits mean when they talked of enmities in a community? They found broadly commensurable situations in every town or city they missionized. There were differences between the nature of the disputes in different communities but they drew upon the same lexicon, grammar, and narrative resources to articulate these situations. Physical attacks stand out as the main reason for states of hatred. Homicides were the most common cause cited by writers of reports followed by woundings. At times they recorded particularly high rates of homicide which had marked towns before the missionaries' arrival. In one unnamed town, they identified 200 homicides, in Camplì eighty, and seventy in Squinzano.[33] Other reasons that enmities prevailed included civil lawsuits, insults, adultery, and other offences to honour.

While nearly all relations discussed various hatreds existing as a result of homicides, certain places were divided more profoundly by enmities. These severe cases tended to be in situations in which many homicides had occurred due to deep factional divisions arising out of public affairs. Soleto, a small town south of Lecce, was found 'almost destroyed' by its enmities in 1668. This had originated in a civil lawsuit between the two most prominent families. Here a 'vengeful heart' was said to beat. Many homicides had resulted from this enmity that had begun with litigation and the inhabitants were said to have kept their hands on their weapons during the early sermons of the mission.[34] Similarly in Morcone, in 1717 they found 'maximam discordiarum'. The popular class were divided and the commune was in conflict with their feudal lord. Unanimity was said to be the reward of the missions. By sharing a soul towards the pursuit of the good they escaped the curse of rivalry. In Morcone the fathers settled lawsuits and the feudal lord provided a remission for the disobedience of the townsmen.[35] In these broader enmities, involving the whole community, aspects of local power relations emerge most clearly. These were factional conflicts that often organized themselves around two large patrician families. Or, instead, between the populace and their feudal lord. These types of hatreds had most potential for disrupting the entire spiritual life of a community. Despite varying situations, the Jesuit accounts do not often go into great detail beyond this broad reason for the enmity. At times even this is not specified. Instead enmities are reduced to their status as a regular feature of un-missionized communities which could be dealt within a single category.

The piling up of lists of the reconciled signalled success. When the Jesuits did probe deeper, some features that interested them included the length of the enmity and the nature of the current relationship between the offended and the offender – did they persecute each other or were they just unwilling to speak and interact?

Hatreds then, with their connections to homicide or other injuries, were inseparable from memory. For the Jesuits, retaining hatred instead of making peace was disordered. Resentment and dwelling on the loss of a relative was harmful. The passage of time and its effects on the nature of an enmity was a regular refrain. The painful memory of a murdered loved one could be 'fresh' or 'present' if recent, or maintain these qualities despite the passage of many years.[36] The difficulties one person who carried hatred had in forgiving were noted as repugnance and 'contradiction in his soul due to the habit, aged over many years, during which the seed of hatred and vendetta was nourished'. Souls were 'cruelly tyrannised' by hatred, so that it seemed 'that they lived with a spirit only for vendetta'.[37] Hatred of another could be sharp and fresh or old and ingrained. Loss dwelt upon grew into poisonous, dominating hatred.

The Jesuits engaged with practices of violence and revenge they found and the material cultures of such bloodshed. Violence was used to avenge offences and to achieve personal ends. In Naples, a large mission of 1642 resulted in penitents bringing arms and other 'instruments' which were 'prepared for taking men's lives' to be destroyed.[38]

Making peace

The Jesuits became specialists in the provision of opportunities to make peace. At their best, they were able to create liminal spaces outside the normal course of events in which peace could be made without the emotional and material costs that forgiveness bore in everyday life. Reconciliation required openness in the sentiments that could be procured through participation in devotional exercises.[39] The missions provided an emotionally charged atmosphere that made the embracing of enemies feasible. They featured mass events, at times carefully choreographed, in which status was achieved by humility and releasing grudges.[40] The extraordinary moment of a mission gave honourable and pious ways out from conflicts that may have become harmful or burdensome. The Jesuits provided a forgiveness that did not shy away from the blood and suffering of grief and revenge. Their devotions centred on the emotions that underpinned revenge. Jesuit peace-making was not modelled on a quiet burial of anger and resentment, forgetting, but instead violent reversals and passionate conversions.

These opportunities followed emotive preaching and were signalled by embraces and the public exchange of the kiss of peace.[41] The Jesuits sought to provide edifying spectacles. They have often been described as both innovators in theatre (and in a more general sense as 'theatrical' in their devotions).[42] Indeed they relished using metaphors that drew from this idea of performance and used vocabularies of theatres, audiences, and viewing. Jennifer Selwyn has argued that Jesuits competed consciously with secular theatre, they were 'vigilant in their efforts to represent their own abilities as equal, if not superior to, those of secular entertainers'.[43] It is also hard to discuss the missions without using the languages of stage-management, choreography, and performance. But of course languages of theatre do not mean their strategies should be understood as knowingly false or solely based in appearances. Instead of dissembling performance, the preaching and manipulation of the sensory world they undertook should be understood as direct attempts to create certain dispositions of the heart; the production of emotion.[44] Attending to the theatrical requires a careful reconstruction of how Jesuits understood both spectacle and audience.[45] Jesuit devotions aimed at the manufacture of certain emotional dispositions and transformations in belief, and from the evidence we can gather, the Jesuits do seem to have been effective at this.[46] Preaching was absolutely central to the Jesuit missions.

One argument in favour of the exercises of the missions was that 'external behaviour creates devotion'.[47] The external mortifications were people whipping themselves bloody on the chest or backs with chains, or walking while chained, with unshod feet, or by wearing crowns of thorns. Bodily pain was an instigation to peace. Such devotions were often drawn as precise opposites of the practices of enmity. The chronicler of a mission in Montesarchio noted that the crowns of thorns that townspeople wore in the procession spilt blood 'not with the effect of enmity, but for encouragement to peace'.[48]

Humiliation was vital. The missions required the lowering of ambition and the greater prize for the people who debased themselves the most rather than those who held worldly pride. It was this competitive humiliation that drew feudal lords to be the most penitent in the missions. But all had to show this humility, many who forgave their enemies threw themselves 'humbly' at the feet of their prior enemies. Public penance was largely concerned with humiliation: the example of King Acab dressed in sackcloth was often cited.[49] An obstinate Greek-speaking community was described as 'not wanting to say one word in humiliation' or 'make one humble step'.[50] This lowering of worldly pride and embracing of the status of slaves was a vital part of the contrition necessary to achieve peace. It also provided an example for others to view and witness the ways in which the Holy Spirit moved within the community.

One of the most cited effects of the sermons, processions, and other 'exercises' of the missions was weeping.[51] The tears of individual penitents were signs of their moved hearts and then came to a symphony with the weeping of others to create the *pianto della città*. The Jesuit emphasis on tears is a clear link to Ignatian spirituality. The first week of Ignatius' *Exercises* was a week of 'contrition, sorrow and tears over their sins'.[52] In other words, exercitants were supposed to provoke themselves to tears by considering Christ on the cross and comparing his death for them with their ill-living. As preachers, Jesuits attempted to create similar sorrow with vivid preaching and drawing from the social scripts of grief and loss. The sobs of many contributed to the soundscapes of the mission, as part of the creation of a sacred 'economy of sentiment'.[53]

In Cardito, a *casale* of Naples, a 'woman went about crying and cutting her face with her nails'. This 'spectacle' increased 'tenderness' in the people who saw her and helped with their conversion during the mission.[54] The *tenerezza* produced by signs of contrition was a state repeatedly emphasized in writings on the mission and the process of 'softening' the hearts of others was a vital part in reconciliation. In Brindisi in 1667 some 5000 people with abundant tears embraced the crucifix 'with such tenderness' and began to pardon their enemies.[55] In Capua, newly reconciled enemies 'kissed each other, embraced each other with abundant tears, and tenderness'. Paolucci notes a man who long had 'hatred in his heart' against his enemy and had pledged 'not to sign a treaty of peace unless it was with the blood of his adversary' but 'the spectacle of this mortificatory multitude softened his heart' and he begged for reconciliation.[56]

One of the key ways in which Jesuits framed their attempts at conciliation was that previous attempts to make peace had failed. The Jesuits talked about themselves as special measures peace-makers, God's ambassadors for reconciliation, able to move in where resident pacifiers had failed. They tackled obstinate enemies and communities where the poison of hatred was everywhere. Those named as the everyday peace-makers were local nobles, notables, and parish priests or, higher up the social ladder, feudal lords, other local title-holders (such as Spanish governors or an *Auditore* of the *Regia Audienza*), or senior clergy ranging from bishops and archbishops to cardinals. During a 1666 mission to Benevento, a woman whose husband had been murdered resisted the pleas of many 'titled' aristocrats and numerous cardinals.[57] The Jesuits identified the attempts of others to make peace most often as through 'their authority'.[58] It was their place in the social hierarchy that endowed them with the presumed power to intervene in differences between other members. In Capua, the prayers and counsels of 'many noble people, of much authority' had failed to achieve the peace-making that the Jesuits were able to in 1649.[59] Notables were those who possessed the vital authority to make peace. The normal path of peace-making, from these accounts, was through the intervention of secular or ecclesiastical elites who attempted to convince those in enmity of the benefits of peace and their duty to forgive. While the level of detail given for any one case is far from enough to establish the exact nature of these quotidian resolutions, it seems that Jesuits may have been requested for partially functional reasons, in situations when internal pacification had reached its limit. In Squinzano, it was apparently Jesuit peace-making that was able to reconcile an archpriest and a vicar who had taken each other to court regularly and who, despite the intervention of the bishop, remained enemies.

'With authenticated writings': Jesuits and notarized peaces

For the Jesuits these emotional and spiritual conversions required integration with the legal system of the Kingdom of Naples. As Paolucci noted, exclamations of forgiveness could be 'like summer storms, that are more terrifying than damaging' so people should be obliged 'with fine writings in their own hand, and other authentications'.[60] Despite, or perhaps all the more because of, their dedication to high emotional drama the Jesuits were concerned about deception and the simulation of forgiveness. It was precisely an integration with notarial, legal frameworks that was necessary in order to fix a peace and extend it into the future.

Part of this can be explained by a concern that the flamboyance of Jesuit mortification misled. Anyone could cry and continue to hate. The emphasis on hearts and sadness in penitence created difficulties in an age when anxieties about dissimulation were high. As Paolucci wrote, the connection between the external and the internal was tightly bound, but deception could still occur.[61] The signing of a remission was an act that did something real: it had concrete effects on peoples' lives that could persist long after the Jesuits had left a town.

More than convenience, however, the Jesuits saw remissions of injuries and the acts of writing and producing documentation of peace as the essence of what they were trying to do: these achievements and the act of signing were the final acts in the ritual of peace. One account given by Paolucci concerned a woman whose husband, a gentleman, had been killed by two other principal citizens. The rich emotional vocabulary used by Paolucci to describe the widow and her feelings is striking. She possessed a visceral determination to remain in a state of hatred towards her husband's killers. She was described as possessing 'manly and resolute courage' and her bitter enmity was born from 'the feeling with which she had tenderly loved her husband' and that, although she was young, her grief, to which she was 'irreparably condemned', led her to remain a widow. She 'would not suffer to hear the name of peace with her enemies' and 'renounced every other pleasure, every other desire' but 'that of vendetta'. Her desires were disordered, perverted by grief that the Jesuits believed should have been laid aside for forgiveness. She was finally persuaded by the priests and monks that dwelt in her town to pardon her enemies and admit that she did not wish them ill but she emphatically would not sign the remission of the injury saying, according to Paolucci: 'Oh that no ... that no, I'm not obliged to do that by the law of Christ, and you cannot demand more of me than God. I am not bound to you, and I should not, nor do I want to, do it; and if I had to do it, I know I could not do so.'[62] Signing the legal instrument of the remission of the injury is presented as a step beyond all other forms of forgiveness: it was too much to ask, outside of the bounds of Christian charity.

Jesuit peace-making had a central place for the officials of justice, they saw the correct end of their peace-making in the arrangement of peaces with the officials of justice. In Squinzano in 1646, some gentlewomen were 'pardoned publicly, and in front of the officials'.[63] A foreign gentleman who had persecuted those who had shot at him, for ten months 'in their lives and their goods', but he pardoned his enemies and kissed the crucifix and he wrote the judicial remission.[64] In 1666 in the Papal enclave of Benevento, a woman made a remission 'with authentic writing'.[65] In another, the 'hand of the notary' was dwelt upon as a key part of the process of remission.

The Jesuits consistently placed an emphasis on 'authenticated writings' as the proper way to track accomplishments. They counted enmities settled by remissions signed in front of a notary. Legal and religious forms of peace-making were intertwined. This is precisely one of the ways in which the Jesuit missions had lasting effects, whether for good or ill. John Bossy has claimed that for Lazarist missions, as opposed from Jesuit ones, '[t]he thing that makes me believe their missions of peace-making were more than a flash in the pan is that they always, so far as I can see, required that the reconciliations they promoted be properly registered by a notary' and that while he thinks Jesuits probably used notaries regularly 'it does not seem to have been part of the strategy'.[66] This judgement should be revised; the Jesuits worked closely with notaries and strongly supported the notarizing of peaces made. It was regularly stressed as central to the practice of the missions.

Resentment and coerced peace

Reconciliation, peace-making, and pardon have almost innately positive connotations. They imply 'getting along' and the collective resolution of disputes. But settlements were far from necessarily events that led to equal satisfaction;

they invariably reinforced unequal power relations. Rather than acts of forgiveness, penitence, and satisfaction, they could instead be events of silencing, forgetting, and coercion. When Jesuits record using their authority to persuade grieving mothers to forgive the murderers of their sons, and label them as obstinate if they refuse, the gap between peace and justice is striking.

A more complex perspective on the morality of peace-making can be gained from recent work on forgiveness during processes of transitional justice in the wake of atrocity or profoundly unequal politico-social regimes. Thomas Brudholm's study of the refusal to forgive is particularly useful and focuses on South Africa and the post-Holocaust writings of Jean Amery.[67] Brudholm highlights the widespread 'assumption that people who have been seriously wronged will be seething with a lust for revenge' which is 'commonly pictured as manifesting in *cycles* of hatred, violence, or revenge, which is one reason why the transformation of victims' emotional responses to injustice and injury is a central concern of efforts to promote reconciliation after mass atrocity'.[68] But this, as Brudholm notes, is framed as 'the overcoming or taming of emotion' through transformation: what he identifies as 'alchemies of reconciliation'.[69] Brudholm's scepticism towards the claims towards the sudden conversion model of reconciliation is instructive. The Jesuits discussions of obstinate grievers matches very well with this belief that cycles of hatred can be escaped through an alchemical, magical conversion experience.

Yet it is not only to modern commentators that we have to turn to find criticism of festivals of peace. Jesuit writers responded to those who criticized their peace-making activities in similar ways. The most sustained account that lets us see a Jesuit ventriloquize the critics of the order (who made such criticisms rarely in print) is a digression by Paolo Segneri in his *Il parocco istruito*. Segneri held the standard position that true peace-making occurred across and through passionate engagement of emotional interiors: it was done 'with tears and embraces, with loving care and with tender kisses'.[70] These were witnesses to the glory of Christian faith. But he soon turned to responded to those 'hardened politicians' who criticized the large-scale peace-making of the missions. He first addressed the question that if 'with such peaces crimes will occur more frequently'.[71] Segneri asks if those who put this objection forward believe that it was a possibility unknown to Christ. For Segneri, those who object in this way have muddled the matter by confusing the act of peace-making with the arrangements of civil peace. Missionaries who make peace have partaken in a spiritual moment which then requires careful administration. It is secular governors who have the responsibility to ensure that the consequences of peace are equitable. Once someone forgives another who has wronged them a whole set of conditions are within the control of governors, rather than missionaries. For example, he suggests that governors should use their discretion regarding whether to allow an outlaw to return to a town even once they have gained a remission from the offended party. Too free a hand with such indulgence would 'loosen public discipline'.[72] He criticizes a slavish reliance upon permissive statutes, advocating changing statutory regulation to allow more flexible reactions to cases where a peace has been made. Too often, he suggests, governors provide indulgence or diminish a penalty because of a statute. 'At the end, such statutes are all human statutes' and if they lead to increased conflict, it is precisely these not the divine, that should be altered.[73]

Segneri's vision of broad spiritual peace-making but careful administration of its aftermath leads him further into a surprisingly acerbic critique of how criminal justice worked in early modern Italian towns. Responding to those 'hardened politicians' who criticized Jesuit festivals of peace, he argued:

> I would want to propose to those oh so zealous defenders of the common good a more suitable target to strike with their eloquent tongues. Strike at those abuses created precisely to save offenders ... Strike at those tribunals, where with prejudice much more than public utility, evil-doers, who merit every punishment, are continually favoured. Strike at those false witnesses, that are everywhere ready to come forward to support such people; those lawyers that defend them; those notaries that cover them up, and those nobles that recommend them; and above all strike at those iniquitous judges, that at the end absolve them, selling justice for vile money, and putting it to market.[74]

But in many other accounts of missions, Segneri's committed vision and broad awareness of the flaws of systems of indulgence is absent. Jesuit accounts of the peace-making in their missions tend to ignore whether resentment may be appropriate. Throughout Paolucci's work, not only the desire for revenge but also the refusal to forgive is made problematic. Segneri's understanding of why peace-making results in domination or injustice draws precisely on a criticism of how justice was administered. He called for a reform of practices of civic government. Such keen-eyed assessments of the flaws of Italian civic government were not often voiced by Jesuits who tended to be very closely associated with those office-holders or nobles who ran local towns. It was the secular governments more than local ecclesiastical authorities who held close relations with Jesuits and asked them to missionize their towns.

A mission to Capua

An account of a Jesuit mission to Capua in 1649 demonstrates the activity of the Jesuits and the Neapolitan state in projects of pacification after 1647–48. Around the time of the mission Capua and its territory had a population of 29,985 based on estimates drawn the numbers of taxable households in 1648.[75]

The mission took place in the aftermath of the rebellion, which the author of the relation of the mission interpreted as part of a broader European crisis, a 'harsh scourge, the heavy blows of which provinces and kingdoms have groaned under'.[76] But it was the Kingdom of Naples, 'perhaps more than any other', that had suffered the three-headed flail of 'war, hunger, and death, with the desolation of many Houses, and the killings of many thousands of its children'.[77] For the author of the relation the Kingdom was being punished not out of *vendetta* but as a remedy and that now, in 1649, God was giving signs that through his clemency the Kingdom had been reconciled to him. The mission in Capua is presented as a sign of this mercy.

Capua experienced considerable internal strife during the 1640s. In 1647–48 there were movements of rebellion and civil struggles. Capuans were proud of their status as a royal city and their illustrious history of having been always 'most faithful' to their kings.[78] The rebellious events of the 1640s were reduced in printed memory to criminal elements. Francesco Granata, writer of the *Storia civile della fedelissima città di Capua*, was

Figure 5.1 An engraving of Capua from Giovan Battista Pacichelli, *Il regno di Napoli in prospettiva diviso in dodici provincie* (1703). Fondo Antiguo, University of Seville.

concerned to promote the steadfast nature of his co-citizens but he admitted there had been rebels among the Capuans, although he described them as wicked and their actions as 'crazed popular tumults'.[79]

These *cattivi* had led an attempted revolt on 5 August 1647, with one Francesco Meo at their head. The forces tried to stop Don Benedetto Tocelles, Marchese di Toraldo and royal governor of Capua, from entering the city. Five executions followed.[80] After these initial internal discords Capua became a key city in the resistance of royal authority against the rebellious *popolani* in the city of Naples. Capua was very close to Naples and well-furnished with protective walls which underscored its strategic value.[81]

Troops were gathered in Capua and it was used as a staging post for excursions into the city by the baronial forces.[82] As it was a fortress-town it was regularly filled with soldiers and in 1648 the Jesuits led a military mission to convert the German (probably Walloon) troops billeted there.[83] The city had suffered the burdens of supporting great numbers of troops and was at the very centre of the disturbances of war. The Jesuits had a permanent residence in Capua that had fourteen members at the beginning of the 1640s.[84] Here they buried silver and other riches during the period of revolt.[85]

The mission of 1649 occurred very soon after this period of strife and military occupation. Like many other of the provincial disturbances of 1647–48, the Capuan discords had long roots in the political organization of the town. A generation before, in 1616, a chronicler reported the 'discords of its citizens'. The viceroy, in response to this disorder, placed officials above the normal *governo* of the town which led the citizens to feel usurped by the 'supervision' placed upon them.[86] Capua itself was governed with a mixture of representatives of the noble *seggi* and the *populani civili*. In line with the general trend of 'closure' across the early modern period, access to this government was continually reduced through a restriction in the numbers of families in both noble and popular classes who were eligible for posts.[87] During the revolt civic divisions degenerated into violent attempts to seize power, disturbing a rough and ready equilibrium between factions.

The mission itself spread across eight days. The chronicler began by recalling all the 'most loyal writers' who had written of Capua before him.[88] But he was far more disdainful of the state of Capua than these past historians; while its history was celebrated and illustrious, by now it was mostly 'fallen greatness'.[89] He made a sharp distinction between the worldly boasts of 'most illustrious Capua' or 'Capua Gentile' and the Christian atmosphere of the mission: the people in sack-cloth, bathed in tears or blood, walking the streets of their town repenting for their own sins. Instead, Capua Penitent overtook these titles, which now seemed worldly flattery in comparison.[90]

Two separate churches were used for the mission: one for the spiritual exercises of the men and the second for the spiritual exercises of the women. In the church for the men, deprived of any light, was 'the spectacle of skulls' in which the bones of the dead were placed atop the altar, which was covered by a black cloth.[91] In front of these funereal objects the exercitants performed their devotions. During the mission they also burnt 'obscene and prohibited books, objects of witchcraft, lascivious letters, hair, silk ribbons, and other similar things'; these were the tools that the devil used to hold 'sensuality' in the souls of many and pull them towards carnal vice and sin.[92]

Don Antonio Navaretta, a Spaniard and governor of Capua, who had played a key role in the military role of Capua in the rebellion, led the penitential procession.[93] In the procession crosses were born on backs, heavy chains on feet, bones of the dead placed in their mouths, skulls in hands, and many hit themselves until they bled. The chronicler saw the procession as one major part of the mission, the other was the preaching. In his account he deploys the notion of the spectacle: telling us the impressive visions of piety that could be viewed from the pulpit. Young men, even young nobles, in humble and penitential dress begged to be given pardon for scandal or bad example they had given. These requests were made 'with great feeling and sorrow' and with loud voices. If in the midst of the congregation they encountered someone whom they had ill-will against in the past they made peace. This *spettacolo* was said to have cancelled in their souls 'any shade of the antique hatred, and any scintilla of the old rancour'.[94]

As in accounts of other missions completed by the Jesuits, the Capuan chronicle notes that the 'major fruit' was the 'arrangements of many notable peaces'. The source also concentrates on how the dangerous effects of gossip had been solved with those who had told lies about others confessing with 'the most profound humility' which made the hearts of the listeners tender.[95] The account notes that the mission was able to achieve things that had not been possible to achieve through the authority of others: nobles had tried and failed to make peace. Again we see flashes of the expected path of events: the use of noble status to settle conflict within a town. The writer distinguishes two reasons that people might have been averse to make peace: the 'most vehement passion of worldly honour' and the 'indomitable fury of vengeance'.[96]

The chronicler moves from individual histories of the passions of hatred to the 'principal motive' that the citizens had requested a mission. This was that between two noble families an 'arrabiata inimicitia' had emerged which had led to bloodshed on both sides. There seemed no way to end it without the destruction of the families involved. The rivalry spread out from these families to the 'many adherents that due to the obligation of kinship, or of friendship, or of self-interest, favoured one or the other' which led, in the end, to the formation of 'two swollen factions'.[97] The city had been full of murders and households were either in fear or in grief. Blood and tears were spilt by one and the other side. Their souls were 'cruelly tyrannised by hatred, and it seemed that they only lived with spirit for vendetta'.[98] In the attempt to return to peace, the 'major forces of the Kingdom' were used: titled nobles, officials, and governors; this was all without effect. The 'Achilles' of one of the factions – young, strong, and vigorous – laughed at the fathers and the work of penitence. But slowly these devotions were said to have worked inside him and softened his view: he went to make peace, laid down his sword, and kissed the crucifix. This was the first success in the 'glorious enterprise of pacifying these families' which the Jesuits accomplished through various interventions. They brought the so-called Achilles to a youthful champion of the opposing faction and reconciled them in the sacristy of the College. An avalanche of peace-making followed.[99]

The mission to Capua is a good representation of the general tenor of Jesuit internal missions. In the account of the mission the reconciling of enemies with each other always occurs in the context of the desire to create a communal peace: to return Capua to an 'bygone amity'.[100] Underlying this public discord or unity was always the souls of men and women; their interior lives, affected by feelings of hatred. Rancour could dominate the heart, spirit and desires. However, Jesuit intervention and their ability to create spectacles which softened the hearts of audiences or quenched 'fires' of hatred meant that they could overcome the factionalism that dominated the town. The next chapter considers directly the background of this mission: the rebellions of 1647–48 and their aftermath.

Notes

1 Archivum Romanum Societatis Iesu [ARSI], *Neap.*, 75, *Brevissimo Racconto della Missione Fatta Nella Città di Trani* (1657), fols. 157^r–180^v.
2 Domenico Beltrano was a printer of Neapolitan origins who married the adopted daughter of the successful Roman printer Lorenzo Valerij, who had a printing career across Puglia from 1619. See Giovanni Beltrani, 'Lorenzo Valerii, tipografo romano in Puglia durante il sec. XVII', *Rassegna pugliese*, 9 (1892), 240–9, 271–81, 365–76.
3 ARSI, *Neap.*, 75, *Brevissimo Racconto*, fol. 9^r.
4 Ibid., fol. 8^r.
5 Ibid., fols. 5^r–6^v: 'affinche con la loro santa predicatione estirpassero dalla Città quei peccati, de'quali si ritrovava macchiata'.
6 Ibid., fol. 11^r.
7 Beltrano had detractors as a result of his rise. On the 24 May 1658, an anonymous letter was written from Trani criticizing the Preside – the Marchese

di Creccia – for having sold the duty of numerating the hearths of Trani for tax purposes to Domenico Beltrano and naming him as a 'printer and low-born man' [stampatore e uomo vile]. There is some evidence for corruption in how Beltrano carried out the numeration. Idamaria Fusco, 'Peste, economia e fiscalità in terra di Bari', *ASPN*, 114 (1996), 34–59 (p. 56).

8 Studies of missionary activities regularly draw from and contribute to the history of the emotions. For example see Laura Stevens, *The Poor Indians: British Missionaries, Native Americans, and Colonial Sensibility* (Philadelphia, University of Pennsylvania Press, 2004); Mary Laven, *Mission to China* (Chatham: Faber & Faber, 2011), pp. 227–30. More generally, the place of affect in the history of early modern religion is more firmly established. See Susan C. Karant-Nunn's study of the varying 'emotive spiritualities' of Catholicism, Lutheranism, and Calvinism, *The Reformation of Feeling: Shaping the Religious Emotions in Early Modern Germany* (Oxford: Oxford University Press, 2010).

9 Jennifer Selwyn, 'Angels of Peace: The Social Drama of Reconciliation in the Jesuit Missions in Southern Italy', in *Beyond Florence: The Contours of Medieval and Early Modern Italy*, ed. by Paula Findlen, Michelle M. Fontaine, and Duane J. Osheim (Stanford: Stanford University Press, 2003); Jennifer Selwyn, *A Paradise Inhabited by Devils: The Jesuits' Civilizing Mission in Early Modern Naples* (Farnham: Ashgate, 2004); Elisa Novi Chavarria, 'L'attività missionaria dei Gesuiti nel Mezzogiorno d'Italia tra XVI e XVIII secolo', in *Per la storia sociale e religiosa del Mezzogiorno d'Italia*, ed. by Giuseppe Galasso and Carla Russo (Naples: Guida, 1980); Elisa Novi Chavarria, *Il governo delle anime: Azione pastorale, predicazione e missioni nel Mezzogiorno d'Italia. Secoli XVI–XVIII* (Naples: Editoriale Scientifica, 2001).

10 Selwyn, *A Paradise Inhabited by Devils*, p. 43

11 David Gentilcore, '"Adapt Yourselves to the People's Capabilities": Missionary Strategies, Methods and Impact in the Kingdom of Naples, 1600–1800', *The Journal of Ecclesiastical History*, 45 (1994), 269–96 (p. 270).

12 Novi Chavarria, 'L'attività missionaria', p. 389.

13 Ibid., p. 389: 'La necessità di una mediazione e di un controllo delle aspre conflittualità e della frattura apertersi tra comunità, nobiltà ed autorità civili e di un'opera di riaggregazione sociale e religiosa determinò il convogliarsi degli interventi operativi della Compagnia sulla capitale e i centri limitrofi'.

14 Nicolò Toppi's *Biblioteca napoletana, et apparato a gli huomini illustri in lettere* (Naples, 1678), pp. 281–2 provides some information on Paolucci. He was a Neapolitan, philosopher, and theologian and 'erudite in belles-lettres' and published various works of devotion.

15 Bodily mortification, particularly in the form of flagellation, had a long history throughout the Middle Ages. On the medieval history of public penance see Mary C. Mansfield, *The Humiliation of Sinners: Public Penance in Thirteenth-Century France* (Ithaca: Cornell University Press, 1995). Jennifer Selwyn has surveyed some mid-seventeenth criticisms of Jesuit penance in her '"Schools of Mortification": Theatricality and the Role of Penitential Practice in the Jesuits' Popular Missions', in *Penitence in the Age of Reformations*, ed. by Katherine Jackson Lualdi and Anne T. Thayer (Aldershot: Ashgate, 2000), pp. 201–20.

16 Paolucci, *Missioni*, p. 37: 'Non sono queste, diceano essi, costumanze da huomini, ma da fiere. Iddio bendetto, che ne vuol salvi, non ne vuol mortir, il morir per Christo s'hà fare alle mani de'tiranni, e manigoldi, non alle nostre: per cancellare le colpè è assai piùatto il pianto del cuore, che'l sangue delle vene'.
17 As it was recorded in the Jesuit yearly report of 1647: 'Publica calamitas, ac seditiosi tumultus, quibus hoc anno, ac sequenti afflictum est universum Neapolitanum Regnum fecerunt, ut cum omnia essent infesta latronibus, seditionibus, suspicionibus, nec literarum, nec spiritualium muerum ad aliquot menses liberum comercium concederetur'. ARSI, *Neap.*, 74a, fol. 219[r].
18 Beyond missions, communities often strongly lobbied for the permanent residence of Jesuits in their towns. The correspondence received by the Jesuits is full of letters petitioning to establish residences. Examples included requests made by Castrovillari in 1621 and Teramo in 1624.
19 ARSI, *Neap.*, 76, fol. 10[v].
20 Ibid., 195, fol. 106[r]: 'La molta divotione, et affetto grande, che tiene questa Città alla Compagnia'.
21 Molfetta, 21 January 1713, *Syndicus petit missionem*. Padre Francesco de Geronimo was one of the most famous preachers and missionaries in the late seventeenth and early eighteenth centuries.
22 Gentilcore, 'Adapt Yourselves to the People's Capabilities'. See Emilio Radius, *I gesuiti: storia della Compagnia di Gesù, da Sant'Ignazio a Teilhard de Chardin* (Rome: Boria, 1967), p. 152.
23 ARSI, *Neap.*, 195, fol. 130[r].
24 Ibid., 195, fols. 343[r–v].
25 Gentilcore, 'Adapt Yourselves to the People's Capabilities', p. 271.
26 ARSI, *Neap.*, 75 fols. 252[r]–254[v]: 'Insiginia pietatis opera, & notabiles reconciliationes'.
27 Selwyn, 'Angels of Peace'.
28 Paolucci, *Missioni*, p. 124: 'la necessità, e l'utilità grandissima, che ne proviene dal pardon de'nostri inimici, s'invite tutto il popolo a praticarlo'.
29 Ibid.: 'quale stima, quale ammiratione si meriti il mirare non uno, o due, anzi non una, o due decine, ma più, e più centinaia, (ove la frequenza delle Città l'hà permesso), d'ogni età, d'ogni sesso, d'ogni qualità, o condition di persone esclamare a gran voci, e con sincerità di cuore, che perdonano qual si sia offesa, qual si sia ignirua a' suoi inimici'.
30 Ibid.: 'si può con ogni verità affermare, che in assai poche Città, e molto di rado son rimaste inimicitie da concordare'.
31 Scipione Paolucci provided numerous accounts of demonic actions; such as a woman being assaulted by demonic forces during the performance of devotions: 'la camera tutta scomposta, le sue vesti buttate in quà, & in là sotto delle tavole, e delle sedie, le lenzuola, e covert del letto strettamente annodate, & ogni cosa posta sossopra'. Paolucci, *Missioni*, p. 204.
32 ARSI, *Neap.*, 74, fol. 7[r].
33 Ibid., 76, fol. 56[v] and 74a, fols. 215[v], 234[v]. These rates of homicides seem, if accurate, considerably high. However, beyond the difficulty of establishing that

166 *States of enmity*

these figures are not marked by exaggeration it is, of course, very hard to see what the annual rate might have been.
34 ARSI, *Neap.*, 76, fols. 53$^{r-v.}$
35 Ibid., fol. 25^r.
36 Ibid., 75, fol. 183^v: 'teneva memoria si presente, e fresca'.
37 Ibid., 74a, fol. 270^v: 'animi tiranneggiati crudelmente dall'odio, parendo che vivessero collo spirito solo della vendetta'.
38 Ibid., 62^r.
39 Ulinka Rublack has discussed the somatic experience of the emotions as understood as flows with disordered blockages in Ulinka Rublack, 'Fluxes: The Early Modern Body and the Emotions', *History Workshop Journal*, 53 (2002), 1–16 (esp. p. 2 and p. 6).
40 While it is surely correct to note the choreography of the Jesuits it was also probably the case that the unfolding of larger missions cannot be placed solely under the rubric of Jesuit control. The audience had its own agency and pressures upon Jesuit missionaries that would rarely surface within the accounts.
41 The Jesuit stress upon the public kiss diverges from the German Lutheran experience discussed by Craig Koslofsky, 'The Kiss of Peace in the German Reformation', in *The Kiss in History*, ed. by Karen Harvey (Manchester: Manchester University Press, 2005), p. 29.
42 See Mario Chiabò and Federico Doglio, eds., *I Gesuiti e I Primordi del Teatro Barocco in Europa* (Rome: Centro Studi sul Teatro Medioevale e Rinascimentale, 1995).
43 Selwyn, 'Schools of Mortification', p. 219.
44 Nevertheless, the risk was high that if missionary spirituality faltered, the Jesuits would fall into mere performance. One Jesuit, Giovanni Battista Cancellotti, was in great turmoil due to the misbehaviour of his Jesuit companions. He wrote to the authorities of the order hoping for this problem to be resolved 'otherwise the missionaries of the Company will be Charlatans of the *piazza*'. ARSI, *Neap.*, 198, fol. 329^v: 'Altrimenti i Missionari della Compagnia saranno Ciarlattiani di piazza'.
45 Recent studies of early modern theatre do not rely on clichéd ideas of the superficiality of performance, instead many consider how performance created affect in theory and practice. The opposition between the 'theatrical' and the creation of emotions is perhaps more apparent than real.
46 Analysing the 'production' of emotion has been a concern of anthropologists: such as Dennis Gaffin's examination of the place of taunting in order to create anger in the Faeroe Islands, 'The Production of Emotion and Social Control: Taunting, Anger, and the Rukka in the Faeroe Islands', *Ethos*, 23 (1995), 149–72.
47 Paolucci, *Missioni*, p. 90: 'lo ... estrinseco portamento spira divotione'
48 ARSI, *Neap.*, 76, 35^v: 'in mirar spargimenti di sangue non per effetto d'inimicitia, ma per affetto alla Pace'.
49 King Acab was also used as a counter-example, according to Paolucci, to a powerful feudal lord who felt that the 'excesses of public penance' [*l'esorbitanze dell'esterne penitenze*] were suitable for 'small towns, and those

were uncultured and rough people live' [*tolerabili in terre picciole, & habitate da gente rozza, & inculta*] but for 'such a noble City' [*città sì nobile*] that there was no need. They replied with the words of Isaiah: *Nonne vidisti humiliatum Acab?* Paolucci, *Missioni*, pp. 37–8.

50 ARSI, *Neap.*, 76, fol. 53^r: 'non voleva ne meno dire una parola d'humilitatione non che far un passo per humiliarsi'.
51 Ignatius of Loyola saw weeping as a religious exercise. See William A. Christian, 'Provoked Religious Weeping in Early Modern Spain', in *Religious Organization and Religious Experience*, ed. by John Davis (London, 1982), pp. 97–114.
52 Ignatius of Loyola, *Spiritual Exercises*, trans. by Joseph A. Munitiz and Philip Endean (London: Penguin, 1996), pp. 281–358.
53 Christian, 'Provoked Religious Weeping', p. 97.
54 ARSI, *Neap.*, 75, fol. 181^r.
55 Ibid., 76, fols. 39^{r-v}: 'con tal tenerezza'.
56 Tenerezza: 'tendernesse, softnesse. Also tender or melting affection'. John Florio, *Queen Anna's New World of Words, or Dictionarie of the Italian and English tongues* (London, 1611), pp. 58–9.
57 ARSI, *Neap.*, 76, fols. 32^v–33^r.
58 Ibid., 74a, fol. 215^v: 'ne anco con l'autorità del Vescovo'.
59 ARSI, *Neap.*, 74a, fol. 223^r.
60 Paolucci, *Missioni*, p. 125: 'come borasca d' state, che hà più terrore, che effetto, si obbligano ovunque è necessario con belle scritte di propria mano, & altre autentiche'.
61 The missions of P. Ignazio Saverio Costanzi and Paolo Segneri Jr were particularly occupied with this problem. P. Costanzi preached that: 'Some weep over their sins, and you see the tears running, but perhaps this is not a sufficient sign of true penitence. Consider how the wood that whines most in the fire is that which burns the least. One needs to have anguish in the heart, so much that it's true that some cannot cry. It's enough that you are one who has truly killed the sin, that is: you have sorrow in your heart and a firm intention [to live without sin]' ('Alcuni piangono i lor peccati, e si vedono uscir le lagrime, ma forse questo non è segno bastante del vero pentimento. Badate quai legna nel fuoco piangano più: son quelle che ardono meno. Bisogna avere il dolore nel cuore, e tanto è ciò vero che indarno alcuni si lagnano di non poter piangere. Basta ben che abbiate quello che veramente uccide il peccato, cioè il dolore nel cuore e il proposito fermo'). Giuseppe Orlandi, 'L. A. Muratori e le missioni di P. Segneri Jr.', *Spicilegium Historicum Congregationis SS.mi Redemptoris*, 20 (1972), 158–294.
62 Paolucci, *Missioni*, p. 53.
63 ARSI, *Neap.*, 74a, fol. 215^r.
64 Ibid., 'fece la remissione giuditiale in scriptis'.
65 Ibid., 76, fol. 33^r: 'con scrittura autentica la remissione alla parte'.
66 John Bossy, *Peace in the Post-Reformation* (Cambridge: Cambridge University Press, 1998), p. 28.

67 Thomas Brudholm, *Resentment's Virtue: Jean Amery and the Refusal to Forgive* (Philadelphia: Temple University Press, 2008).
68 Ibid., p. 6.
69 Ibid., p. 4.
70 Paolo Segneri, *Il parrocco istruito, opera in cui si dimostra à qualsisia Curato novella il debito, che lo strigne, e la via da tenersi nell'adempirlo* (Naples, 1693), p. 442: 'con lagrime e con amplessi, con accarezzamenti e con baci di tenerezza'.
71 Ibid., p. 444: 'si moltiplicheranno I delitti con tante paci'; 'Se da tali paci avviene giammai la moltiplicazion dei delitti (cosa che può più presumersi, che provarsi) avviene per accidente)'
72 Ibid.: 'allentare la publica discipline'.
73 Ibid.
74 Ibid., pp. 441–5: 'Frattanto io vorrei proporre a questi così fervidi zelatori del ben comune un bersaglio più atto ad essere saettato dalle loro lingue eloquenti. Saettino tanti abusi ordinati direttamente a salvare i rei, non gli occorsi indirettamente. Saettino quei tribunali, dove con pregiudizio molto maggiore della pubblica utilità, si favoriscono del continuo persone facinorose, le quali meriterebbeno ogni supplizio. Saettino quei testimonj falsi, che vengono quivi addotti a giustificare tali persone; quegli avvocati che le difendono; quei notai che le ricuoprono, e quei nobili che le raccomandano; e sopratutto saettino quei giudici iniqui, che al fine le assolvono, vendendo la giustizia per vil danaro, e cambiandolo in mercimonio.'
75 Idamaria Fusco, *Peste, demografia e fiscalità nel regno di Napoli del XVII secolo* (Milan: FrancoAngeli, 2007), p. 3.
76 ARSI, *Neap.*, 74a, fol. 260^r: 'rigido flagello ha fatto gemere sotto al peso delle gravissime percosse le provincie, et i regni'.
77 Ibid.
78 Francesco Granata, *Storia civile della fedelissima città di Capua* (Naples, 1752), p. 269: 'sempre fedelissima a'suoi Re'.
79 The motives of these *cattivi* were described as envy of wealth, success and morality Granata, *Storia civile*, p. 269: 'álcuni d'ignotissimo nome, e ne'più vili ministerij esercitati, o per invidia delle fortune de'ricchi, o per malvagità de'proprj costumi, odiando i buoni, o pure persuadendosi di migliorar condizione in questi insani popolari tumulti'.
80 Ibid., p. xxvii
81 Rosario Villari, *Un sogno di libertà: Napoli nel declino di un impero* (Milan: Mondadori, 2012), p. 520.
82 The great barons of the Kingdom were charged with raising armies during the revolt.
83 ARSI, *Neap.*, 74a, fol. 223^r.
84 Filippo Iappelli, 'Il Collegio dei Gesuiti a Capua (1611–1767)', in *Roberto Bellarmino arcivescovo di Capua. Teologo e pastore della riforma cattolica* (Capua: Istituto superiore di scienze religiose, 1990), I, p. 504–5.

85 ARSI, *Neap.*, 74a, fol. 249[v]: 'Capuae aucta est sacra suppellex pluribus tum argenteis vasis, tum sevicis, lineisque vestibus'.
86 The diary of Francesco Zazzera. London, British Library, Add MS 8668, fol. 17[v]: 'sopraintendenza'.
87 The eligible families numbered seventy-two in the sixteenth century, fifty at the end of the seventeenth, and forty in 1738. Gérard Delille, *Famiglia e potere locale: una prospettiva mediterranea* (Bari: Edipuglia, 2011), p. 280.
88 ARSI, *Neap.*, 74a, fol. 260[r]: 'fedellissimi scrittori'.
89 Ibid: 'in gran parte cadute grandezze'.
90 Ibid: 'Ma tutte le prerogative, come che illustrissime, di Capoua gentile, delle quali son gravidi i libri e ricche l'historie, non meritano d'essere paragonate a quelle della medesima christiana, e penitente'.
91 Ibid., fol. 263[r]: lo spettacolo di teschi, ossa di morti, sparse per tutto l'altare, coverto di un gran panno nero, e la vista di un divotissimo crocefisso, innanzi al quale assistevano i divoti esercitanti'.
92 Ibid., fol. 267[r]: 'il numero de'libri osceni, e prohibiti, fattuchiarie, lettere lascive, capelli, lacci nastri di seta, e cose simili, che molti sembravano appresso di se, et erano l'esca, con cui il Demonio teneva sempre dentro il fuoco della sensualità ne gli animi di molti infangati miseramente nel vitio, e diletto carnale'.
93 Don Antonio Navaretta was a high-achieving Spanish administrator. In 1640 he had been the *uditor generale* of the army as well as a judge in the *Vicaria*, see Domenico Arena, 'Istoria delli disturbi e Revolutioni accaduti nella Città di Cosenza e Provincia nelli anni 1647 e 1648', ed. by Giuseppe de Blasi, *ASPN*, 4 (1879), 3–32 (p. 32). He was also father of Francesco Navaretta who featured in chapter 4.
94 ARSI, *Neap.*, 74a, fol. 265[r].
95 Ibid., fol. 266[r].
96 Ibid., fol. 267[v]: 'la furia indomabile della vendetta'.
97 Ibid., fol. 270[v].
98 Ibid.: 'parendo che vivessero collo spirito solo della vendetta'.
99 Ibid., fol. 271[r].
100 Ibid., 'per ridurle all'antica amistà'.

6

The politics of hatred in the aftermath of 1647–48

In November 1649 the earth shook in Naples. Vesuvius belched forth smoke and fire. Fear spread in the streets of the capital city, as the people feared a repeat of the deadly eruption of 1631.[1] Soon afterwards an anonymous pamphlet was published, titled *Prodigiosi portenti del monte Vesuvio*, which indicted the viceroy the Count of Oñate was a tyrant, and argued that the volcanic activity was a signal of God's displeasure with the Spanish regime.[2]

Just over two years before, on 7 July 1647, riots had broken out on the *piazza del mercato* in Naples. The spark that ignited this was the reimposition of a tax on the sale of fruit. The burden of fiscal impositions of all sorts had becoming more and more onerous as the Spanish Crown hunted ever more desperately for money and men to feed the Thirty Years' War. But this tax held a symbolic weight: the authorities had pledged that it would not be imposed again. The fish-seller Masaniello, for nine days, led the rioters until he was assassinated. While Masaniello has attracted the majority of attention, especially in English-language scholarship, and also captured the early modern European imagination as a disturbing personification of social upheaval, his involvement was short-lived.[3] In fact, the revolt quickly connected with longstanding *popolo* complaints about their marginalized role in civic government. One of the more significant figures behind the development of the revolt was the eighty-year-old Giulio Genoino. This *éminence grise* had been only recently released from twenty years of imprisonment in a Spanish fortress in north Africa. Before his exile, Genoino had held the office of *eletto di popolo* from which he was removed and arrested due to aristocratic objections over his reform agenda and his supposed collaboration with the putative conspiracy of the viceroy Osuña. The city had already returned to an uneasy peace when John of Austria arrived and bombarded the city in a show of strength. The riots thereby morphed into an uprising of the *popolo* class of Naples, led by the gunsmith Gennaro Annese under Genoino's counsel. In the provinces, a variety of uprisings occurred and pre-existing conflicts between vassals and lords accelerated into conflagrations. Hunger had well prepared the ground for dissent.

News of the revolt of the *Mercato* spread in only a few days around the provinces in July. Soon began the provincial uprisings that would occur in every province of the kingdom by 1648. Among the earliest was Cosenza which rose up in revolt on 14 July, then many more urban centres followed such as Bitonto, Melito, and Monopoli on 17 July and Nardò on 20 July. Scores of local uprisings would eventually occur in every province of the kingdom. Back in the capital, an initial loyal protest against bad government had given way to outright resistance and, in October 1647, a Royal Neapolitan Republic was declared with the French Duke of Guise its intended leader. Across the winter of 1647–48 the city of Naples was divided between rebel- and Spanish-controlled portions guarded by military force on both sides. On all sides of the rebellion themes of vengeance, hatred, and betrayal framed the events. For critics the rebellion itself was unrestrained vengeance; the rebels were pursuing enmities unjustly and rabidly.[4]

The language of vendetta was grasped by observers to understand the chaotic events of the summer. It was through the idiom of offence, resentment, and violent revenge that the conflicts between social orders was interpreted. For instance, the cleric and loyalist Gabriele Tontoli described Masaniello and his companions as 'animated to vendetta'.[5] The Spaniard Diego Amatore used the plot of vendetta to understand the development of the revolt in his work *Napoli sollevata*. He described the people as 'engulfed in a ferocious rage, and a burning desire for vengeance' and that Masaniello was their 'minister of vendettas'.[6] Indeed, the word vendetta appears scores of times in Amatore's account of the rebellion. For observers, it made sense to plot the events as revenge. The question of whether such revenge was justified and righteous or unjustified and savage depended upon perspective. But the animating force of enmity and revenge was everywhere to be seen.

Returning to the ominous rumblings of Vesuvius in 1649, the cleric and scholar Camillo Tutini, identified in scholarship as the author of the pamphlet, called the viceroy Oñate a tyrant precisely for his policies of pacification of the revolt. The phrase repeated again and again in this pamphlet is: 'The earth cries out!' (*'Terra Clamat!'*). The shaking of the earth and the spewing of smoke and fire was a sign that: 'the earth … is saying that it can suffer no more from the tyrannical Spanish dominion'. Tutini argued that the Neapolitans had been betrayed. They had been forced into rebellion through impossible financial burdens, that reduced them to desperation. Then, they laid down their arms under assurances that Oñate agreed with this interpretation of their actions, that he would come and pardon them all. Oñate had violated an oath given under the 'royal word' and the Spanish had come lying back to domination, with peace on their lips and vendetta in their hearts. Vesuvius was now called upon to perform 'revenge on these Moors, these Barbarians, revenge our injuries and martyrdoms, and the Mountain seems to say to the Count of Oñate, do you think to root Spanish Domination in the kingdom by spilling so much innocent blood?'[7]

While a portion of this usage of the language of enmity and revenge can be attributed to poetics, rhetoric, or social chauvinism on the part of some commentators, it should not be discarded as a lens through which to interpret the chaotic events of 1647–48. Rather, using the analytical lens on the dynamics of enmity and peace-making assists in understanding the course of the rebellion and, especially, the difficult period of pacification. This chapter argues that the politics of enmity, peace-making, and associated issues of justice must be considered in historical interpretations of the events of 1647–48 and their pacification. Without attending to the category of enmity, and its relationship to criminal justice, we have a limited view of why and how the events of 1647–48 and their aftermath unfolded as they did.

Enmities and the events of 1647–48

The outbreak of rebellion in July depicted just how fragile the social peace of the kingdom was. When authority shook, private enmities easily took the form of outright warfare. The events of 1647–48 demonstrate the connections between feudal authority and its discontent, the militarization of the kingdom, and the practices of inimical rivalry.

In the days after the rioting, many outlaws entered the suburbs and centre of Naples. The rebels quickly adopted the right to deliver justice, especially executions, to these outlaws, whose loyalties – if any – probably lay with feudal barons resident in Naples. But by some it was reported that chaotic revolutionary justice was an opportunity to revenge private enmities. For instance, Giovanni Battista Piacente repeated a rumour that the gathering of a 'quantity of heads of bandits' to be displayed around the capital and its suburban settlements (*borghi*) was in fact a demonstration of how political upheaval was used to revenge private enmities: 'it was discussed that among the multitude of the slaughtered, the majority had been decapitated for the reason of private enmities, not for having conspired with the Duke of Madaloni'.[8] The Duke of Madaloni was accused of having connections with bandits including Perrone and Grasso, igniting a paramilitary incursion into the city of Naples with rumours that these bandits were behind such actions as poisoning fountains and grain-stores.[9]

In the provinces the revolt played out in a number of ways, with some municipal revolts attempting to unite against feudal lords, supported by troops loyal to the republican cause. However, internal divisions within communities were also highly important. The context of a kingdom-wide disturbance allowed for pre-existing enmities to reach fever pitch in the total breakdown of provincial order.

Unsuccessful initial attempts to settle the rebellion in 1647 demonstrated some of the core objections of the rebellion to the practices of justice in the kingdom. The rebels demanded that all those in galley service who had, in fact, finished their sentence be released immediately. Further, that Masaniello and those who accompanied him into the Church of Santa Maria di Constantinopoli be included in a general indulgence. Item 12 of the document demonstrates the significance of the category of 'delinquenti et contumaci Napoletani' who the people were strongly in support of reintegrating into society. The inclusion of this demand stresses the significant social impact of the system of contumacy and outlawing upon the capital city.[10] The rigors of justice were objectionable to the rebels, many of whom must have known those who had to flee the capital in the preceding years. The item argues that every Neapolitan should be free and indulged for every crime, regardless of whether they had remissions of the offended party or not. If it was truly necessary for them to obtain this, they would be given ten years to accomplish the remission. The special tribunals known as *giunte* were picked out as especially negative, notably the *giunta* concerned with contraband and smuggling. Similarly, trials held during royal visits were noted as needing to be included in the same acts of mercy.

At the heart of the initial uprising, therefore, was a hope for the yoke of judicial inquisitions and outlawing to be removed from the inhabitants of the capital, demonstrating a sentiment that the practice of justice had become onerous, unjust, and damaging. As this compromise order was issued in July 1647, far from the end of the revolt, it would not stand, but it provides a useful account of what was desired at the outset.

Some of the leaders of the revolutionary movement were motivated by their enmities and resentments. For a leading example of this, we can take Francesco Salazar, the Duke of Vaglio. Salazar, born in 1606, had lost the feudal land of Vaglio in 1632 when it was seized for sale against his wishes due to his debts. One of the many bankrupted feudal lords of the first half of the seventeenth century, he never forgave this and set about engaging in offensives. In 1646 he entered Vaglio and sacked the palace and possessions of the new feudal lord Giovanni Battista Massa di Ventimiglia. Arrested for this, he was imprisoned in the *Vicaria* from whence he was freed by the Duke of Guise to serve as leader of the revolutionary armies in Terra di Bari, Principato Citra, and Basilicata. Many of the leaders of provincial revolutionary moves were raised in the internecine conflicts of cities. Such struggles shaped their worldview and became the lens through which the crisis of 1647–48 was viewed. One leader of the revolutionary movement in Cosenza, Giuseppe Gervasi was involved in the struggles of his family against the Sambiase family who had blocked the Gervasis' entrance into the ranks of the patriciate.[11]

The revolutionary upheaval did not only pit feudal lords against rebellious *università*, it also escalated pre-existing enmities between feudal lords and within patriciate orders. These could take the form of assaults against another lord's vassals, an act which would be received with much displeasure. The Marchese of Buonalbergo led an assault on the town of Casa d'Albore, in the feudal lands of Francesco Carafa, as revenge for offences he had received. Hearing that Buonalbergo had led such an assault and 'that from this event many bad consequences could have arisen due to the power and valour of these lords and for their large followings, the Duke of Salza, *preside* of this province left with all haste to solve the problem and put out this fire'.[12] The way in which he tried to fight this potential fire and division within the feudal nobility was first by speaking to both of the aristocrats on their own and then bringing them together 'not finding between them anything that would impede the peace, having the one and other displayed their choler, the peace was made by placing the *fede regia* between them'.[13] The ability to mediate was a key resource of the successful *Preside* and here we see a stress on mediation after the noble licence to vent their rage.

Attempts at pacification had begun very soon after protests began. Peter Burke has reconstructed how religious processions aimed to quell the rioting crowds.[14] On all sides uncertainty and fear of betrayal was the dominant tone of the febrile early days of the revolt. By the time Gennaro Annese took control of the revolutionary leadership in the same month, the aspirations of the republican branch of the *Popolo* had scorned reconciliation. The initial loyalty of the rebellion, with its cries of 'long live the King, and death to bad government' had faded. In November 1647, the *popolo* rebels printed a decree that some people against the 'common will' promoted 'peace with the Spanish ministers'.[15] The risk, they believed, was that the Spanish would betray the peace with violence.[16] They had already gone against their word and the rebels attempted to shore up their resistance by imposing a death penalty for those who sought peace with the Spanish. Peace with the Spanish was seen as welcoming later betrayal with open arms; the Spanish would revenge themselves under a facade of capitulation.

Yet despite the arrival of the Duke of Guise the prospects of successful revolt faded. Instead the rebels suffered military defeats and fatigue from armed stand-off in the city of Naples grew. Indeed, the presence of the Duke of Guise and his forces led to conflict between various parts of the rebellious forces. When the hopes of republican Naples became clear fantasy, attempts at gaining indulgence became a more attractive avenue out of the situation.

The offer of indulgences of crimes was at the heart of the ending of the rebellion. But a ceasefire required credible assurances or it was voluntary surrender to execution. The rebels feared vengeance caused by the enmity of the aristocracy and the Spanish towards them. In late January 1648 a group of barons and nobles published a memorial recognizing that 'some of the *Popolo* hold suspicions that the nobility will pursue vendetta of the presumptuous offences, that some have committed to their goods, and lives'. Instead the aristocrats sought to reassure that they had forgotten all such offences: 'forgiving all of them, actually burying them in perpetual oblivion, as Christian piety and the generosity of their blood, and the desire for public good all require'. They also showed how they 'live so far from hatreds, and rancour against the *Popolo*' that they requested 'infinite graces' be given to them.[17] They desired 'public Peace' and denied the existence of hatred or enmity.

The promise that offences would be forgotten was at the centre of attempts to make peace. On 5 April Don John of Austria occupied the *Popolo* controlled areas of the city. He had been dispatched by Madrid to pacify Naples. His entrance into the city was met mostly by cries of *pace*.[18] This denial of what had happened was an attempt to stop cycles of hatred and recrimination building. Instead, the 'total and perfect quiet and peace of this City and Kingdom' should be maintained by 'receiving them in our arms as vassals born this day, and as if such crimes had never occurred'.[19] Pacification required oblivion.

On 11 April an indulgence was issued that offered reasonably broad forgiveness for crimes committed. But it also ordered that the rebellion itself should be forgotten. The decree instructed 'that in no way should anyone speak' or write of the offences of the rebellion; as this would 'disturb the total and perfect quiet' of the city and Kingdom.[20] However, the wording of this grace was not enough to convince everyone and did not include the desired total removal of penalties.[21] Another indulgence was issued on 20 April under the authority of Don Giovanni with far wider absolution.[22] But very little was forgotten; a violent crackdown on rebels began. Scores of rebels were executed.[23] Then on 9 August 1648 a further general indulgence was issued. In 1650 a further general pardon was issued, that spanned all crimes from 1647 to the day of publication on 27 April 1650 for anyone who presented themselves in Fondi, ready to sign up for three years' service in the Spanish armies.

Many feudal lords of Puglia united to put down the rebellion in collaboration with royal forces. The union of arms between Francesco Boccapianola, *Governatore delle armi* of the provinces of Terra d'Otranto and Bari, and the Count of Conversano was the major operation against the tumults in the region. They gathered a considerable number of smaller barons along with their followers, including the ill-fated Bartilotti, the Prince of Presicce. They also had pieces of artillery which they used to infuse fear in the local populations, threatening total destruction if they did not give up the chief rebels in chains.[24]

As well as reprisals, the relevance of the politics of enmity to the events can be seen in the pacification projects that operated in the aftermath. For instance, the peace-making activities of the Jesuits increased as part of a strategy to address tensions. Similarly, the use of general indulgences was an attempt to return the kingdom to a state of tranquillity. In 1648 Oñate issued a further indulgence. The main target of such indulgences was not the leaders of popular rebellions but rather the squadrons of outlaws that had gathered throughout the countryside. The use of indulgence also opened up opportunities for abuse and extortion.

Civil war in Puglia: the pacification of Altamura

We can take the town Altamura and the provinces of the Terra di Bari more generally as a telling example for the politics of enmity in the revolt of 1647. The major feudal lords of the Terra di Bari included the Count of Conversano. Altamura was, instead, held by the Farnese lords of Parma. From 1646 the feudatory was the teenage Ranuccio II Farnese, Duke of Parma, son of the vindictive hero of the Thirty Years' War Odoardo Farnese. In the aftermath of the rebellion, Ranuccio was involved in a failed attempt to sell the fief of Altamura.

For individual communities the general indulgence of 1648 also opened up problems. The town of Altamura lies about fifty kilometres southwest of Bari in Puglia. It was a proud town with a robust and enmity-prone patrician nobility. In the early years of Spanish rule, in the 1530s, Altamura had purchased its liberty at the price of 20,000 ducats to become part of the royal demesnial lands. However, spiralling debts led to its sale only eight years later to the Farnese Duke of Parma. Altamura is a very useful case because a range of material concerning its governance survives in the Farnese archive. Gérard Delille, and before him Giovanni Masi, have profited much from the consultation of this material and placing it in conversation with other records to examine the kinship dynamics of factionalism.[25]

Altamura was a difficult fief to govern. For decades, it had been troubled by two major factions that gathered around two families: the De Angelis and the Viti. These noble factions were involved in the most vicious enmities. By the middle of the seventeenth century, the situation was that the de Angelis had managed to bully the Viti out of municipal control, leading to a situation of disorder. Like many communities in the Kingdom of Naples, the solution was supposed to be balance – the periodic exchange of control of the posts of government between the two factions. Tenure of posts in the city government was a year, leading to constant struggle.

The crisis of 1648 had hit Altamura hard. In 1650 the agent of the Duke of Parma in Naples reported the intense difficulties of extracting revenue from feudal lands in the aftermath of the rebellion. It was a miracle, he related, that anything be gained from the feudal lands due to the lack of spare money. He noted that 'the times are so tight that if anyone has a little money, he thinks it a lot'.[26]

In the aftermath of the Neapolitan rebellion, Ranuccio II Farnese had only recently emerged from his minority after the death of his father Odoardo in 1646. The teenage duke, therefore, was provided with much information on the situation in his Neapolitan holding of Altamura. Marco Aurelio Massarenghi, resident agent of the Farnese in Naples wrote extensive reports on the situation in Altamura:

> The *Governo* of this city consists of a Mayor [*Sindico*] who is the chief, six noble *eletti*, six from the *Popolo*, and a chamberlain who all have a year's tenure; the city is divided into two factions: the Angelis and their followers, the Viti and their followers each of which should be part of the government but this doesn't happen as only the Angelis govern because of this there have been and there are most capital enmities.

The enmities stretched back decades: in 1599, Ranuccio's grandfather and eponym Ranuccio I was informed that 'the city is very troubled by debts and full of infinite discords because everyone wants to manage in their own manner the public purse, which is the cause of all their enmities'.[27]

The ability to escape the penalties of the state was a theme that produced recrimination: Alberto Di Via, before the revolt, wrote that:

> criminals are not followed and taken, but when they are advised if it's suspected that officials are looking for them. Wherefore from any crime, the nobles, the rich, their friends, their relatives, the adherents of the noble or the rich, stand secure. From which it is impossible to verify any crime, being in this way the peasants and poor terrified by the powerful, that not only do they dare not to accuse anyone, but it's impossible to extract the truth from their mouths. And if, by fortune, you manage to clarify a crime, there is no shortage of false witnesses in defence.

The upshot of this situation was that '[i]t is impossible that justice has its place here'.[28] Similar despairing sentences can be found throughout, with one governor having a sword held at his throat. Alberto di Via, at any rate, advised the Farnese the best thing to do would be to sell Altamura, and fast.

In August 1650 Masserenghi argued that with the Count of Oñate returning from Portolongone 'full of glory'; that is, having driven away French forces from Elba, thereby securing the kingdom further. The extraordinary rejoicing of the city of Naples was a sight to see, with fireworks dancing above the riveria of Posillipo. But now, Masserenghi wrote, we can hope that 'apply himself to the conciliation of many troubled municipal problems [*tante travagliate imprese civile*], relics of the passed revolutions'.[29]

By 1651, the situation had become so extreme that Ranuccio ordered a visit to be completed by a trusted official Alessandro Pencolini. Masserenghi, the resident in Naples, then composed a long set of instructions for Pencolini, to familiarize him with the situation in Altamura. These instructions reveal very interesting points: within them it is noted that it was the viceroy Oñate's policy of general pardon that utterly transformed the situation on the ground in Altamura. In his instructions, Masserenghi recounted the feudal politics of Altamura. He wrote that:

> In Altamura there are two factions, the most capital enemies, each of which pretends to Dominion and to hold the government of the town. However, the de Angelis party has always been superior, and the other party, the Viti, has been protected in the past by ministers of His Highness, for good politics so as to balance the power of the faithless de Angelis.[30]

He then recounted the events of 1638, when Altamura was returned to Farnese control after a three-year period of sequester because of Odoardo Farnese's alliance with the French. In Naples, Masserenghi was friends with the *procurator-fiscal* of the Vicaria, the central criminal court of the Kingdom of Naples. His friend subsequently provided the Farnese administration with 'notable services'. This service was the licensing of a commission from the *Vicaria* with viceregal authority. This commission, composed of twenty-five armed men, came to Altamura and proceeded to launch criminal prosecutions against the 'principal' members of the faction as part of a strategy for regaining control of the community.[31]

Then less than a decade later came the rebellion, and after the rebellion, the general pardons went against this avenue of policy. Masserenghi wrote:

> After the revolutions, everything changed so much that it was even necessary to change policy [*politica*], since His Majesty had pardoned with a general indulgence all the crimes, then all the heads of this faction were released from the many inquisitions with which they were kept quarrelling [*con le quali li teneva litigati*].

This is a very clear statement of the use of criminal proceedings as a tool for keeping factions wrapped up in long-running inquisitions, that attempted to stop them escalating into larger problems. But the general indulgence, in Masserenghi's account, changed everything.[32]

The main consequence of this was a transformation of the stakes of factionalism in Altamura, Masserenghi continued:

one side has given themselves to the protection of the Count of Conversano, and the Duke delle Noci his son, the other to the duke of Andria their enemies, as each of them wants dominon over these provinces and to be *padroni* not only of the lands of other title-holders and barons but also over the cities and lands of the king.

A vicious civil war had unfolded in Puglia during the rebellion and afterwards, with Giangirolamo d'Acquaviva, the Count of Conversano, and Carlo Carafa, the Duke of Andria, in a vicious struggle for control over the region. Such a situation caused trouble at the very height of the Spanish regime in Naples. Massarenghi had convinced the viceroy Oñate to summon all the heads of each faction to appear in Naples, and under the oversight of the Regent of the Collateral Council Zuffia be united and re-pacified – as well as being forced, under the heaviest of fiscal penalties, to renounce their noble protectors.

This was not deemed a large enough measure: and instead, Spanish troops had already dispatched in May to occupy the city along with the trusted Parman courtier, the Marchese Lampugnani.[33] In this letter it is explicitly the enmities that remained between the Count of Conversano and the dukes of Andria that form one of the relics left by the revolt, which are said to continue more than ever and required intervention from the viceroy.[34] On the 18 May 1651 Lampugnani wrote to Ranuccio noting the division of the town into two factions, each pledged to a feudal lord, writing:

> I'll try my best as far as possible to make them notice of their harm, and truly this was high-time for a visit, so that they may know, that the Lord Duke, and not the subjects, are their Lord, and I already see that things are walking in such a way that we can hope for a good result.

At the end of May, he reported that the Altamurans were 'very enraged' against Massarenghi because they blamed him for the coming of the Spanish troops 'they swear they have certainty that they came for his ends … and they say incredible things about it' but that 'anyway I have in great part pacified them'.[35]

While intriguing and violence continued in Altamura, the imprisonment of Conversano and, in 1655, the assassination of Carlo Carafa reduced the extreme risks of this situation. In 1653, Oñate was replaced by Garçia de Haro, the Count of Castrillo. This new viceroy was reputed as less fierce than his predecessor. In the next year, the Duke of Guise would again try to press his claim through his blood-right but fail in the attempt.

The 1650s were a period of considerable instability and the politics of enmity, in which strong emotions, especially hatred, were of great importance. Masserenghi repeated a saying that he attributed to the viceroy Oñate: 'that this is a new world, and that there is no kingdom any more'. These complex results from central policies in local areas, intersecting with long internal struggles of feuding and violence, are not easy to recover: indeed, as most governing records from local communities are lost it is not easy to place the case of Altamura in direct comparison with others. But the use of criminal proceedings as a tool of government, as a way to restrain factions, was obviously widespread even if it was a totally inadequate tool for any solution to cycles of vindicatory violence, able to create truce more than peace. The policy of pardoning crimes had consequences, even if not the ones predicted and even if rebels were often punished.

Altamura was but one community participating in the complex and violent politics of Puglia in this period. It is also useful to analyse the case of Nardò, which opposed attempts to be brought to heel by Conversano in the 1630s and 1640s at courts in Naples and Spain. But even in Nardò there were partisans for the house of Conversano. The case of Nardò makes clear that there should be no simple division between feudal lord and vassal, rather, the conflicts and enmities were complex and multiple, involving various parties. In Nardò, the enmity between the Falconi and the Carignani was a primary division that then could search around for exogenous forces that could be drawn in to accomplish local goals. On 12 August 1639 Francesco Maria Manieri was murdered by a forest guard of the Count of Conversano. In the 1640s royal justice was instrumentalized by Acquaviva to imprison some of his opponents, such as Alessandro Campilongo, Giandonato Ri, Scipione Puzzovivo.[36]

The case of Nardò provides a good example of the ways in which the control over communal institutions created violence. The events in Nardò in the 1630s and 1640s set the stage for a violent confrontation with the Count of Conversano. Nardò was a city with notable fiscal resources and does not represent poor agricultural vassals; they pursued their case against Conversano in the 1630s and 1640s at courts in Naples and Spain. In August 1647, a host of summary executions and imprisonments took place in Nardò and the surrounding territories. The imprisonment of many who were not involved, led many to leave Nardò for safer places, notably Gallipoli.[37] Every pot of *materia medica* in the pharmacy of the Venetian Antonio Corilli was smashed to pieces and he narrowly escaped with his life, as he had made it known he thought revolt was shameful.[38] On 20 August six men were killed by arquebus then their heads were chopped off, on the orders of the Count of Conversano. The chronicler recorded how the smoke from the muskets made it impossible to see while the executed, mostly clerics, chanted in Latin: 'Forgive them father, for they know not what they do.'[39]

The government of Nardò was controlled by those opposed to the Count of Conversano in the 1650s. In December 1653 news came of the murder of Mario Antonio Puzzovivo; Cosimo Acquaviva, the Duke of Noci, was accused of the murder. In 1654, after the arrest of Conversano, agents of the *audienza* of Otranto came to arrest some of the supporters of the count. Some managed to hide in the church. Others were interrogated about the arrest of Mario Antonio Puzzovivo.

The continuation of upheaval

Despite the defeat of the Duke of Guise and the surrender of the rebels there was not a total return to peace after 1648. The Prince of Carignano, Tommaso Francesco di Savoia, was in charge of a fleet of French ships that stayed in the Neapolitan gulf after Guise's departure and even led a land invasion of the Kingdom in August with the cooperation of bandit chiefs, albeit one that was soon routed.[40] Aristocratic ties with bandits had increased during 1647–48 and had significant political effects in the 1650s, in sharp distinction to the wider Italian trend.[41] In the tumultuous 1650s bandits and barons cooperated with political aims: seeking to grab power in the strange aftermath of a rebellion that had disrupted local equilibrium. These nobles were often supporters of French power and the French embassy in Rome was a nexus for the exchange of information and a site where plots were arranged.[42] The viceroys of this period had to return adequate peace to the kingdom and oppose certain aristocratic parties. These parties had formed to oppose popular revolt but had transformed into loose coalitions that could equally challenge Spanish dominion. The pursuit of private enmities intensified in these years, and the violence in the wake of the failed revolt was notable.

The immediate aftermath of the failure of the Duke of Guise's first invasion and the fall of the Neapolitan republic in 1648 was not a swift return to peace. Pacification was hesitant and partial until the cold winter of 1648–49 set in and forced the swollen bandit armies to disband for survival. By the end of February 1649 there was no significant open rebellion in the Kingdom. But disaffected nobles, *capi popoli* and bandit-chiefs all remained on the political scene.[43]

The revolt and its initial pacification had left the kingdom in a woeful state. In the memorials that flowed to the Collateral Council, many authors referred to the tragedies that had befallen the kingdom. Manuel Vaaz de Andrada wrote noting the 'universal calamity caused by the late revolutions'.[44] The viceroy Oñate pursued repression with a vigour that unsettled many in the kingdom. The diarist Fuidoro argued that 'the harshness of his rule, does nothing but reopen the wounds that had healed only shortly before'.[45]

Figure 6.1 The viceroy Oñate, from Domenico Antonio Parrino, *Teatro eroico, e politico de'governi de'vicere del Regno di Napoli* (Naples, 1692). Biblioteca Nacional De España.

In 1653, Oñate was replaced by Garçia de Haro, the Count of Castrillo. This new viceroy was less fierce than his predecessor, although he was dedicated to strengthening royal authority as far as was possible, and made some attempts to oppose baronial criminality and to tackle the problem of criminals taking asylum in churches.[46]

In the next year, the Duke of Guise re-invaded the Kingdom, landing at Castellammare di Stabia, again trying to press his claim through his bloodright. Thousands of French troops and Neapolitan outlaws supported this attempt.[47] Yet as Silvana d'Alessi has argued, the general reaction as seen through print culture was of parody. History repeating itself, the second time as farce. But the reality for those involved was not satirical.

The viceroy the Count of Castrillo issued a law that noted how

> plotting various betrayals ... seeking by illicit means, and exceeding their natural duty, to disturb the peace and to create unrest in this Kingdom, as is shown and proven by the invasion of the French armada, lured by foolish hopes, and promises made by the said rebels, with great prejudice to the credit and fidelity that they always held and hold as vassals of this Kingdom; being that it has been seen clearly, that with various inventions they have presumed to create many innovations in the Abruzzi, in order to disturb the public, and the universal quiet, not only of this Kingdom, but of all of Italy.[48]

Nonetheless, a general indulgence was issued. The necessity of issuing indulgences in order to counter rebellion created many opportunities for those accused of homicide, that did not need to have anything to do with the events in Castellammare to seek forgiveness. For instance, we can take a letter written by Bartolomeo Guaragnone who complains of an abusive use of the indulgence. He wrote that Marcello de Iorito, imprisoned in the Vicaria for the murder of his own brother and 'the most grave injuries' to Guaragnone, was using the indulgence, with support of a group of unnamed powerful men to escape punishment.

The failed attempt at stealing the Kingdom from the Spanish was not the end of conspiratorial movements in the 1650s. In 1657, a plot apparently orchestrated by Carlo Antonio Guevara, the Duke of Bovino was revealed. The nature of this 'conspiracy' underscores the connections between nobles, bandits, and international politics in the uneasy 1650s. It also points to the deeply personal nature of these connections, in which the relations between lords and bandits was modelled after patronage and also tied to certain aristocratic aspirations to dominion. The evidence for the conspiracy comes from the efforts of the *giunta degli banditi* dedicated to the extirpation of bandits, which in the late 1650s began a concerted effort to counter aristocratic protection of bandits.[49] The actual records of the *giunta* no longer survive but a manuscript report provides some information on the activities of the subcommittee.[50] This note records that from the arrests and interrogations of four notorious bandit chiefs and more than twenty other bandits 'the discussions that the aforesaid bandits had for the loss of this Kingdom with the help, that they expected from the armies of France' were proven.

The records of the *giunta* show that Bovino made contact with bandit-chiefs who had legitimate military experience. The Neapolitan *cavalieri* still prided themselves on the warlike spirit of their noble blood.[51] For the Duke of Bovino, friendship with one Carlo Petriello and the bandit chief Paolo Fioretti was key to the conspiracy. Petriello had travelled widely across the peninsula in his career. He had been a captain of cavalry for the Duke of Modena, fighting against invading Spanish forces. After this period of service, he had assisted in the plot of the Marchese di Acaya to take the Kingdom. With encouragement both from Acaya and the French ambassador in Rome, he led armed men into the Kingdom 'to embolden the foray', that is, the planned landing of troops in Puglia.[52] In 1657–58, the viceroy the count of Castrillo published two pragmatics aimed directly at these *capobanditi*.[53] Huge sums were promised for those who presented them alive or dead to the court; 10,000 ducats for both of them or 5000 a head.[54]

From interrogations, Bovino was said to have addressed them: 'What demon has you? Be happy! Shortly the French armada will come, and you will all be lords.' The duke was said to have believed that he was prophesied to lead the Kingdom and that he cared nothing for the will of the *popolo*.[55] Fioretti and Petriello then made contact with 'various bandit chiefs around the Kingdom'.[56] They gathered a force nearly 200 men strong on Mount Matese. In the next months they met the Duke near Bovino many times, in 'secret congresses', where the Duke gave them food and drink as well as firearms.[57]

Beyond Guevara, the Duke of Maddaloni, the Prince of Isernia, the Marchese di Cammorota, and the Baron of Rocca Gloriosa as well as many others were implicated in protecting bandits.[58] In the late 1650s, then, it was clear that a considerable group of powerful barons would have given their support to any invading French forces and some were actively participating in conspiracy. Their belief in their ability to determine the rule of the Kingdom was heightened by their decisive role in putting down the Neapolitan republic and the associated provincial uprisings.[59] Castrillo's viceroyalty had not been successful in opposing banditry. Indeed, outlaw politics increased. Bandits controlled towns close to Naples, including Somma and Nola. Cardinal Buoncompagni was forced to use an outlaw-issued safeguard to travel across the kingdom. In 1656 a new calamity befell the kingdom. A plague swept through the city and kingdom of Naples, leading to hundreds of thousands of dead and a further blow to the state capacity of the Spanish regime.

The civil conflicts of the period 1647–56, which continued to smoulder afterwards, must be understood through the lens of the politics of enmity. The particular aspects of this that were most important were the politicized nature of justice in the early seventeenth century, the complex interconnection of municipal, feudal, and provincial politics and the ways in which private enmities could easily become public in the fervid atmosphere of the mid-seventeenth century. The betrayal of indulgence was received as evidence of the unforgiving nature of the Spanish. When Vesuvius erupted in 1649 it was described by Camillo Tutini in his *Prodigiosi portenti* as vengeance in turn for such 'false oaths' of reconciliation and indulgence given by the Spanish.

Notes

1 Indeed, the eruption of 1631 led to large amounts of dissenting literature and has been studied in Domenico Cecere, Chiara De Caprio, Lorenza Gianfresco, and Pasquale Palmieri, *Disaster Narratives in Early Modern Naples: Politics, Communication and Culture* (Rome: Viella, 2018).
2 'Prodigiosi portenti del monte Vesuvio', *Archivio storico per le province Napoletane*, 2.1 (1877), 161–75.
3 Peter Burke, 'The Virgin of the Carmine and the Revolt of Masaniello', *Past & Present*, 99 (1983), 3–21; Silvana d'Alessio, *Masaniello: The Life and Afterlife of a Neapolitan Revolutionary* (Amsterdam: Amsterdam University Press, 2023).
4 Alain Hugon, *La insurrección de Nápoles 1647–1648: la construcción del acontecimiento* (Zaragoza: Prensas de la Universidad de Zaragoza, 2014), p. 306.
5 Gabriele Tontoli, *Il Mas'Aniello, overo discorsi narrative la Sollevatione di Napoli* (Naples, 1648), p. 6.
6 Diego Amatore, *Napoli sollevata narratione degli accidenti occorsi in detta Città dalli 7. Luglio 1647 sino li 20. Marzo 1648* (Bologna, 1650), p. 26: 'sommerso in una ferocita rabbia, & ardente desiderio di vendetta'.
7 *Prodigiosi portenti*, p. 168.
8 Giovanni Battista Piacente, *Le rivoluzioni del Regno di Napoli negli anni 1647–1648 e l'assedio di Piombino e Portolongone* (Naples: Giuseppe Guerrera, 1861), p. 49.
9 Alessandro Giraffi, *Le rivolutioni di Napoli* (Venice, 1648), p. 93.
10 Item, che li delinquenti et contumaci Napolitani sieno liberi, et indultati da qualsivoglia loro inquisition et delitti, ancorchè non tenessero.
11 Pier Luigi Rovito, *La rivolta dei notabili: ordinamenti municipali e dialettica dei ceti in Calabria citra, 1647–1650* (Naples: Jovene, 1988), p. 59.
12 Ursino Scoppa, *Relazione delle cose seguite in Ariano nel 1648* (Naples, 1839), pp. 10–11: 'che da questo successo potevano nascere molte male conseguenze

per la potenza ed il valore di detti signori e per le comuni aderenze, il duca di Salza, preside di quella provincia, partì con ogni velocità per rimediarvi e smorzare questo fuoco'.

13 Ibid.: 'non ritrovandosi cosa che impedisse la quiete, avendo l'uno e l'altro mostrato la loro bizzarria, si stipulò la pace con interponersi la fede regia'.
14 Burke, 'The Virgin of the Carmine', pp. 11–12.
15 Piacente, *Le rivoluzioni del Regno di Napoli*, p. 220.
16 Ibid.: 'è bene noto per l'istorie che con altri popoli, con li quali ebbero forse minor differenza, dopo una conclusa, e lunga pace di più anni sfogarono la loro ira, e vendetta, con farne ammazzare più di quarantamila persone'.
17 ARSI, *Neap.*, 74a, fol. 385[r]: 'Et essendosi presentiti i sospetti, che tengono alcuni particulari del Popolo, che la Nobiltà debba prender vendetta delle pretese offese, che alcuni gli han fatto nelle robbe, e nelle vite, offeriscono a S.M. & a V.A. di dover affatto scordarsi di tutti li pretesi eccessi, che nelle presenti revolutioni così in generale, com'in particolare'.
18 Francesco Capecelatro, *Diario di Francesco Capecelatro: contenente la storia delle cose avvenute nel reame di Napoli negli anni 1647–1650*, ed. by Angelo Granito (Naples: G. Nobile, 1852), p. 27.
19 'De Abolitionibus Criminum XII', in Lorenzo Giustiniani, ed., *Nuova collezione delle prammatiche del Regno di Napoli* (Naples, 1803), I, p. 20: 'totale e perfetta quiete e pace di questa Città e Regno'.
20 Capecelatro, *Diario*, p. 202: 'che in nessun modo si possa parlare'.
21 Giuseppe Galasso, *Napoli spagnola dopo Masaniello: politica, cultura, società* (Florence: Sansoni, 1982), I, p. 5.
22 Ibid.
23 Aurelio Musi, *La rivolta di Masaniello nella scena politica barocca* (Naples: Guida, 2002), pp. 237–8.
24 Capecelatro, *Diario*, p. 146.
25 Giovanni Masi, *Altamura Farnesiana* (Bari: Cressati, 1959) and Gérard Delille, *Le maire et le prieur: Pouvoir central et pouvoir local en Méditerranée occidentale (XVe–XVIIIe siècle)* (Paris: EHESS, 2003).
26 ASN, Farnese, 2016.
27 ASN, Farnese, 2015.
28 Masi, *Altamura Farnesiana*, p. 110.
29 ASN, Farnese, 2016.
30 Ibid.
31 Ibid.
32 Ibid.
33 Ibid., letter of 23 August 1650.
34 Ibid.
35 Ibid.
36 Gio. Battista Biscozzo, 'Libro d'annali de successi accaduti nella Città di Nardò, notati da D. Gio: Battista Biscozzo di detta Città', *Rinascenza salentina*, 4 (1936), 7–44.
37 Ibid.

38 Ibid.
39 Ibid.
40 Galasso, *Napoli spagnola dopo Masaniello*, I, p. 9.
41 This claim is based on readings that suggest a general trend away from direct ties in many parts of Italy. For example, Irene Fosi argues that the '[n]obles' blatant and massive participation in banditry vanished, but their violence went on via the use of country thugs to do misdeeds and pursue vendettas against enemy lords, and to afflict the locals in countless ways', *Papal Justice: Subjects and Courts in the Papal State, 1500–1750* (Washington, DC: Catholic University Press of America, 2011), pp. 102–3.
42 For this history see Giuseppe Coniglio, *Il viceregno di Napoli nel sec. XVII: notizie sulla vita commercial e finanziaria secondo nuove ricerche negli archive italiani e spagnoli* (Rome: Edizioni di Storia e Letteratura, 1955), p. 281 and Maria Grazia Maiorini, *Il viceregno di Napoli: introduzione alla raccolta di documenti curata da Giuseppe Coniglio. Con indici* (Naples: Giannini, 1992), pp. 30, 52.
43 Niccola Palma, *Storia ecclesiastica e civile della regione più settentrionale del Regno di Napoli* (Teramo, 1832–36), III, p. 137.
44 ASN, Consiglio Collaterale, Affari Diversi, I, 105r.
45 'L'asprezza del suo governo e non esaperasse più le piaghe che poco prima erano state guarite'.
46 Galasso, *Napoli spagnola dopo Masaniello*, I, pp. 28–9.
47 Ibid., I, p. 8.
48 Biagio Aldimari, *Pragmaticae, edicta, decreta, regiaeque sanctiones Regni Neapolitani* (Naples, 1682): 'De Abolitionibus', XII, pp. 13–14: 'machinare diversi tradimenti … procurando per mezzi illeciti, e fuora della loro natural obbligazione l'inquiete, e sollevazion di questo Regno, conforme si è esperimentato per l'invasione fatta in esso dall'armata di Francia, sollecitata dalle vane speranze, e promesse di detti Ribelli, con molto pregiudizio al credito, e fedeltà, che sempre hanno tenuto, e tengono come vassalli di esso Regno; essendosi attualmente visto, che con varie invenzioni han preteso far molte novità per le provincie d'Apruzzo, per inquietar la pubblica, ed universal quiete, non solo di questo Regno, ma di tutti l'Italia'.
49 British Library, Add MS 20924, fols. 171r–174v: 'Stato della Giunta de Banditi formata dal Signor Conte di Castrillo sotto il 3 di Dicembre 1657'. The only use of this manuscript by another historian that I have found is in Salvo Mastellone, *Pensiero politico e vita culturale nel seconda metà del seicento* (Messina: Casa Editrice d'Anna, 1965), pp. 18–19.
50 This also makes understanding its history more complicated. Giovanni Muto has found traces of its existence from as early as 1560. But whether its existence or functions were constant is harder to establish. Giovanni Muto, 'Apparati finanziari e gestione della fiscalità nel Regno di Napoli dalla seconda metà del '500 alla crisi degli anni '20 del sec. XVII', in *La Fiscalité et ses implications sociales en Italie et en France aux XVIIe et XVIIIe siècle. Actes du colloque de Florence (5–6 décembre 1978)* (Rome: École Française de Rome, 1980), p. 126.

51 This 'warlike spirit' is taken from the title of *Il Genio Bellicoso di Napoli. Memorie istoriche d'alcuni Capitani Celebri Napolitan, c'han militato per la fede, per lo Rè, per la Patria nel secolo corrente* by Raffaele Maria Filamondo (Naples, 1694).
52 BL, Add Ms, 20924: 'per dar'calore al sbarco'.
53 'De Abolitionibus Criminum LXXXIV', in *Nuova collezion delle prammatiche*, I, p. 143.
54 Ibid.
55 BL, Add MS, 20924, fol. 171[r]: 'l'intentione, che haveva esso Duca d'impadronirsi del'Regno, dicendo che cossi l'era stato pronosticato, e oltre poi doveva esser'strascinato à furor di Popolo, del'che non si curava, purche fusse stato padrone del Regno'.
56 Ibid.: 'diversi capi di Banditi per il Regno'.
57 Ibid., fol. 171[v]: 'congressi secreti'.
58 Ibid., fol. 174[r].
59 Ibid.

Conclusion

Let us return to the case with which this book opened: the murder of Carlo Bartolotti, the Prince of Presicce. The case can now be seen through the interpretative lenses established in the body of this monograph. It demonstrates the unity of the themes explored: the relevance of the first half of the seventeenth century, culminating in the rebellion of 1647–48 in making private enmities more violent and more tightly held; the role of banditry in such actions as resource and refuge; the place of the legal system and especially its composition and indulgences; the emotions attended to revenge, most well catered to by the Jesuits; the complex political geographies of enmity and their intersection with municipal and feudal politics. The multiple assassination attempts in 1648 and 1649 further illustrate the disturbances of the period of attempted pacification after the revolt.

For a second concluding episode let us turn to another, less prominent murder in 1653. That is the death of Rutilio di Pinto in Candela near Foggia in 1653. Rutilio was a sub-deacon in Candela. One day his mother, as she testified to the *Audienza*, was working in her home when she heard Rutilio cry out for help. She looked out the window and she saw him fall to the ground. Three men stood over him and she saw one stab him with a knife. Her son died the next day, despite the attentions of two surgeons from a nearby city.[1]

Other witnesses talked of the aftermath within Rutilio's house; where many relatives gathered to cry and lament Rutilio's fate and where his mother wept and tore out her hair 'as all the other mothers do when their children die', one witness recalled.[2] While a trial was occurring in her land she wrote to the *Regia Audienza* and in the letter she wrote of the fear she had as a poor widow, against the 'potency' of those who had committed the crime; she felt that their pre-eminence in the town and power over the court of Candela meant that she would never achieve justice there. She recounted that they were day and night pressuring her to sign a remission.[3] This was a domineering faction who had been Rutilio's enemies for years.

This communal pressure and the influence they had over the officials of justice led her to avoid pursuing the offenders in the court of Candela. But in the laws of the Kingdom her status as a widow allowed her to seek first instance justice from the *Regia Audienza*.

But this recourse held no satisfaction for Rutilio's mother. As the *Audienza* gathered information on the event a fat packet of letters arrived in which many illustrious noblemen certified that the murderer had assisted the Crown in military service. In particular the provincial revolts of 1648, which were referred to as the 'wars of the Abruzzi'.[4] As such, the *Audienza* indulged his crime; notwithstanding that she had never given the remission of the parties to him. The offender's endorsement by nobles and past loyal service, in the wake of the general indulgences of Oñate, outweighed her claim as grieving relative. The empowerment that her status as widow and offended party gave her was contingent and could quickly be overridden by other factors.

Historians should attend to the ways in which vocabularies of hatred and pacification were used to represent social and political relations both within their towns and villages but also when communicating with state and ecclesiastical authorities. It underscored how the representation of these relationships was a central part of the interaction between centre and locality in Naples. Maladministration was understood to produce enmity. The languages of these emotional states were used in recourse to authorities. But it also stressed that the institutions of local power obscure much everyday peace-making that only comes to light in accidental ways. The ways in which enmities are described in the sources are evidence themselves of the mediation of power relations, inequalities and the micropolitics of communities.

Chapter 2 reconstructed the significance of the legal system and its political oversight in the experience of enmity and peace-making in the Kingdom. It showed that the legal instrument of the remission of the offended party was a very significant part of the social, emotional, and legal history of peace-making but also an institution that was exposed to numerous abuses. Moral and legal thought about offended parties was central to the practice of administration. Yet respect for offended parties was often easily overridden when other policy goals seemed more important. Moreover, legal arrangements that were intended to be in the favour of those whose family members had been killed were often instead exposed to extortion or pressure. There were numerous paradoxes, contradictions, and unintended consequences of the attempt to administer a plural legal system from the compound heart of a labyrinthine polity. A conclusion to be drawn is that, especially for the Kingdom of Naples, accounts of state monopolization of peace pacts abridge a more tortuous narrative that must recognize the recurring failures of delegated governance.

Chapter 4 traced how banditry was one of the most significant problems in early modern Naples. The social history of the Kingdom is deficient if outlaws are not considered as central characters. Banditry informed many of the understandings of enmity and of peace-making in early modern Naples. Both the life experiences of bandits and the policy tools aimed at punishing or pardoning them need to be understood. The prior lack of detailed study of banditry has led to a relative lack of understanding of its important role. The experience of 1647–48 shaped the character of banditry in the 1650s. It became more political as aristocratic resentment merged with international relations and the enmities of bandits. Violence rose in this period as local enmities fused with aristocratic conspiracies.

In Chapter 5 the Jesuit missions in southern Italy were studied. It was underscored in this chapter that enmity had its broadest purchase in civic disorder. It was these manifestations of hatred that the viceregal regime and the Jesuits aimed to resolve. This focus on the enmities of those who wielded some sort of authority points to the ways in which hating and reconciling were structured by power and authority. The Jesuits believed peace-making was accomplished through devotions that were understood to both affect the humours and therefore 'softened' hearts. The peace-making of the Jesuits reminds us of the significance of the memory of injuries given in communities. Rituals of peace were used to knit together divided communities. Accounts of grieving women and men being harassed into providing *remissioni* encourage an interpretation of these events as serving the powerful rather than the weak.

One contribution was in establishing the connections between enmity as a legal concept and enmity in practice in Naples. This looks at the discussion of 'enmity' in jurisprudence and juridical practice, both as evidence towards guilt but also how the notion was embedded in the process by which the Neapolitan state attempted to rule through justice. Local disputes were reflected, refracted, and distorted through jurisprudential languages of enmity. But the legal aspects of enmity were also central to how it was experienced as a relationship. The institution of the remission shaped the aftermaths of violent crimes. There were relationships between what happened to bereaved relatives and certain decisions made in the Collateral Council. These relationships were far from simple and peace pacts were not easy to grasp as tools of policy. It was more a case of unintended consequences unleashed when an indulgence was granted with the proviso that remissions be presented. A season of extortion was opened.

In direct relation to this then, this book has been a study of the ways governance was shaped by attempts to keep the Kingdom tranquil. The administration of criminal justice and good government were inseparable. Enmities were problems that could be addressed by political intervention or missions of the Jesuits. But the Spanish regime did not have tight control on the mechanisms of justice. The weakness of the viceregal regime in the face of the challenges of the rural world – feudal power, widespread banditry, inaccessible terrain – meant that viceroys tried to govern through surrendering the right to punish by offering very broad indulgences and regular pardons. Many of these policy options resulted in unintended consequences or the persecution of victims. The search for public quiet defined many of the decisions made by the viceroys in the seventeenth century. It was a fragmented and difficult search that created many painful ironies for southern Italians. Fundamentally this was because unlike other areas of Italy, such as Venice, a well-managed project of rural pacification was impossible in Naples.[5] The barrier was the feudal nobility. The dispatch of legates or other officials of royal justice was not a possible option. Indeed the representatives of royal justice in the provinces, the *presidi*, were drawn from the feudal aristocracy.

This book has argued that the political and legal history of the Kingdom must be seen as also a history of the emotions. Love, friendship, forgiveness, and hatred were integral parts of state and legal processes of peacemaking. The overlap between law and the emotions is clearly seen in the value that the Jesuits placed on the notarial recording of forgiveness and the variety of grief, resentment, and hatreds that fractured any southern Italian community. This history of offences, hatred, grief, and reconciliation is central to understanding the early modern Kingdom of Naples. Any of the themes and topics covered in this book could be studied with greater depth. Nonetheless, I hope the way in which this book ranges over these different topics is useful in itself, although deficient as a study of any individual topic. Demonstrating some of the connections and interrelations between local politics, banditry, criminal policy, ecclesiastical peace-making, and the mid-century disorder of the Kingdom has been a goal of this work.

Naples is well known as one example of an early modern European state with high levels of violence, weak state institutions, and a high level of elite (baronial) autonomy. It is by no means unique in having many of these characteristics, the Papal States in particular had very similar challenges, but the combination of a non-resident monarch, the persistence (and revitalization) of feudal control over institutions of justice, and the Spanish regime's interest in fiscal exploitation above 'buon governo' led to an absence of effective projects of pacification or the reliable extension of justice to all subjects of the Crown for much of this period. No other part of Italy rivalled Naples in the extent and depth of the domination of feudal rule. But the lack of striking efficacy in these projects does not mean they were totally absent or had no effects. Indeed, their weak, partial, corrupted, and undermined aspects have been the explicit focus of this monograph. The always compromised search after public order, and the limited ways in which it was achieved, along with the variety of sorts of compromises that undermined the vaunted aims of authorities, created a world of social interactions, the richness of which deserve to be attributed a significance beyond a limited account of failure and absence.

Notes

1 ASL, Regia Udienza, Processi Penali, busta 1, fasc. 5, fols. 33^r–34^v.
2 Ibid., fol. 40^r.
3 Ibid. fol. 42^r.
4 Ibid., fol. 95r.
5 Compare to the Venetian case outlined by Edward Muir, 'The Sources of Civil Society in Italy', *Journal of Interdisciplinary History*, 29 (1999), 379–406 (p. 392).

Bibliography

Printed primary sources (pre-1800)

Albergati, Fabio, *Del modo di ridurre a pace le inimicitie private* (Bergamo, 1587)
Aldimari, Biagio, *Pragmaticae, edicta, decreta, regiaeque sanctiones Regni Neapolitani* (Naples, 1682)
Aldimari, Tobia, *Raccolta di varie notitie historiche non meno appartenenti all'historia del Summonte che curiose* (Naples, 1675)
Amatore, Diego, *Napoli sollevata narratione degli accidenti occorsi in detta Città dalli 7. Luglio 1647 sino li 20. Marzo 1648* (Bologna, 1650)
Bagnati, Simone, *Vita del servo di Dio P. Francesco di Geronimo della Compagnia di Gesu* (Naples, 1705)
Baiardi, Giovanni Battista, *Praticam criminalem* (Frankfurt, 1622)
Baronio, Francesco, *De effectibus inimicitiae, seu de inimicitia eiusque causis, et effectibus* (Palermo, 1656)
—— *De effectibus inimicitiae, tomus secundus* (Palermo, 1658)
Battaglini, Marco, *Annali del sacerdozio e dell'imperio intorno all'intero secolo decimosettimo di nostra salute* (Venice, 1701)
Bethel, Slingsby, *The Interest of the Princes and States of Europe* (London, 1694)
Boccalini, Traiano, *La bilancia politica di tutte le opera di Traiano Boccalini parte prima dove si tratta delle osservazioni politiche sopra I sei Libri degli Annali di Cornelio Tacito* (Castellana, 1678)
Caccini, Giulio, *Le nuove musiche* (Florence, 1602)
Campanile, Giuseppe, *Notizie di Nobiltà* (Naples, 1672)
Capaccio, Giulio Cesare, *Il Forastiero. Dialogi di Giulio Cesare Capaccio* (Naples, 1634)
Carafa, Gregorio, *De monomachia seu duello opus theologico-morale* (Naples, 1647)
Caravita, Prospero, *Commentaria super ritibus Magna Curiae Vicariae Regni Neapolis* (Naples, 1601)
Cavalcanti, Bartolomeo, *La Retorica* (Venice, 1559)
Celano, Carlo, *L'ardito vergognoso* (Naples, 1676)
—— *Sopra l'ingannator cade l'inganno* (Naples, 1696)
Chioccarello, Bartolomeo, *Archivio della Reggia Giurisdizione del Regno di Napoli* (Venice, 1721)
Costacciaro, Lodovico Carbone de, *De pacificatione et dilectione inimicorum iniuriarumque remissione* (Florence, 1583)
De Gaeta, Gaspar Cervantes, *Constitutioni Sinodali della Chiesa Metropolitana di Salerno* (Rome, 1568)

De Jorio, Francesco, *Introduzione allo studio delle prammatiche del Regno di Napoli* (Naples, 1777)
De Lellis, Carlo and Domenico Confuorto, *Discorsi Postumi di alcune poche nobili famiglie con l'Annotationi in esse, e Supplimento di altri Discorsi Genealogici di Famiglie Nobili della Città, e Regno di Napoli* (Naples, 1701)
De Luca, Giovanni Battista, *Il principe cristiano pratico di Gio: Battista de Luca. Abbozzato nell'ozio Tusculano Autunnale del 1675. Accresciuto, e ridotto a diversa forma ne'spazij estivi, avanzati alle occupazioni del Quirinale nel 1679* (Rome, 1680)
De Santis, Tommaso, *Historia del tumulto di Napoli* (Leiden, 1652)
Della Porta, Giambattista, *La fisionomia dell'huomo et la celeste* (Venice, 1652)
Delli statuti criminali di Genova (Genoa, 1590)
Dizionario delle leggi del Regno di Napoli (Naples, 1788)
Doria, Paolo Mattia, *Massime del governo spagnolo a Napoli*, ed. by Vittorio Conti (Naples: Guida, 1973)
────── *Relazione dello stato politico, economico e civile del Regno di Napoli nel tempo ch'è stato governato da i Spagnuoli* (Naples, 1707)
Ercolani, Francesco *De cautione de non offendendo* (Venice, 1569)
Farinacci, Prospero, *Praxis et theoricae criminalis* (Frankfurt, 1597)
Filamondo, Raffaele Maria, *Il Genio Bellicoso di Napoli. Memorie istoriche d'alcuni Capitani Celebri Napolitani, c'han militato per la fede, per lo Rè, per la Patria nel secolo corrente* (Naples, 1691)
Florio, John, *Queen Anna's New World of Words, or Dictionarie of the Italian and English tongues* (London, 1611)
Follerio, Pietro, *Canonica criminalis praxis* (Venice, 1583)
────── *Practica criminalis* (Leiden, 1556)
Gatta, Diego, *Regali Dispacci nelli quali si contengono le Sovrane Determinazioni de'Punti Generali o che servono di norma ad altri simili casi nel Regno di Napoli* (Naples, 1776)
Giannone, Pietro, *Istoria Civile del Regno di Napoli* (Haya, 1753)
Giraffi, Alessandro, *Le rivolutioni di Napoli* (Venice, 1648)
Giustiniani, Lorenzo, *Dizionario Geografico-ragionato del Regno Di Napoli* (Naples, 1797)
Granata, Francesco, *Storia civile della fedelissima città di Capua* (Naples, 1752)
Grimaldi, Ginesio, *Istoria delle leggi e magistrati del Regno di Napoli, continuata da Ginesio Grimaldi* (Naples, 1771)
Grimaldi, Gregorio, *Istoria delle leggi e magistrati del Regno di Napoli* (Naples, 1749)
Guazzini, Sebastiano, *Tractatus de pace, treuga, verbo dato alicui principi, vel alteri persone nobili, & de cautione de non offendendo* (Rome, 1610)
Guicciardini, Francesco, *La historia d'Italia* (Geneva, 1636)
Howell, James, *Epistolae Ho-Elianae: Familiar Letters Domestic and Forren; Divided into sundry SECTIONS, Partly Historicall, Politicall, Philosophicall upon Emergent Occasions* (London, 1655)
Lamento, et morte di Benedetto Mangone Capo di Banditi, nel Regno di Napoli. Con li crudelissimi assassinamenti, che lui faceva in Campagna. Come fu pigliato in Alessandria dalla Paglia vestito da Pellegrino, e condotto a Napoli, dove fu attanagliato, & arrotato (Florence, 1599)
Les memoires de feu Monsieur le Duc de Guise (Paris, 1668)
Lithgow, William, *Nineteen Years Travels Through the Most Eminent Places in the Habitable World* (London, 1682)

Machiavelli, Niccolò, *Florentine Histories*, trans. by Laura F. Banfield and Harvey C. Mansfield Jr. (Princeton: Princeton University Press, 1990)
Mancino, Geronimo, *Utili instruttioni et documenti per qualsivoglia persona che ha da eligere officiali circa il regimento de populi et anco per officiali che seranno eletti, et università da quelli gubernate con li Riti della Vicaria, e Pragmatiche Vulgari* (Naples, 1590)
Marciano, Giovanni, *Memorie historiche della Congregatione dell'Oratorio* (Naples, 1693)
Marini, Biagio, *Affetti musicali* (Venice, 1618)
Mazzella, Scipione, *Descrittione del Regno di Napoli* (Naples, 1601)
Muratori, Ludovico Antonio, *Introduzione alle paci private* (Modena, 1708)
Nova situatione de pagamenti fiscali de carlini 42 à foco delle Provincie del Regno di Napoli, & Adohi de Baroni, e Feudatarij dal primo di Gennaro 1669 avanti (Naples, 1670)
Novario, Giovanni Maria, *Novissimae decisiones civiles, criminales & canonicae: tam regii tribunalis audientiae provinciarum Capitanate, Apuleae, & Comitatus Mollisij Regni Neapolis, quam causarum delegatrum* (Geneva, 1637)
—— *Tractatus de vassallorum gravaminibus* (Geneva, 1686)
Paolacci, Domenico, *Pensieri Predicabili sopra tutti gl'evangelii* (Venice, 1641)
Paolucci, Scipione, *Missioni de Padri della Compagnia di Giesu nel Regno di Napoli* (Naples, 1651)
Parrino, Domenico Antonio, *Compendio istorico, o sian memorie delle notizie più vere e cose più notabili, e degne da sapersi, accadute nella felicissima entrata delle sempre gloriose Truppe Cesaree nel Regno, ed in questa Città di Napoli* (Naples, 1708)
—— *Teatro eroico, e politico de'governi de'vicerè del Regno di Napoli* (Naples, 1694)
Privilegii et capitoli con altre gratie concesse alla fidelissima Città di Napoli, & Regno per li Serenissimi Rì di Casa de Aragona. Confirmati, & di nuovo concessi per la Maestà Cesarea dell'Imperator Carlo V et Re Filippo Nostro Signore. Con tutte le altre Gratie concesse per tutto questo presente Anno MDLXXXVII. Con nuove addizioni, & la tavola delle cose notabili e di nuovo ristampati con le nuove Gratie, e Privilegii conceduti e confirmati dalla Sacra Cesarea et Cattolica Maesta di Carlo VI Imperadore sino all'anno 1720 (Milan, 1720)
Privilegii et capitoli con altre gratie concesse alla Fidelissima Città di Napoli, & Regno per li Serenissimi Rì di Casa de Aragona. Confirmati, & di nuovo concessi per la Maestà Cesarea dell'Imperator Carlo V et Re Filippo Nostro Signore con tutte le altre gratie concesse per tutto questo presente Anno MDLXXXVII (Venice, 1588)
Ray, John, *Travels Through the Low-Countries, Germany, Italy, France with curious observations natural, topographical, moral, physiological* (London, 1738)
Reassunto de servitii ottenuti nel felicissimo Governo dell'Eccellentissimo Sinor Marchese de los Velez (Naples, 1682)
Sandys, George, *A Relation of a Journey Begun Anno Domini 1610* (London, 1615)
Savelli, Marco Antonio, *Pratica universale del Dottor Marc'Antonio Savelli* (Parma, 1633)
Schinosi, Francesco, *L'Istoria della Compagnia di Giesu, Appartenente al Regno di Napoli* (Naples, 1711), II.

Scialoya, Angelo, *Praxis Foriudicatoria, seu de modo procedendi in Regno Neapolitano ad sententiam foriudicationis contra reum absentum in eius contumacia vigore Constitutionis Regni poenam eorum* (Naples, 1645)
Segneri, Paolo, *Il confessore istruito* (Venice, 1672)
—— *Il parrocco istruito, opera in cui si dimostra à qualsisia Curato novella il debito, che lo strigne, e la via da tenersi nell'adempirlo* (Naples, 1693)
Segni, Giovan Battista, *Trattato sopra la carestia e la fame* (Bologna, 1602)
Serrao, Giacinto, *Direttorio e prontuario utilissimo per l'essercitio della santa missione* (Naples, 1669)
Siri, Vittorio, *Il Mercurio overo Historia de'correnti tempi* (Casale, 1668)
Summonte, Giovanni Antonio, *Dell'historia della citta, e regno di Napoli* (Naples, 1675)
Tarcagnota, Giovanni, *Del sito, et lodi della città di Napoli con una breve historia de gli re suoi, e delle cose piu degne altrove ne'medesimi tempi avenute di Giovanni Tarchagnota di Gaeta* (Naples, 1566)
Tomani, Buoso, *Della Compagnia de'Tagliacantoni, descrittione universale. Nella quale à pieno si scuopre l'origine, & progresso della vita loro* (Venice, 1601)
Tontoli, Gabriele, *Il Mas'Aniello, overo discorsi narrative la Sollevatione di Napoli* (Naples, 1648)
Toppi, Nicolò, *De origine ominium tribunalium nunc in Castro Capuano fidelissimae civitatis Neapolis existentitum* (Naples, 1655–66)
—— *Biblioteca napoletana, et apparato a gli huomini illustri in lettere* (Naples, 1678)
Torelli, Carlo, *Lo splendore della nobiltà napoletana, ascritta ne'cinque seggi* (Naples, 1678)
Torriano, Giovanni, *The Italian Reviv'd* (London, 1673)
Valmarana, Giulio, *Modo del far pace in via calvaresca e christiana per sodisfattion di parole, nelle ingiurie frà privati* (Vincenza, 1619)
Vannozzi, Bonifazio, *Della suppellettile degli avvertimenti politici, morali, et christiani* (Bologna, 1610)
Varius, Domenicus Alfenus, ed., *Pragmaticae, edicta, decreta, interdicta, regiaeque sanctiones Regni Neapolitani* (Naples, 1772)
Wright, Thomas, *Passions of the Minde in Generall* (London, 1604)

Printed primary sources (post-1800)

Ajello, Raffaele, *Una società anomala: il programma e la sconfitta della nobiltà napoletana in due memoriali cinquecenteschi* (Naples: Edizioni scientifiche italiane, 1996)
Albèri, Eugenio, ed., *Le relazioni degli ambasciatori veneti al senato* (Florence, 1863)
Basile, Giambattista, *Giambattista Basile's The Tale of Tales, or Entertainment for Little Ones*, ed. and trans. by Nancy L. Canepa (Detroit: Wayne State University Press, 2007)
Briganti, Tommaso, ed., *Pratica criminale raccolta dal dottor Tommaso Briganti* (Naples, 1842)
Bulifon, Antonio, *Giornali di Napoli dal MDXLVII al MDCCVI*, ed. by Nino Cortese, 2 vols. (Naples: Società napoletana di storia patria, 1932)
Bulletino delle leggi del Regno di Napoli (Naples, 1813)

Campanella, Tommaso, *Del senso delle cose e della magia* (Soveria Mannelli: Rubbettino, 2003)
—— *Opere di Tommaso Campanella*, ed. by Alessandro d'Ancona (Turin: Cugini Pomba, 1854)
Capecelatro, Francesco, *Degli annali della Città di Napoli (1631–1640)* (Naples: Tipografia di Reale, 1849)
—— *Diario di Francesco Capecelatro: contenente la storia delle cose avvenute nel reame di Napoli negli anni 1647–1650*, ed. by Angelo Granito (Naples: G. Nobile, 1852)
Confuorto, Domenico, *Giornali di Napoli dal MDCLXXIX al MDCIC*, 2 vols. (Naples: Società napoletana di storia patria, 1930–31)
Covino, Luca, *Baroni del 'buon governo': istruzioni della nobiltà feudale nel Mezzogiorno moderno* (Naples: Liguori, 2004)
D'Onofrio, Vincenzo [Innocenzo Fuidoro], *Giornali di Napoli dal MDCLX al MDCLXXX*, ed. by Franco Schlitzer, Antonio Padula, and Vittoria Omodeo, 3 vols. (Naples: Società napoletana di storia patria, 1934–39)
De Capua, Donato Antonio, *Cronaca inedita della famiglia Labini in Bitonto* (Bitonto: Liantonion, 1992)
De Marino, Virgilio, *Apprezzo della città di Gravina, trascrizione e note* (Gravina: Fondazione Ettore Pomarici Santomasi, 1979)
De Rosa, Gabriele, ed., *Clero e mondo rurale nel sinodo di Policastro del 1633* (Venosa: Edizioni Osanna Venosa, 1987)
Del Tufo, Giovan Battista, *Ritratto o modello delle grandezze, delitie et maraviglie della nobilissima Città di Napoli* (Naples: Agar, 1959)
Di Cicco, Pasquale, 'Una Cronaca Bovinese del Seicento', La Capitanata (1986), 53–91
—— *Libro Rosso di Foggia* (Foggia: Amministrazione Provinciale di Capitanata, 1965)
Evelyn, John, *Diary and Correspondence of John Evelyn F.R.S.*, vol I (London: George Bell and Sons, 1878),
Firpo, Luigi, *Il supplizio di Tommaso Campanella* (Rome: Salerno Editrice, 1985)
Garcia Garcia, Bernardo Jose, ed., *Una relazione vicereale sul governo del Regno di Napoli agli inizi del '600* (Naples: Bibliopolis, 1993)
Giustiniani, Lorenzo, ed., *Nuova collezione delle prammatiche del Regno di Napoli*, 15 vols. (Naples, 1803–08)
Keppel Craven, Richard, *Excursions in the Abruzzi and Northern Provinces of Naples* (London, 1838)
Le Relazioni degli Ambasciatori Veneti al Senato, ed. by Eugenio Alberì (Florence: Società Editrice Fiorentina, 1853)
Mastrini, Raffaele, *Dizionario geografico-storico-civile del Regno delle Due Sicilie* (Naples, 1838)
Moroni, Gaetano, *Dizionario di erudizione storico-ecclesiastica da S. Pietro sino ai nostri* (Venice: Tipografia Emiliana, 1854)
Palermo, Francesco, ed., *Narrazioni e documenti sulla storia del Regno di Napoli dall'anno 1522 al 1667* (Florence: Gio. Pietro Vieusseux, 1846)
Ravenna, Bartolomeo, *Memorie istoriche della città di Gallipoli* (Naples, 1836)
Romano, Marcello, *Gli apprezzi e le plate dell'Archivio Caracciolo di Torella come fonte per la ricostruzione del paesaggio e della 'forma Urbis' medievali degli insediamenti del Vulture* (Potenza: Olita, 2004)

Secondary sources

Ajello, Raffaele, *Il problema della riforma giudiziaria e legislativa nel Regno di Napoli durante la prima metà del secolo XVIII* (Napoli: Jovene, 1961)

Amabile, Luigi, *Fra Tommaso Campanella ne'castelli di Napoli, in Roma ed in Parigi* (Naples: Cav. Antonio Morano, 1887)

Ambron, Daniela, 'Il banditismo nel Regno di Napoli alla fine del XVII secolo tra istituzioni regie e protezioni baronali', in *Banditismi mediterranei, secoli XVI–XVII*, ed. by Francesco Manconi (Rome: Carocci, 2003), pp. 379–400

—— 'Le carceri regie del Regno di Napoli tra capital e province (XVII–XVIII secolo)', in *Carceri, carcerieri, carcerati. Dall'antico regime all'Ottocento*, ed. by Livio Antonielli (Soveria Mannell: Rubbettino, 2006), pp. 145–64

Angelozzi, Giancarlo and Cesarina Casanova, *La nobiltà disciplinata: violenza nobiliare, procedure di giustizia e scienza cavalleresca a Bologna nel XVII secolo* (Bologna: CLUEB, 2003)

—— *La giustizia criminale in una città di antico regime. Il tribunale del Torrone di Bologna (sec. XVI–XVII)* (Bologna: CLUEB, 2007)

Antichi, Valerio, 'Giustizia consuetudinaria e giustizia d'apparato nello Stato pontificio', in *Stringere la pace: teorie e pratiche della conciliazione nell'Europa moderna (secoli XV–XVIII)*, ed. by Paolo Broggio and Maria Pia Paoli (Rome: Viella, 2011), pp. 229–75

Arena, Domenico, 'Istoria delli disturbi e Revolutioni accaduti nella Città di Cosenza e Provincia nelli anni 1647 e 1648', ed. by Giuseppe de Blasi, *ASPN*, 3 (1878), 255–90, 425–69, 646–76, and 4 (1879), 3–32

Astarita, Tommaso, *The Continuity of Feudal Power: The Caracciolo di Brienza in Spanish Naples* (Cambridge: Cambridge University Press, 1992)

—— *Village Justice: Community, Family, and Popular Culture in Early Modern Italy* (Baltimore: Johns Hopkins University Press, 1999)

—— *Between Salt Water and Holy Water: A History of Southern Italy* (New York: W. W. Norton, 2006)

Barletta, Laura, *La regolata licenza: il carnevale a Napoli* (Messina: G. D'Anna, 1978)

Barnett, Gregory, 'Form and Gesture: Canzona, Sonata and Concerto', in *The Cambridge History of Seventeenth-Century Music*, ed. by Tim Carter and John Butt (Cambridge: Cambridge University Press, 2005), pp. 479–532

Bartlett, Robert, '"Mortal Enmities": The Legal Aspect of Hostility in the Middle Ages', in *Feud, Violence and Practice: Essays in Medieval Studies*, ed. by Tracey Billado and Belle Tuten (Farnham: Ashgate, 2010), pp. 197–212

Bellabarba, Marco, *La giustizia ai confini: Il principato vescovile di Trento agli inizi dell'età moderna* (Bologna: Il Mulino, 1996)

—— 'Pace pubblica e pace privata: linguaggi e istituzioni processuali nell'Italia moderna', in *Criminalità e giustizia in Germania e in Italia: pratiche giudiziarie e linguaggi giuridici tra tardo medioevo e prima età moderna/Kriminalität und Justiz in Deutschland und Italien: Rechtspraktiken und gerichtliche Diskurse in Spätmittelalter und Früher Neuzeit*, ed. by Marco Bellabarba, Andrea Zorzi, and Gerd Schwerhoff (Bologna: Il Mulino, 2001), pp. 189–213

—— *La giustizia nell'Italia moderna: XVI–XVIII secolo* (Rome: Laterza, 2008)

Beltrani, Giovanni, 'Lorenzo Valerii, tipografo romano in Puglia durante il sec. XVII', *Rassegna pugliese*, 9 (1892), 240–9, 271–81, 365–76

Beneduce, Sabrina, 'Inimicizia capitale. La ricusazione del giudice nel Sacro Regio Consiglio (1601–1701)' (unpublished Laurea thesis, Università degli Studi di Napoli Federico II, 1992)

Benigno, Francesco, 'Aristocrazia e Stato in Sicilia nell'epoca di Filippo II', in *Signori, patrizi, cavalieri: in Italia centro-meridionale nell'Età moderna*, ed. by Maria Antonietta Visceglia (Rome: Laterza, 1992), pp. 76–93

Biscozzo, Gio. Battista, 'Libro d'annali de successi accaduti nella Città di Nardò, notati da D. Gio: Battista Biscozzo di detta Città', *Rinascenza salentina*, 4 (1936), 7–44

Black, Christopher, *Early Modern Italy: A Social History* (London: Routledge, 2001)

Bock, Gisela, *Thomas Campanella. Politisches Interesse und philosophische Spekulation* (Tübingen: Niemeyer, 1974)

Bossy, John, 'The Social History of Confession in the Age of the Reformation', *Transactions of the Royal History Society*, 25 (1975), 21–38

―――― 'Postscript', in *Dispute and Settlements: Law and Human Relations in the West*, ed. by John Bossy (Cambridge: Cambridge University Press, 1983), pp. 287–94

―――― 'The Social Miracle' in his *Christianity in the West, 1400–1700* (Oxford: Oxford University Press, 1985)

―――― *Peace in the Post-Reformation* (Cambridge: Cambridge University Press, 1998)

Brancaccio, Giovanni, *'Nazione genovese': consoli e colonia nella Napoli moderna* (Naples: Guida, 2001)

―――― *Il Molise medievale e moderno: storia di uno spazio regionale* (Naples: Edizioni scientifiche italiane, 2005)

Braudel, Fernand, *The Mediterranean and the Mediterranean World in the Age of Philip II*, 2 vols. (New York: Fontana, 1975)

Broggio, Paolo, 'Linguaggio religioso e disciplinamento nobiliare: Il "modo di ridurre a pace l'inimicitie private" nella trattatistica di età barocca', in *I linguaggi del potere: politica e religione nell'età barocca*, ed. by Francesca Cantù (Rome: Viella, 2009), pp. 275–317.

Brudholm, Thomas, *Resentment's Virtue: Jean Amery and the Refusal to Forgive* (Philadelphia: Temple University Press, 2008)

Burke, Peter, 'The Virgin of the Carmine and the Revolt of Masaniello', *Past & Present*, 99 (1983), 3–21

Caeser, Mathieu, ed., *Factional Struggles: Divided Elites in European Cities and Courts (1400–1750)* (Leiden: Brill, 2017)

Calabria, Antonio *The Cost of Empire: The Finances of the Kingdom of Naples in the Time of Spanish Rule* (Cambridge: Cambridge University Press, 1991)

―――― 'The South Pays for the North: Financing the Thirty Years' War from Naples, 1622–1644', *Essays in Economic & Business History*, 20 (2002), 1–20

―――― and John A. Marino, eds., *Good Government in Spanish Naples* (New York: Peter Lang, 1990)

Campennì, Francesco, *La patria e il sangue: Città, patriziati e potere nella Calabria moderna* (Manduria: Lacaita, 2004)

Cancila, Rosella, ' "Per la retta amministratione della giustitia": la giustizia dei baroni nella Sicilia moderna', *Mediterranea Ricerche storiche*, 16 (2009), 315–52

Canosa, Romano and Isabella Colonnello, *Storia del carcere in Italia dalla fine del Cinquecento all'Unità* (Rome: Sapere 2000, 1984)

Carraway, Joanna, 'Contumacy, Defense Strategy, and Criminal Law in Late Medieval Italy', *Law and History Review*, 29 (2011), 99–132

Carroll, Stuart, 'The Peace in the Feud in Sixteenth and Seventeenth-Century France', *Past & Present*, 178 (2003), 74–115

—— *Blood and Violence in Early Modern France* (Oxford: Oxford University Press, 2006)

—— 'Peace-making in Early Modern Europe: Towards a Comparative History', in *Stringere la pace: teorie e pratiche della conciliazione nell'Europa moderna (secoli XV–XVIII)*, ed. by Paolo Broggio and Maria Pia Paoli (Rome: Viella, 2011), pp. 75–92

—— 'The Rights of Violence', *Past and Present*, 214 (2012; supplement 7), 127–62

—— 'Revenge and Reconciliation in Early Modern Italy', *Past and Present* 233.1 (2016), 101–42

—— *Enmity and Violence in Early Modern Europe* (Cambridge: Cambridge University Press, 2023)

Casey, James, 'Bandos y bandidos en la Valencia moderna', in *Homenatge al doctor Sebastià García Martinez* (Valencia: Universitat de València, 1988), I, pp. 407–422

Castiglione, Caroline, 'Adversarial Literacy: How Peasant Politics Influenced Noble Governing of the Roman Countryside during the Early Modern Period', *The American Historical Review*, 109 (2004), 783–804

—— *Patrons and Adversaries: Nobles and Villagers in Italian Politics, 1640–1760* (Oxford: Oxford University Press, 2005)

Cecchi, Dante, 'Sull'istituto della pax: dalle costituzioni Egidiane agli inizi del secolo XIX nella Marca di Ancona', *Studi maceratesi*, 3 (1968), 103–62

Cecere, Domenico, Chiara De Caprio, Lorenza Gianfresco, and Pasquale Palmieri, *Disaster Narratives in Early Modern Naples: Politics, Communication and Culture* (Rome: Viella, 2018)

Cernigliaro, Aurelio, *Sovranità e feudo nel Regno di Napoli, 1505–1557* (Naples: Jovene, 1983)

Chiabò, Mario and Federico Doglio, eds., *I Gesuiti e i primordi del teatro barocco in Europa* (Rome: Centro Studi sul Teatro Medioevale e Rinascimentale, 1995)

Chittolini, Giorgio, 'The "Private", the "Public", the State', in *The Origins of the State in Italy, 1300–1600*, ed. by Julius Kirshner (Chicago: University of Chicago Press, 1995), pp. 34–61

Christian, William A., 'Provoked Religious Weeping in Early Modern Spain', in *Religious Organization and Religious Experience*, ed. by John Davis (London: Academic Press, 1982), pp. 97–114

Cocco, Sean, *Watching Vesuvius: A History of Science and Culture in Early Modern Italy* (Chicago: University of Chicago Press, 2013)

Cohen, Thomas, *Love and Death in Renaissance Italy* (Chicago: University of Chicago Press, 2004)

Colapietra, Raffaele, *Vita pubblica e classi politiche del viceregno napoletano (1656–1734)* (Rome: Edizioni di storia e letteratura, 1961)

—— 'Il baronaggio napoletano e la sua scelta spagnola: il "Gran Pescara"', *ASPN*, 107 (1989), 7–71

Coniglio, Giuseppe, *Il viceregno di Napoli nel sec. XVII: notizie sulla vita commercial e finanziaria secondo nuove ricerche negli archive italiani e spagnoli* (Rome: Edizioni di Storia e Letteratura, 1955)

—— *I vicerè spagnoli di Napoli* (Naples: Fausto Fiorentino, 1967)

Contigliozzi, Domenico, ed., *Calendario d'Oro* (Rome, 1899)
Corcione, Marco, *Modelli Processuali nell'Antico Regime: La giustizia penale nel tribunale di Campagna di Nevano* (Frattamaggiore: Istituto di Studi Atellani, 2002)
Covino, Luca, 'Le carceri baronali del Regno di Napoli nel Settecento', in *Carceri, carcerieri, carcerati. Dall'antico regime all'Ottocento*, ed. by Livio Antonielli (Soveria Mannell: Rubbettino, 2006), pp. 165–94
Croce, Benedetto, 'Duelli nel seicento', *ASPN*, 20 (1895), 543–58
—— 'Il tipo del napoletano nella commedia' in his *Saggi sulla letteratura italiana del seicento* (Bari: Laterza, 1911), pp. 262–314
—— *Montenerodomo: storia di un comune e di due famiglie* (Bari: Laterza, 1919)
—— *Un paradiso abitato da diavoli* (Naples: Adelphi, 2006)
D'Agostino, Guido, *La capitale ambigua: Napoli dal 1458 al 1580* (Naples: Guida, 1979)
—— *Parlamento e società nel Regno di Napoli: secoli XV–XVII* (Naples: Guida, 1979)
—— 'Napoli capitale', in *Storia del Mezzogiorno*, ed. by Giuseppe Galasso and Guido d'Agostino (Rome: Editalia, 1994), pp. 15–94
—— *L'ultimo parlamento generale del regno di Napoli nell'età spagnolo* (Naples: La Valle del Tempo, 2022)
d'Alessio, Silvana, *Masaniello: The Life and Afterlife of a Neapolitan Revolutionary* (Amsterdam: Amsterdam University Press, 2023)
Dandelet, Thomas James, *Spanish Rome, 1500–1700* (New Haven: Yale University Press, 2001)
Danker, Uwe, 'Bandits and the State: Robbers and the Authorities in the Holy Roman Empire in the Late Seventeenth and Early Eighteenth Centuries,' in *The German Underworld: Deviants and Outcasts in German History*, ed. by Richard J. Evans (London: Routledge, 1988), pp. 75–107
De Simoni, Alberto, *Del furto e sua pena* (Florence, 1813)
De Waele, Michel, 'Un Modèle de clémence: le Duc d'Albe, lieutenant-gouverneur des Pays-Bas, 1567–1573', *Cahiers d'histoire: la Revue du département d'histoire de l'Université de Montréal*, 16 (1996), 21–32
Dedola, Marco, ' "Tener Pistoia con le parti": Governo fiorentino e fazioni pistoiesi all'inizio del '500', *Ricerche storiche*, 22 (1992), 239–59
Del Bagno, Ileana, 'Reintegrazione nei Seggi napoletani e dialettica degli "status" ', *ASPN*, 102 (1984), 189–204
Del Vasto, Valeria, *Baroni nel tempo: i Tocco di Montemiletto dal XVI al XVIII secolo* (Naples: Edizioni scientifiche italiane, 1995)
Delille, Gérard *Famiglia e proprietà nel Regno di Napoli, XV–XIX secolo* (Turin: Einaudi, 1988)
—— *La maire et le prieur: Pouvoir central et pouvoir local en Méditerranée occidentale (XVe–XVIIIe siècle)* (Paris: EHESS, 2003)
—— *Famiglia e potere locale: una prospettiva mediterranea* (Bari: Edipuglia, 2011)
Dessì, Rosa Maria, 'Pratiques de la parole de paix dans l'historie de l'Italie urbaine', in *Prêcher la paix et discipliner la société: Italie, France, Angleterre (XIIIe–XVe siècle)*, ed. by Rosa Maria Dessì (Turnhout: Brepols, 2005), pp. 245–78
Di Zio, Tiziana, 'Il tribunale criminale di Bologna nel sec. XVI', *Archivi per la storia*, 1–2 (1991), 125–36
Dodds Pennock, Caroline, Robert Antony, and Stuart Carroll, eds., *The Cambridge World History of Violence: Volume III 1500–1800CE* (Cambridge: Cambridge University Press, 2020)

Donati, Claudio, 'Scipione Maffei e la "Scienza chiamata cavalleresca": saggio sull'ideologia nobiliare al principio del settecento', *Rivista storica Italiana*, 90 (1978), 30–7

Donvito, Luigi and Bruno Pellegrino, *L'organizazzione ecclesiastica degli Abruzzi, Molise e della Basilicata nell'età post-tridentina* (Florence: Sansoni, 1973)

Douglass, William 'The Joint Family Household in Eighteenth Century Southern Italian Society (Molise)', in *The Family in Italy from Antiquity to the Present*, ed. by David Kertzer and Richard Saller (New Haven: Yale University Press, 1991), pp. 286–303

Ebner, Pietro, *Chiesa, baroni e popolo nel Cilento* (Rome: Edizioni di storia e letteratura, 1982)

——— *Storia di un feudo del Mezzogiorno: La Baronia di Novi* (Rome: Edizioni di Storia e Letteratura, 2004)

Edelmayer, Friedrich, 'Delincuencia nobiliaria en un territorio de frontera: la Carniola en la segunda mitad del siglo XVI', in *Banditismi mediterranei, secoli XVI–XVII*, ed. by Francesco Manconi (Rome: Carocci, 2003), pp. 359–67

Edigati, Daniele, 'La pace nel processo criminale: il caso toscano in età moderna', in *Stringere la pace: teorie e pratiche della conciliazione nell'Europa moderna (secoli XV–XVIII)*, ed. by Paolo Broggio and Maria Pia Paoli (Rome: Viella, 2011), pp. 369–410

Eisner, Manuel, 'Modernization, Self-Control and Lethal Violence: The Long-Term Dynamics of European Homicide Rates in Theoretical Perspective', *British Journal of Criminology*, 41 (2001), 618–38

Elliott, John, 'Reform and Revolution in the Early Modern Mezzogiorno', *Past & Present*, 224 (2014), 283–96

Epstein, David F., *Personal Enmity in Roman Politics, 218–43 BC* (London: Croom Helm, 1987)

Erspamer, Francesco, *La biblioteca di Don Ferrante: duello e onore nella cultura del cinquecento* (Rome: Bulzoni, 1982)

Fabris, Dinko, *Music in Seventeenth-Century Naples: Francesco Provenzale (1624–1704)* (Farnham: Ashgate, 2007)

Faggion, Lucien, 'La pacificazione e il notaio nel vicariato di Valdagno nel secondo Cinquecento', *Acta histriae*, 21 (2013), 93–106

Ferrario, Giulio, *Il costume antico e moderno* (Florence: Vincenzo Batelli, 1832)

Fiorilli, Sonia, 'Poteri, economia e stili di vita di una famiglia feudale. Il caso di Sinforosa Mastrogiudice marchesa di Pietracatella (1675–1743)' (unpublished doctoral thesis, Università degli Studi del Molise, 2010)

Forclaz, Betrand, 'Local Conflicts and Political Authorities in the Papal State in the Second Half of the Seventeenth Century', in *Empowering Interactions: Political Cultures and the Emergence of the State in Europe*, ed. by Willem Pieter Blockmans, André Holenstein, and Jon Mathieu (Farnham: Ashgate, 2009), pp. 65–78

Foscarini, Amilcare, *Armerista e Notiziario delle famiglie nobili, notabili e feudatarie di Terra d'Otranto* (Lecce: La Modernissima, 1927)

Fosi, Irene, *La società violenta: il banditismo nello Stato pontificio nella seconda metà del Cinquecento* (Rome: Edizioni dell'Ateneo, 1985)

——— 'Il banditismo nello Stato Pontificio nella seconda metà del cinquecento', in *Bande armate, banditi, banditismo e repressione di giustizia negli stati europei di antico regime*, ed. by Gherardo Ortalli (Rome: Jouvence, 1986), pp. 67–85

────── *Papal Justice: Subjects and Courts in the Papal State, 1500–1750* (Washington, DC: Catholic University Press of America, 2011)
Fusco, Idamaria, 'Peste, economia e fiscalità in terra di Bari', *ASPN*, 114 (1996), 34–59
────── *Peste, demografia e fiscalità nel regno di Napoli del XVII secolo* (Milan: FrancoAngeli, 2007)
────── 'Banditismo e sacheggi in tempo di epidemia: il Regno di Napoli nella seconda metà del Seicento', in *Nella morsa della guerra: assedi, occupazioni militari e sacheggi in età preindustriale*, ed. by Guido Alfani and Mario Rizzo (Milan: FrancoAngeli, 2013), pp. 111–28
Gaffin, Dennis, 'The Production of Emotion and Social Control: Taunting, Anger, and the Rukka in the Faeroe Islands', *Ethos*, 23 (1995), 149–72
Galasso, Giuseppe, *Napoli spagnola dopo Masaniello: politica, cultura, società*, 2 vols. (Florence: Sansoni, 1982)
────── 'Lo stereotipo del napoletano e le sue variazioni regionali', in his *L'altra Europa: per un'antropologia storica del Mezzogiorno d'Italia* (Milan: Mondadori, 1982)
────── 'Unificazione italiana e tradizione meridionale' in *Il brigantaggio postunitario nel Mezzogiorno d'Italia* (Naples: Società per la Storia Patria: 1984)
────── *Economia e società nella Calabria del Cinquecento* (Naples: Guida, 1992)
────── *Alla periferia dell'impero: il Regno di Napoli nel periodo spagnolo (sec. XVI–XVII)* (Turin: Giulio Einaudi, 1994)
────── *Napoli capitale: identità politica e identità cittadina* (Naples: Electa Napoli, 2003)
────── ed., *Le città del Regno di Napoli nell'età moderna: studi storici dal 1980 al 2010* (Naples: Editoriale Scientifica, 2011)
Gallant, Thomas W., 'Honor, Masculinity, and Ritual Knife Fighting in Nineteenth-Century Greece', *The American Historical Review*, 105 (2000), 359–82
Garnot, Benoît, 'Justice, infrajustice, parajustice et extrajustice dans la France d'ancien régime', *Crime, histoire, société*, 41 (2000), 103–20
Gaskill, Malcolm, *Crime and Mentalities in Early Modern England* (Cambridge: Cambridge University Press, 2009)
Gaudioso, Francesco, *Il potere di punire e perdonare: banditismo e politiche criminali nel Regno di Napoli* (Naples: Congedo, 2006)
Gentilcore, David, *From Bishop to Witch: The System of the Sacred in Early Modern Terra d'Otranto* (Manchester: University of Manchester Press, 1992)
────── '"Adapt Yourselves to the People's Capabilities": Missionary Strategies, Methods and Impact in the Kingdom of Naples, 1600–1800', *The Journal of Ecclesiastical History*, 45 (1994), 269–96
Gentile, Marco 'La vendetta di sangue come rituale: Qualche osservazione sulla Lombardia fra Quattro e Cinquecento', in *La morte e i suoi riti in Italia tra Medioevo e prima età moderna*, ed. by Francesco Salvestrini, Gian Maria Varanini, and Anna Zangarini (Florence: Firenze University Press, 2007), pp. 209–41
Gérard, Philippe, François Ost, and Michel Van De Kerckhove, eds., *Droit négocié, droit imposé?* (Brussels: Publications universitaires Saint Louis, 1996)
Giudice, Gianfranco, *Benedetto Croce* (Rimini: Luisè, 1994)
Gluckman, Max, 'The Peace in the Feud', *Past and Present*, 8 (1955), 1–14
Grubb, James S., 'Catalysts for Organized Violence in the Early Venetian Territorial State', in *Bande armate, banditi banditismo e repressione di giustizia negli stati europei di antico regime*, ed. by Gherardo Ortalli (Rome: Jouvence, 1986)

Guarino, Gabriel, 'The Reception of Spain and its Values in Habsburg Naples: A Reassessment', in *Exploring Cultural History: Essays in Honour of Peter Burke*, ed. by Joan Pau Rubiés, Melissa Calaresu, and Filippo de Vivo (Farnham: Ashgate, 2010), 93–112

—— *Representing the King's Splendour: Communication and Reception of Symbolic Forms of Power in Viceregal Naples* (Manchester: Manchester University Press, 2010)

—— 'Public Rituals and Festivals in Naples, 1503–1799', in *A Companion to Early Modern Naples*, ed. by Tommaso Astarita (Leiden: Brill, 2013), pp. 257–80

Hanlon, Gregory, *The Twilight of a Military Tradition: Italian Aristocrats and European Conflicts, 1560–1800* (London: UCL Press, 1998)

—— 'Violence and its Control in the Late Renaissance', in *A Companion to the Worlds of the Renaissance*, ed. by Guido Ruggiero (Blackwell: London, 2002), pp. 139–57

Head, Randolph C., 'Modes of Reading, Community Practice and the Constitution of Textual Authority in the Thurgau and Graubünden, 1520–1660', in *Empowering Interactions: Political Cultures and the Emergence of the State in Europe*, ed. by Willem Pieter Blockmans, André Holenstein, and Jon Mathieu (Farnham: Ashgate, 2009), pp. 115–30

Herrup, Cynthia, 'Negotiating Grace', in *Politics, Religion and Popularity in Early Stuart Britain: Early Stuart Essays in Honour of Conrad Russell*, ed. by Thomas Cogswell, Richard Cust, and Peter Lake (Cambridge: Cambridge University Press, 2002), pp. 124–42

Hugon, Alain, *La insurrección de Nápoles 1647–1648: la construcción del acontecimiento* (Zaragoza: Prensas de la Universidad de Zaragoza, 2014)

Hyams, Paul R., 'Nastiness, Wrong, Rancor, Reconciliation', in *Conflict in Medieval Europe: Changing Perspectives on Society and Culture*, ed. by Warren Brown and Piotr Górecki (Farnham: Ashgate, 2003), pp. 195–218

—— *Rancor and Reconciliation in Medieval England* (Ithaca: Cornell University Press, 2003)

Iappelli, Filippo, 'Il Collegio dei Gesuiti a Capua (1611–1767)' in *Roberto Bellarmino arcivescovo di Capua. Teologo e pastore della riforma cattolica*, ed. by Gustavo Galeota (Capua: Istituto superiore di scienze religiose, 1990)

Intorcia, Gaetana, *La comunità beneventana nei secoli XII–XVIII: Aspetti istituzionali. Controversie giurisdizionali* (Naples: Edizioni scientifiche italiane, 1996)

Jamison, Evelyn, 'The Administration of the County of Molise in the Twelfth and Thirteenth Centuries', *The English Historical Review*, 177 (1930), 1–34

Janora, Michele, *Memorie storiche, critiche e diplomatiche della Città di Montepeloso (oggi Irsina)* (Matera: F. P. Conti, 1901)

Janssens, Gustaaf, ' "*Superexcellat autem misericordia iudicium*": The Homily of François Richardot on the Occasion of the Solemn Announcement of the General Pardon in the Netherlands (Antwerp, 16 July 1570)', in *Public Opinion and Changing Identities in the Early Modern Netherlands*, ed. by Judith Pollmann and Andrew Spicer (Leiden: Brill, 2007), pp. 107–23

Johnson, Christopher H. and David Warren Sabean, 'From Siblingship to Siblinghood: Kinship and the Shaping of European Society (1300–1900)', in *Sibling Relations and the Transformations of European Kinship, 1300–1900*, ed. by Christopher H. Johnson and David Warren Sabean (New York: Berghahn, 2011), pp. 1–30

Kagan, Richard, *Lawsuits and Litigants in Castile, 1500–1700* (Chapel Hill: University of North Carolina Press, 1981)
Karant-Nunn, Susan C., *The Reformation of Feeling: Shaping the Religious Emotions in Early Modern Germany* (Oxford: Oxford University Press, 2010)
Kesselring, Krista J., *Mercy and Authority in the Tudor State* (Cambridge: Cambridge University Press, 2003)
—— *Making Murder Public: Homicide in Early Modern England* (Oxford: Oxford University Press, 2019)
Koslofsky, Craig, 'The Kiss of Peace in the German Reformation', in *The Kiss in History*, ed. by Karen Harvey (Manchester: Manchester University Press, 2005), pp. 18–35
Kuehn, Thomas, *Law, Family, and Women: Toward a Legal Anthropology of Renaissance Italy* (Chicago: University of Chicago Press, 1991)
Labrot, Gérard, *Baroni in città: residenze e comportamenti dell'aristocrazia napoletana 1530–1734* (Naples: SEN, 1979)
—— 'La città meridionale' in *Storia del mezzogiorno*, ed. by Giuseppe Galasso, vol VIII-1 (Rome: Editalia, 1994), pp. 215–92
Lacchè, Luigi, *Latrocinium: giustizia, scienza penale e repressione del banditismo in antico regime* (Milan: Giuffrè, 1988)
Lacey, Helen, *The Royal Pardon: Access to Mercy in Fourteenth-Century England* (York: York Medieval Press, 2009)
Lambet, Thomas Benedict and David W. Rollason, *Peace and Protection in the Middle Ages* (Durham: Durham University, 2009)
Largier, Niklaus, *In Praise of the Whip: A Cultural History of Arousal* (New York: Zone Books, 2007)
Lauro, Agostino, *Il giurisdizionalismo pregiannoniano nel Regno di Napoli: problema e bibliografia (1563–1723)* (Rome: Edizioni di Storia e Letteratura, 1974)
Laven, Mary, *Mission to China* (Chatham: Faber & Faber, 2011)
Laven, Peter, 'Banditry and Lawlessness in the Venetian Terraferma', in *Crime, Society and Law in Renaissance Italy*, ed. by Trevor Dean and Kate Lowe (Cambridge: Cambridge University Press, 1994), pp. 221–48
Le Goff, Jacques, 'Saint Louis et la parole royale', in *Le nombre du temps: en hommage à Paul Zumthor*, ed. by Emmanuelle Baumgartner (Paris: Libr. H. Champion, 1988), pp. 127–36
Lepre, Aurelio, *Storia del mezzogiorno d'Italia: la lunga durata e la crisis (1500–1656)* (Naples: Liguori, 1986)
Levi, Giovanni, *Inheriting Power: The Story of an Exorcist*, trans. by Lydia Cochrane (Chicago: Chicago University Press, 1988)
Lewis, Mark A., 'The Development of Jesuit Confraternities in the Kingdom of Naples in the Sixteenth and Seventeenth Centuries', in *The Politics of Ritual Kinship: Confraternities and Social Order in Early Modern Italy*, ed. by Nicholas Terpstra (Cambridge: Cambridge University Press, 200), pp. 210–27
Liruti, Gian-Giuseppe, *Notizie delle vite ed opere scritte da'letterati del Friuli* (Venice, 1830)
Macfarlane, Alan, *The Justice and the Mare's Ale: Law and Disorder in Seventeenth Century England* (Oxford: Blackwell, 1981)
Maffei, Elena, *Dal reato alla sentenza: il processo criminale in età comunale* (Rome: Edizioni di storia e letteratura, 2005)
Maiorini, Maria Grazia, *Il viceregno di Napoli: introduzione alla raccolta di documenti curata da Giuseppe Coniglio. Con indici* (Naples: Giannini, 1992)

Manconi, Francesco, ed., *Banditismi mediterranei, secoli XVI–XVII* (Rome: Carocci, 2003)
Mansfield, Mary C., *The Humiliation of Sinners: Public Penance in Thirteenth-Century France* (Ithaca: Cornell University Press, 1995)
Mantelli, Roberto, *Il pubblico impiego nell'economia del Regno di Napoli: retribuzioni, reclutamento e ricambio sociale nell'epoca spagnuola (secc. XVI–XVII)* (Naples: Istituto italiano per gli studi filosofici, 1986)
Marin, Brigitte, 'Town and Country in the Kingdom of Naples, 1500–1800', in *Town and Country in Europe, 1300–1800*, ed. by Stephen R. Epstein (Cambridge: Cambridge University Press, 2001)
Marino, John A. *Pastoral Economics in the Kingdom of Naples* (Baltimore: Johns Hopkins University Press, 1988)
—— 'Wheat and Wool in the Dogana of Foggia: An Equilibrium Model for Early Modern European History', *Mélanges de l'Ecole française de Rome. Moyen-Age, Temps modernes*, 100 (1988), 871–92
—— 'The Rural World in Italy under Spanish Rule', in *Spain in Italy: Politics, Society, and Religion 1500–1700*, ed. by Thomas James Dandelet and John A. Marino (Leiden: Brill, 2007), pp. 405–29
—— 'The Zodiac in the Streets: Inscribing "Buon Governo" in Baroque Naples', in *Embodiments of Power: Building Baroque Cities in Europe*, ed. by Gary B. Cohen and Franz A. J. Szabo (New York: Berghahn, 2008), pp. 203–29
—— 'Solidarity in Spanish Naples: *Fede Pubblica* and *Fede Privata* Revisited', in *Sociability and its Discontents: Civil Society, Social Capital, and their Alternatives in Late Medieval and Early Modern Europe*, ed. by Nicholas Terpstra and Nicholas Eckstein (Turnhout: BREPOLS, 2009), pp. 193–212
—— *Becoming Neapolitan: Citizen Culture in Baroque Naples* (Baltimore: Johns Hopkins University Press, 2011)
—— 'Problems and Methods in Neapolitan History', in *A Companion to Early Modern Naples*, ed. by Tommaso Astarita (Leiden: Brill, 2013), pp. 11–34
Marrone, Giovanni, *Città, campagna e criminalità nella Sicilia moderna* (Palermo: Palumbo, 2000)
Martino, Aurora, 'Giovan Girolamo II Acquaviva d'Aragona (1604–c.1665). Signore feudale del Mezzogiorno spagnolo' (unpublished PhD thesis, Universidad de Valladolid, 2012)
Masi, Gino, 'Il sindicato delle magistrature comunali nel sec. XIV (con speciale riferimento a Firenze)', *Rivista italiana per le scienze giuridiche*, 5 (1930), 43–115, 331–411
Masi, Giovanni, *Altamura Farnesiana* (Bari: Cressati, 1959)
Mastellone, Salvo, *Pensiero politico e vita culturale nel seconda metà del seicento* (Messina: Casa Editrice d'Anna, 1965)
Mauro, Achille, *Le fortificazioni nel Regno di Napoli* (Naples: Giannini Editore, 1998)
Mazur, Peter, *The New Christians of Spanish Naples 1528–1671: A Fragile Elite* (Basingstoke: Palgrave Macmillan, 2013)
Medick, Hans and David Warren Sabean, 'Introduction', in *Interest and Emotion: Essays on the Study of Family and Kinship*, ed. by Hans Medick and David Warren Sabean (Cambridge: Cambridge University Press, 1984), pp. 9–27
Miletti, Marco Nicola, 'Strade di banditi, banditi di strada: Criminalità e comunicazioni nel Mezzogiorno del Cinquecento', *Frontiera d'Europa*, 6 (2000), 49–114
Morelli, Giorgio, 'Contributi ad una storia del brigantaggio durante il vicereame spagnolo', *ASPN* (1968–69), 293–328

Morgan, Victor, 'A Ceremonious Society: An Aspect of Institutional Power in Early Modern Norwich', in *Institutional Culture in Early Modern Society*, ed. by Anne Goldgar and Robert I. Frost (Leiden: Brill, 2004), pp. 133–63

Mostaccio, Silvia, *Early Modern Jesuits between Obedience and Conscience during the Generalate of Claudio Acquaviva (1581–1615)* (Farnham: Ashgate, 2014)

Muchembled, Robert, *A History of Violence from the End of the Middle Ages to the Present* (Cambridge: Polity, 2012)

Muir, Edward, *Mad Blood Stirring: Vendetta and Factions in Friuli during the Renaissance* (Baltimore: Johns Hopkins University Press, 1993)

—— 'The Sources of Civil Society in Italy', *Journal of Interdisciplinary History*, 29 (1999), 379–406

—— 'The Idea of Community in Renaissance Italy', *Renaissance Quarterly*, 55 (2002), 1–18

Muldrew, Craig, 'The Culture of Reconciliation: Community and the Settlement of Economic Disputes in Early Modern England', *The Historical Journal*, 39 (1996), 915–42

Musi, Aurelio, *Finanze e politica nella Napoli del '600: Bartolomeo d'Aquino* (Naples: Guida, 1976)

—— *Mezzogiorno spagnolo: la via napoletana allo stato moderno* (Naples: Guida, 1991)

—— *La rivolta di Masaniello nella scena politica barocca* (Naples: Guida, 2002)

—— *Benevento tra Medioevo ed età moderna* (Manduria: Lacaita, 2004)

—— *La Campania: Storia Sociale e Politica* (Naples: Guida, 2006)

—— 'The Kingdom of Naples in the Spanish Imperial System', in Thomas James Dandelet and John A. Marino, eds., *Spain in Italy: Politics, Society, and Religion 1500–1700* (Leiden: Brill, 2007), pp. 73–98

Muto, Giovanni, 'Apparati finanziari e gestione della fiscalità nel Regno di Napoli dalla seconda metà del '500 alla crisi degli anni '20 del sec. XVII', in *La Fiscalité et ses implications sociales en Italie et en France aux XVIIe et XVIIIe siècle. Actes du colloque de Florence (5–6 décembre 1978)* (Rome: École Française de Rome, 1980), pp. 125–50

—— 'Il regno di Napoli sotto la dominazione spagnola', in *Storia della società italiana*, ed. by Giovanni Cherubini et al., 25 vols (Milan: Teti, 1987), XI, pp. 225–316

—— 'Istituzioni dell'universitas e ceti dirigenti locali', in *Storia del Mezzogiorno*, ed. by Giuseppe Galasso and Rosario Romeo (Naples: Edizioni del Sole, 1991), IX, 2, pp. 19–67.

—— '"I segni d'honore": rappresentazioni delle dinamiche nobiliari a Napoli in età moderna', in *Signori, patrizi, cavalieri in Italia centro-meridionale nell'età moderna*, ed. by Maria Antonietta Visceglia (Rome: Laterza, 1992), pp. 171–92

—— 'Pouvoirs et territoires dans l'Italie espagnole', *Revue d'histoire moderne et contemporaine* 45 (1998), 42–65

—— 'Il Patriziato napoletano e il governo della città capitale', in *Patriziato Napoletano e Governo della Città*, ed. by Giovanni Muto, Enzo Capasso Torre delle Pastene, and Pierluigi Sanfelice di Bagnoli (Naples: Cappella del Tesoro, 2005), pp. 19–25

—— 'Fedeltà e patria nel lessico politico napoletano della prima età moderna', in *Storia sociale e politica: omaggio a Rosario Villari*, ed. by Alberto Merola, Giovanni Muto, Elena Valeri, and Maria Antonietta Visceglia (Milan: FrancoAngeli, 2006), pp. 495–522

―― 'Strategie e Strutture del Controllo Militare del Territorio nel Regno di Napoli nel Cinquecento', in *Guerra y Sociedad en la monarquía hispánica: política, estrategia y cultura en la Europa moderna (1500–1700)*, ed. by Enrique García Hernán and Davide Maffi (Madrid: Laberinto, 2006), pp. 153–70

―― 'Noble Presence and Stratification in the Territories of Spanish Italy', in *Spain in Italy: Politics, Society, and Religion 1500–1700*, ed. by Thomas James Dandelet and John A. Marino (Leiden: Brill, 2007), pp. 251–98

―― 'Urban Structures and Population', in *A Companion to Early Modern Naples*, ed. by Tommaso Astarita (Leiden: Brill, 2013), pp. 35–62

―― 'Fidelidad, política y conflictos urbanos en el Reino de Nápoles (siglos XVI–XVII)', in *Ciudades en conflicto. Siglos XVI–XVIII*, ed. by José Ignacio Fortea Perez and Juan Eloy Gelabert González (Madrid: Marcial Pons Historia, 2008), pp. 371–395

Niccoli, Ottavia, 'Giustizia, pace, perdono: a proposito di un libro di John Bossy', *Storica*, 25–6 (2003), 195–207

―― 'Pratiche sociali di perdono nell'Italia della Controriforma', in *I linguaggi del potere: politica e religione nell'età barocca*, ed. by Francesca Cantù (Rome: Viella, 2009), pp. 249–73

―― 'Rinuncia, pace, perdono. Rituali di pacificazione nella prima età moderna', *Studi storici*, 40 (1999), 219–61

―― *Perdonare: idee, pratiche, rituali in Italia tra Cinque e Seicento* (Rome: Laterza, 2007)

Nicolini, Niccola, *Quistioni di dritto* (Naples: Tipografia Salita, 1839)

Noto, Maria Anna, *Viva la Chiesa, mora il tiranno: il sovrano, la legge, la comunità e i ribelli (Benevento 1566)* (Naples: Guida, 2010)

Novi Chavarria, Elisa, 'L'attività missionaria dei Gesuiti nel Mezzogiorno d'Italia tra XVI e XVIII secolo', in *Per la storia sociale e religiosa del Mezzogiorno d'Italia*, ed. by Giuseppe Galasso and Carla Russo (Naples: Guida, 1980)

―― *Il governo delle anime: Azione pastorale, predicazione e missioni nel Mezzogiorno d'Italia. Secoli XVI–XVIII* (Naples: Editoriale Scientifica, 2001)

O'Malley, John W., *The First Jesuits* (Cambridge, MA: Harvard University Press, 1993)

Orlandi, Giuseppe, 'L. A. Muratori e le missioni di P. Segneri Jr.', *Spicilegium Historicum Congregationis SS.mi Redemptoris*, 20 (1972), 158–294

―― 'S. Alfonso Maria de Liguori e l'ambiente missionario napoletano nel settecento: La Compagnia di Gesu', *Spicilegium Historicum Congregationis SSmi Redeptoris*, 38 (1990), 5–195

Ortalli, Gherardo, ed., *Bande armate, banditi, banditismo e repressione di giustizia negli stati europei di antico regime. Atti del Convegno – Venezia 3–5 novembre 1983* (Rome: Jouvence, 1986)

Osbat, Anna, ' "E il perdonar magnanima vendetta": i pacificatori tra bene comune e amor di Dio', *Ricerche di storia sociale e religiosa*, 53 (1998), 121–46

Padoa-Schioppa, Antonio, 'Delitto e pace privata nel pensiero dei legisti bolognesi: brevi note', *Studia Gratiana*, 20 (1976), 269–87

Palazzo, Donato, 'Del "truglio" e delle sue applicazioni in Puglia', in *Studi di storia pugliese in onore di Giuseppe Chiarelli*, ed. by Michele Paone (Galatina: Congedo Editore, 1977), VI, pp. 59–113

Palazzolo, Giorgia Alessi, *Prova legale e pena: la crisi del sistema tra evo medio e moderno* (Napoli, Jovene: 1987)

Palma, Niccola, *Storia ecclesiastica e civile della regione più settentrionale del Regno di Napoli*, 5 vols. (Teramo, 1832–36)

Panico, Guido, *Il carnefice e la piazza: crudeltà di stato e violenza popolare a Napoli in età moderna* (Naples: Edizioni scientifiche italiane: 1985)

Papagna, Elena, *Sogni e bisogni di una famiglia aristocratica: i Caracciolo di Martina* (Milan: FrancoAngeli, 2002)

—— 'Ordine pubblico e repressione del banditismo nel Mezzogiorno d'Italia (secoli XVI–XIX)', in *Corpi armati e ordine pubblico in Italia (XVI–XIX sec.)*, ed. by Livio Antonielli and Claudio Donati (Soveria Mannelli: Rubbettino, 2003), pp. 49–72

—— 'Avversari, nemici, … anzi parenti: i rapporti tra famiglie delle nobilità napoletana nella prima età moderna', *Società e storia*, 116 (2007), 273–91

Pastor, Ludwig von, *The History of the Popes from the Close of the Middle Ages; Vol. XXIV: Clement VIII (1592–1605)* (London: Routledge, 1952)

Pedìo, Tommaso, *Napoli e Spagna nella prima metà del Cinquecento* (Bari: Caccuci, 1971)

Pepe, Gabriele, *Il Mezzogiorno d'Italia sotto gli Spagnoli* (Florence: Sansoni, 1952)

Petkov, Kiril, *The Kiss of Peace; Ritual, Self, and Society in the High and Late Medieval West* (Leiden: Brill, 2003)

Peytavin, Mireille, 'Naples, 1610: comment peut-on être officier?', *Annales: Histoire, Sciences Sociales*, 52.2 (1997), 265–91

—— *Visite et gouvernement dans le royaume de Naples (XVIe–XVIIe siècles)* (Madrid: Casa de Velázquez, 2003)

Piacente, Giovanni Battista, *Le rivoluzioni del Regno di Napoli negli anni 1647–1648 e l'assedio di Piombino e Portolongone* (Naples: Tipografia di Giuseppe Guerrera, 1861)

Polecritti, Cynthia, *Preaching Peace in Renaissance Italy: Bernardino of Siena and His Audience* (Washington, DC: Catholic University of America Press, 2000)

Pomara Saverino, Bruno, *Bandolerismo, violencia y justicia en la Sicilia barroca* (Madrid: Fundación Española de Historia Moderna, 2011)

—— 'Tra violenze e giustizie: La società del mondo mediterraneo occidentale e cattolico in antico regime', *Il palindromo: storie al rovescio e di frontiera*, 3 (2011), 83–110

Povolo, Claudio, *L'intrigo dell'Onore: poteri e istituzioni nella Repubblica di Venezia* (Verona: Cierre, 1997)

Prodi, Paolo, *Il sacramento del potere: Il giuramento politico nella storia constituzionale dell'Occidente* (Bologna: Mulino, 1992)

Prosperi, Adriano, *Giustizia bendata: Percorsi storici di un'immagine* (Turin: Einaudi, 2008)

Putnam, Robert D., with Robert Leonardi and Raffaella Y. Nanetti, *Making Democracy Work: Civic Traditions in Modern Italy* (Princeton: Princeton University Press, 1993)

Radius, Emilio, *I gesuiti: storia della Compagnia di Gesù, da Sant'Ignazio a Teilhard de Chardin* (Rome: Boria, 1967)

Raggio, Osvaldo, 'La politica della parentela: conflitti locali e commissari in Liguria orientale (secoli XVI–XVII)', *Quaderni storici*, 21 (1986), 721–57

—— *Faide e Parentele: Lo stato Genovese visto dalla Fontanabuona* (Turin: Einaudi, 1990)

Reddy, William, *The Navigation of Feeling: A Framework for the History of Emotions* (Cambridge: Cambridge University Press, 2004)

Resta, Patrizia, *Parentela ed Identità Etnica: Consanguineità e Scambi Matrimoniali in Una Comunità Italo-Albanese* (Milan: FrancoAngeli, 1991)
Reumont, Alfred, *Naples Under Spanish Dominion: The Carafas of Maddaloni and Masaniello* (London: George Bell & Sons, 1853)
Ricci, Roberto, ed., *Lo stato degli Acquaviva d'Aragona, duchi di Atri: atti di convegno* (L'Aquila: Colacchi, 2012)
Rispoli-Ciasca, Carolina, 'Aspetti della vita dell'Italia meridionale nei secoli XVII e XVIII', *Vita e Pensiero*, 34 (1951), 304–9
Roberts, Penny, *Peace and Authority During the French Religious Wars, 1560–1600* (London: Palgrave, 2013)
Romeo, Giovanni, *Aspettando il boia: condannati a morte, confortatori e inquisitori nella Napoli della Controriforma* (Florence: Sansoni, 1993).
—— *Amori proibiti: I concubini tra Chiesa e Inquisizione* (Rome: Laterza, 2008)
Roodenburg, Herman, 'Social Control Viewed from Below: New Perspectives', in *Social Control in Europe: 1500–1800*, ed. by Herman Roodenburg and Pieter Spierenburg (Columbus, OH: Ohio State University Press, 2004), pp. 145–58
Rose, Colin, *A Renaissance of Violence: Homicide in Early Modern Italy* (Cambridge: Cambridge University Press, 2019)
Rosenwein, Barbara, 'Problems and Methods in the History of Emotions', *Passions in Context*, 1 (2010), 1–32
Rossi, Maria Clara, 'Polisemia di un concetto: la pace nel basso medioevo. Note di lettura', in *La pace fra realtà e utopia* (Sommacampagna: Cierre, 2005), pp. 9–46
Rovito, Pier Luigi, *Respublica dei togati: giuristi e società nella Napoli del Seicento* (Naples: Jovene, 1981)
—— *Il viceregno spagnolo di Napoli: ordinamento, istituzioni, culture di governo* (Naples: Arte Tipografica, 2003)
—— *La rivolta dei notabili: ordinamenti municipali e dialettica dei ceti in Calabria citra, 1647–1650* (Naples: Jovene, 1988)
Rublack, Ulinka, 'Fluxes: The Early Modern Body and the Emotions', *History Workshop Journal*, 53 (2002), 1–16
—— 'Interior States and Sexuality in Early Modern Germany', in *After The History of Sexuality: German Genealogies with and beyond Foucault*, ed. by Scott Spector, Helmut Puff, and Dagmar Herzog (New York: Berghahn, 2012), pp. 43–62
Ryder, Alan Frederick Charles, *The Kingdom of Naples Under Alfonso the Magnanimous: The Making of a Modern State* (Oxford: Clarendon Press, 1976)
Sabean, David, *Power in the Blood: Popular Culture and Village Discourse in Early Modern Germany* (Cambridge: Cambridge University Press, 1984)
Sakellariou, Eleni, *Southern Italy in the Late Middle Ages: Demographic, Institutional and Economic Change in the Kingdom of Naples, c. 1440–c.1530* (Leiden: Brill, 2011)
Sabatini, Gaetano, 'Economy and Finance in Early Modern Naples', in *A Companion to Early Modern Naples*, ed. by Tommaso Astarita (Leiden: Brill, 2013), pp. 87–107
Sallmann, Jean-Michel, *Chercheurs de trésors et jeteuses de sorts: La quête du surnaturel à Naples au XVIe siècle* (Paris: Aubier, 1986)
Sánchez, Carlo José Hernando, 'Una visita a Castel Sant'Elmo: famiglie, città e fortezze a Napoli tra Carlo V e Filippo II', *Annali di Storia moderna e Contemporanea*, 6 (2000), 39–89

—— 'Immagine e cerimonia: la corte vicereale di Napoli nella monarchia di Spagna', in *Cerimoniale del viceregno spagnolo e austriaco di Napoli: 1650–1717*, ed. by Attilio Antonelli (Soveria Mannelli: Rubbettino, 2012), pp. 37–80

—— 'Nation and Ceremony: Political Uses of Urban Space in Viceregal Naples', in *A Companion to Early Modern Naples*, ed. by Tommaso Astarita (Leiden: Brill, 2013), pp. 153–76

Sánchez, Carlos José Hernando, *El Reino de Nápoles en el Imperio de Carlos V: la consolidación de la conquista* (Madrid: Sociedad Estatal para la Commemoración de los Centenarios de Felipe II y Carlos V, 2001)

Sandberg, Brian, *Warrior Pursuits: Noble Culture and Civil Conflict in Early Modern France* (Baltimore: Johns Hopkins University Press, 2010)

Sans, Xavier Torres i, 'Faide e banditismo nella Catalogna dei secoli XVI e XVII', in *Banditismi Mediterranei, secoli XVI–XVII*, ed. by Francesco Manconi (Rome: Carocci, 2003), pp. 35–52

Sbriccoli, Mario, 'Brigantaggio e ribellismi nella criminalistica dei secoli XVI–XVIII', in *Bande armate, banditi, banditismo e repressione di giustizia negli stati europei di antico regime*, ed. by Gherardo Ortalli (Rome: Jouvence, 1986), pp. 479–500

—— 'Legislation, Justice and Political Power in Italian Cities, 1200–1400', in *Legislation and Justice*, ed. by Antonio Padoa-Schioppa (Oxford: Clarendon, 1997), pp. 37–55

—— 'Justice négociée, justice hégémonique: L'émergence du pénal public dans les villes italiennes des XIIIe et XIVe siècles', in *Pratiques Sociales et Politiques Judiciares dans les villes de l'occident à la fin du moyen âge*, ed. by Jacques Chiffoleau, Claude Gauvard, and Andrea Zorzi (Rome: Publications de l'École française de Rome, 2007), pp. 389–421

Scaduto, Mario, 'Le carceri della Vicaria di Napoli agli inizi del Seicento', *Redenzione umana*, 6 (1968), 393–412

Scatigna Minghetti, Gaetano, 'I figli di S. Paolo della Croce a Ceglie Messapica: scansioni socio-storiche di un'esperienza centenaria', in *I Passionisti a Ceglie Messapica: 1897–1997*, ed. by Carmelo Turrisi (Empoli: Barbieri, 2003)

—— and Luigi Ricci, 'Ferruzzo nella storia di Casa Allegretti', *Riflessioni: Umanesimo della Pietra*, 9 (1986), 113–17

Schipa, Michelangelo, 'Un grido di libertà nel seicento', in *Studii dedicati a Francesco Torraca nel XXXVI anniversario della sua laurea* (Naples: Francesco Perrella, 1912)

Scoppa, Ursino, *Relazione delle cose seguite in Ariano nel 1648* (Naples, 1839)

Selwyn, Jennifer, ' "Schools of Mortification": Theatricality and the Role of Penitential Practice in the Jesuits' Popular Missions', in *Penitence in the Age of Reformations*, ed. by Katherine Jackson Lualdi and Anne T. Thayer (Aldershot: Ashgate, 2000), pp. 201–20

—— 'Angels of Peace: The Social Drama of Reconciliation in the Jesuit Missions in Southern Italy', in *Beyond Florence: The Contours of Medieval and Early Modern Italy*, ed. by Paula Findlen, Michelle M. Fontaine, and Duane J. Osheim (Stanford: Stanford University Press, 2003), pp. 160–76

—— *A Paradise Inhabited by Devils: The Jesuits' Civilizing Mission in Early Modern Naples* (Farnham: Ashgate, 2004)

Senatore, Francesco, 'The Kingdom of Naples', in *The Italian Renaissance State*, ed. by Andrea Gamberini and Isabella Lazzarini (Cambridge: Cambridge University Press, 2012), pp. 30–49

Sharpe, James A., *Crime in Early Modern England 1550–1750* (London: Routledge, 1998)
Sicilia, Rosanna, *Un Consiglio di spada e di toga: Il Collaterale napoletano dal 1443 al 1542* (Naples: Guida, 2010)
Sirago, Maria, 'Il Feudo Acquaviviano in Puglia (1575–1665)', *Archivio Storico Pugliese*, 37 (1984), 73–122
—— 'Due esempi di ascensione signorile: i Vaaz conti di Mola e gli Acquaviva conti di Conversano tra '500 e '600 (Terra di Bari)', *Studi storici*, 36 (1986), 169–213
—— 'Il Feudo Acquaviviano in Puglia (1665–1710)', *Archivio Storico Pugliese*, 39 (1986) 215–254
Smail, Daniel Lord, 'Telling Tales in Angevin Courts', *French Historical Studies*, 20 (1997), 183–215
—— *The Consumption of Justice: Emotions, Publicity, and Legal Culture in Marseille, 1264–1423* (Ithaca: Cornell University Press, 2003)
Snyder, Jon R., *Dissimulation and the Culture of Secrecy* (Oakland: University of California Press, 2009)
Soccio, Pasquale, *Pauperismo, brigantaggio ed emigrazione in Terra di Capitanata* (Foggia: Sentieri Meridiani, 2008)
Sodano, Giulio, 'Governing the City', in *A Companion to Early Modern Naples*, ed. by Tommaso Astarita (Leiden: Brill, 2013), pp. 109–31
Sole, Giovanni, *Breve storia della Reale Salina di Lungro* (Cosenza: Edizioni Brenner, 1981)
Spagnoletti, Angelantonio, 'Potere amministrativo ed élite nelle "università" del Regno di Napoli (sec. XVI–XVII)', in *Congreso internacional espacios de poder: Cortes, ciudades y villas (s.XVI–XVIII)*, ed. by Jesús Bravo (Madrid: Universidad Autónoma de Madrid, 2002), pp. 69–78
—— 'The Naples Elites Between City and Kingdom', in *A Companion to Early Modern Naples*, ed. by Tommaso Astarita (Leiden: Brill, 2013), pp. 197–214
Spierenburg, Pieter, *The Prison Experience: Disciplinary Institutions and their Inmates in Early Modern Europe* (New Brunswick: Rutgers University Press, 1991)
—— 'Faces of Violence: Homicide Trends and Cultural Meanings: Amsterdam, 1431–1816', *Journal of Social History*, 27 (1994), 701–16
—— 'Masculinity, Violence, and Honor: An Introduction', in *Men and Violence: Gender, Honor, and Rituals in Modern Europe and America*, ed. by Pieter Spierenburg (Columbus, OH: Ohio State University Press, 1998), pp. 1–29
Stevens, Laura, *The Poor Indians: British Missionaries, Native Americans, and Colonial Sensibility* (Philadelphia: University of Pennsylvania Press, 2004)
Tavilla, Carmelo Elio 'Paci, feudalità e pubblici poteri nell'esperienza del ducato estense (secc. XV–XVIII)', in *Duelli, faide e rappacificazioni: Elaborazioni concettuali, esperienze storiche: Atti del seminario di studi storici e girudici (Modena 14 gennaio 200)*, ed. by Marco Cavina (Milan: Giuffrè, 2001), pp. 285–318
Terpstra, Nicholas and Nicholas Eckstein, eds., *Sociability and its Discontents: Civil Society, Social Capital, and their Alternatives in Late Medieval and Early Modern Europe* (Turnhout: BREPOLS, 2009)
Thompson, E. P., *The Poverty of Theory and Other Essays* (Pontypool: Merlin Press, 1978)
Throop, Susanna A. and Paul R. Hyams, eds., *Vengeance in the Middle Ages: Emotion, Religion and Feud* (Farnham: Ashgate, 2010)
Tilly, Charles, 'Invisible Elbow', *Sociological Forum* 11 (1996), 589–601

Torre, Angelo, 'Faide, fazioni e partiti, ovvero la ridefinizione della politica nei feudi imperiali della Langhe tra Sei e Settecento', *Quaderni Storici*, 63 (1986), 796–810

Tracey, James D., *Charles V, Impresario of War: Campaign Strategy, International Finance and Domestic Politics* (Cambridge: Cambridge University Press, 2002)

Valiente, Francisco Tomás, 'El perdon de la parte ofendida en el derecho penal castellano (siglos XVI, XVII, y XVIII)', *Anuario de historia del derecho español*, 31 (1961), 55–114

Vallerani, Massimo, 'Pace e processo nel sistema giudiziario del comune di Perugia', *Quaderni Storici*, 101 (1999), 315–54

—— *Medieval Public Justice*, trans. by Sarah Rubin Blanshei (Washington, DC: Catholic University of America Press, 2012)

Villani, Pasquale, 'Ricerche sulla proprietà e sul regime fondiario nel Lazio', *Annuario dell'Istituto Storico Italiano per l'età moderna e contemporanea*, 12 (1960), 97–263

Villari, Rosario, 'Baronaggio e finanza a Napoli alla viglia della rivoluzione del 1647-8', *Studi Storici*, 3 (1962), 259–305

—— 'La feudalità e lo Stato napoletano nel secolo XVII', *Clio*, 1 (1965), 555–75

—— 'Congiura aristocratica e rivoluzione popolare' *Studi Storici*, 8 (1967), 37–112

—— 'Banditismo sociale alla fine del Cinquecento', in his *Riformatori e ribelli dal XVI al XVIII secolo* (Rome: Editori Uniti, 1979), pp. 69–81

—— *Elogio della dissimulazione: la lotta politica nella Seicento* (Bari: Laterza, 1987)

—— *The Revolt of Naples* (Cambridge: Polity, 1993)

—— *Per il re o per la patria: la fedeltà nel Seicento con 'Il Cittadino Fedele' e altri scritti politici* (Rome: Laterza, 1994)

—— *Un sogno di libertà: Napoli nel declino di un impero* (Milan: Mondadori, 2012)

Visceglia, Maria Antonietta, 'Un groupe social ambigu: Organisation, stratégies et représentations de la noblesse napolitaine XVIe–XVIIIe siècles', *Annales. Économies, Sociétés, Civilisations*, 48 (1993), 819–51

—— 'Factions in the Sacred College in the Sixteenth and Seventeenth Centuries', in *Court and Politics in Papal Rome, 1492–1700*, ed. by Gianvittorio Signorotto and Maria Antonietta Visceglia (Cambridge: Cambridge University Press, 2002), pp. 99–131

Volpicella, Scipione 'D. Giovanni Orefice, Principe di Sanza decapitato in Napoli nel 1640', *ASPN*, 3 (1878), 713–742

Von Lobstein, Franz, 'La presa di possesso di un territorio da parte del feudatorio', *Rassegna storica dei comuni. Periodico di studi e di ricerche storiche locali*, 1 (1969).

Wiener, Leo, *Commentary to the Germanic Laws and Medieval Documents* (Cambridge, MA: Harvard University Press, 1915)

Willoweit, Dietmar, 'The Holy Roman Empire as Legal System', in *Legislation and Justice*, ed. by Antonio Padoa-Schioppa (Oxford: Oxford University Press, 1997), pp. 123–30

Withington, Phil, 'The Semantics of "Peace" in Early Modern England', *Transactions of the Royal Historical Society*, 23 (2013), 127–53

Würgler, Andreas, 'Voices from Among the "Silent Masses": Humble Petitions and Social Conflicts in Early Modern Central Europe', in *Petitions in Social History*, ed. by Lex Heerma van Voss (Cambridge: Cambridge University Press, 2001), pp. 11–34

Zazo, Alfredo, 'Bandi e repressioni per i "confugientes" in Benevento nei secoli XIV–XVII', in *Ricerche e studi storici*, ed. by Alfredo Zazo (Naples: Istituto della Stampa, 1961)

Zemon Davis, Natalie, *Fiction in the Archives: Pardon Tales and their Tellers in Sixteenth-Century France* (Stanford: Stanford University Press, 1987)

Zilli, Ilaria, 'Per una storia della città e delle città del Molise', in *Le città del Regno di Napoli nell'età moderna*, ed. by G. Galasso (Naples, 2011), pp. 577–603

Zorzi, Andrea, 'The Judicial System in Florence in the Fourteenth and Fifteenth Centuries', in *Crime, Society and the Law in Renaissance Italy*, ed. by Trevor Dean and Kate Lowe (Cambridge: Cambridge University Press, 1994), pp. 40–58

—— 'Legislation, Justice and Political Power in Italian Cities, 1200–1400', in *Legislation and Justice (The Origins of the Modern State in Europe, 13th to 18th Centuries)*, ed. by Antonio Padoa Schioppa (Oxford: Clarendon Press, 1997), pp. 37–55

—— *La trasformazione di un quadro politico: ricerche su politica e giustizia a Firenze dal comune allo Stato territoriale* (Florence: Firenze University Press, 2008)

—— 'I conflitti nell'Italia comunale: Riflessioni sullo stato degli studi e sulle prospettive di ricerca', in *Conflitti, paci e e vendette nell'Italia comunale*, ed. by Andrea Zorzi (Florence: Firenze University Press, 2009), pp. 7–43

Index

Acquaviva d'Aragona 46–8
Albanian minority in Italy 106
   in Rossano 49
Altamura 15, 95, 176–7
Altomonte 106, 109
Amatore, Diego 171
Annese, Gennaro 170, 174
aristocracy 44–8
   Caracciolo clan 46
   coachmen and livery-wearers 48
   feudal power 14
   Seggi of Naples 16
   seventeenth-century expansion 44
assassination 46, 102
asylum 36, 50, 67, 133

banditry 34, 62, 66, 78
   civic defence against 128
   comparisons with soldiers 129
   definitions and identities 118–19
   Domenico Allegretti and his gang 132–8
   from the Marche 120
   giunta degli banditi 183
   kidnap for ransom 124
   organization and ranks 120
   reception of bandits 127
   role in 1647–48 172
   supporters of 71
   travellers accounts of 34
   use of explosives 125
Bari 100
Baronio, Francesco 7
Basile, Giambattista 65
battaglione (militia) 100
Beltrano, Domenico 146

Benevento 122, 135, 155, 157
   as *confugium* 137
Bethel, Slingsby 35
Bitonto 171
Boccapianola, Francesco 175
Bossy, John 9, 21, 157

Calcabottaccio 66
Campanella, Tommaso 9, 79
Capecelatro, Francesco 74
Capua 155, 159–63
Caracciolo, Giulio Cesare 38
Cardito 155
Carroll, Stuart 34
Casa d'Albore 174
Charles V 39, 78, 80
Collateral Council 16, 22, 43, 77, 81, 181
   attempts to counter violence 60
   difficult relations with the Vicaria 73
   involvement in aristocratic conflict 45
Conversano 51, 69, 105
Cosenza 171, 174
Council of Italy 17, 43
criminal justice
   accusations (*querele*) 68
   ad modum belli 64
   aristocratic complaints about 38
   cautions and sureties 79
   composition of crimes 60
   delays 64
   as factor in rebellions of 1647–48 173
   flight from 66
   general indulgences 176, 178

pardoning for violent criminals 50
remissions of the offended party *see*
   remissions of the offended party
sources for the Neapolitan
   history of 36
summary execution 63
torture 62

D'Alessi, Silvana 183
D'Avalos, Bonaventura 71
Delille, Gérard 16, 95, 96, 108
Della Porta, Giambattista 9
Doria, Paolo Mattia 18, 76
duelling 34

ecclesiastical criminal courts 64
enmity
   banditry's relationship to 125
   caused by financial interests 100
   as civic problem 94
   as emotional practice 22
   everyday signs of 6
   inimicitia as legal concept 8
   in jurisprudence 7–8
   metaphors of 7
   as problem for governors 106
   as proxy battles between
     authorities 3
   as reason for human mobility 50
   role in rebellions of 1647–48 172
   tackled in Jesuit missions 147
Evelyn, John 35
excommunication 104, 105
extorsion 103

factionalism 6
   civil conflict between Count of
     Conversano and Duke of
     Andria 179
   patrician nobility 152
feudalism
   criminal authority of feudal lords 62
   feudal right to compose crimes 74
   governance of communities 98
   local politics of 101–2
   mero et misto impero 74
   open feudal land market 42
   royal sale of demenial lands 41
feuding 50

firearms 2, 46, 50, 103
   extorsion of forgiveness with 72
Foggia 66, 122, 149
folkore 4
Follerio, Pietro 8, 69

Genoa 35
government of the countryside 128, 131
Gragnano 104
Guazzini, Sebastiano 79

hatred 100, 104
   disrupting local government 101
   Jesuit understandings of 153
   memory practices 153
Howell, James 42

inquisition 69
Italian Wars 11, 37

jealousy 52
Jesuit missions
   burning of superstitious objects 162
   criticisms of 158
   diabolic presence 151
   Ignatian spirituality 155
   notarial practice 157
   physical mortification and penitence
     149, 154
   requested by communities 149
   theatrical techniques 154
jurisdiction 117
   complex geographies of 36
   conflict between secular and
     ecclesiastical 67, 103
   conflict within towns 101
   debates over bandits 135

Kingdom of Naples
   finances 71
   parliament of 39
   ritual celebrations 44
   seven offices of 39
   stereotypes of 10, 37

Lecce 150
Lepre, Aurelio 49
litigation 44, 62, 109
Lucera 64, 66

Marino, John A. 19
Masaniello 170
Mastrodatti 63, 73
Melito 171
Molise 97, 132
Monopoli 15, 150, 171
Montepeloso 76
Montorio 131
Morcone 51, 72, 152
Muir, Edward 19
Muratori, Ludovico Antonio 6
murder
   as cause of enmity 152
   committed by the bishop of
     Isernia 49
   debated incidence in Genoa 35
   many in Novi 36
   memory practices 149
   poisoned Soup 2

Naples (city)
   Castel Nuovo 65
   population growth 49
Nardò 180
Navaretta, Antonio 162
Navaretta, Francesco 131
Nocera 67
Novario, Giovanni Maria 76

oaths on the royal word 78–81
   banditry 83
   criticized as too widely used 83
office-holding 99
   reviews of tenure (*sindicato*) 101
Ottoman Empire
   fear of invasion by 41

Paolucci S.J., Scipione 148, 151
patrician nobility 98
peace
   ideology of 5
peace-making 4–5, 108, 134
   as fruit of penitence 150
   magic and scandal 51
   as occasion for violence 50
   penance 151
Petriello, Carlo 184
Presicce 1–3

prisons and imprisonment 66–7
Prodi, Paolo 79
Putignano 149

Raggio, Osvaldo 21, 94
rebellions of 1647–48 2, 63, 149, 161
   role of Masaniello 170
Reggio Calabria 106
Regie Audienze 99, 146, 189
   kinship investigations 3
   overview of structure and
     functions 62–4
   Regia Audienza of Lucera 121, 122
remissions of the offended party 73–4
   as explanation for violence 74
Rosario Villari 18, 122, 126
Rose, Colin 34
royal audiences (*Regie Audienze*) 17

Salazar, Francesco 173
Salerno 150
Sandys, George 44
Sant'Elia 66
Sciarra, Marco 78, 122
Segneri, Paolo 7, 158
sheep customshouse of Puglia
   (*Dogana*) 123
soldiers
   unpopularity of 130
Soleto 152
Spanish Army 44
   as yoke for the Kingdom 42
   billetting in the Kingdom of
     Naples 41
   Walloon soldiers 161
Squinzano 152

Thirty Years' War 5, 37
   fiscal burdens on Naples 43
togati 39, 43
Toledo, Pedro de 38
   criminal justice policy 68
Tontoli, Gabriele 171
travellers to early modern Italy 33
tribunali della campagna 64
Tutini, Camillo 171

Università *13, 15*, 95–7

Vaglio 173
vendetta 33
　in confession 7
　everyday signs of 7
　kinship obligation to 45
　legal measures against 42
　in rebellions of 1647–48 171
　in southern Italy 34
Vesuvius 170
Vicaria, Great Court of 17, 60, 76, 178, 183
　as instrument of Spanish rule 62
　prisons of 67
　Viceroy's pardoning in 70
Viceroys of Naples
　Alcalá, Duke of 73
　Arcos, Duke of 74
　Castrillo, Count of 183
　grace and pardoning of crimes 70
　Lannoy, Charles de 39
　Lemos, Count of 80
　Medina, Duke of 45
　Oñate, Count of 179, 180
　Osuña, Duke of 41, 77
　political power 43–4
　Cardona, Ramon de 39
　relation with Collateral Council *see* Collateral Council
　Toledo, Pedro de *see* Toledo, Pedro de
violence
　blamed on nocturnal music 49
　crisis of 1620s 42
　duelling 34
　historical explanations of 36
　in churches 50
　potential causes of 34
　travellers 34

www.ingramcontent.com/pod-product-compliance
Ingram Content Group UK Ltd.
Pitfield, Milton Keynes, MK11 3LW, UK
UKHW022039050325
4871UKWH00004B/81